THE RESURRECTION IN KARL BARTH

Many, perhaps most, of the major advances in the interpretation of Barth's work have stemmed from close reading of the texts, attending both to their scope and to their details, and alert to their place in the overall shape of Barth's account of the Christian faith. What follows offers just this kind of account ... As he grew older, Barth was increasingly captivated by one single fact, namely that, by virtue of his resurrection, Jesus Christ is utterly alive, utterly real and limitlessly present: 'He is the reality!' This lent an air of cheerfulness, confidence and calm to what he had to say, as well as a pastoral and spiritual helpfulness which no reader ought to miss. Dawson certainly doesn't miss these things, and not the least of the virtues of his study is its pervasive sense that, in the domain of the resurrection, theology is the most joyful of all the sciences.

From the Foreword by Professor John Webster

How does what happened a long, long time ago in Jesus become real for me? Many modern theologians have answered this question by reflecting on human selfhood. For Karl Barth, it becomes an occasion for a profound series of meditations on the resurrection of Jesus Christ from the dead. Dale Dawson draws us into the very heart of Barth's thinking on resurrection. The result is a fresh and insightful account of a rich theme.

Joseph L. Mangina, Wycliffe College, Toronto School of Theology

Karl Barth repeatedly spoke of the centrality and unparalleled significance of the resurrection of Jesus Christ for his theological understanding, yet a clear grasp of its nature and scope in Barth continues to find little expression in scholarly literature. This book seeks to draw out the theological substance and systematic implications of Barth's thinking on this theme. Barth's mature understanding of the resurrection concentrates upon the transition from the objective achievement of reconciliation culminating in the crucifixion and death of Jesus Christ to its subjective appropriation in the life of the believer, all within a thoroughly christological context. The resurrection may be described as the way of the crucified Lord to others, and is, for Barth, the essential and efficient link between christology proper and the extension of Christ's saving work to others.

D0219595

Barth Studies

Series Editors

The work of Barth is central to the history of modern western theology and remains a major voice in contemporary constructive theology. His writings have been the subject of intensive scrutiny and re-evaluation over the past two decades, notably on the part of English-language Barth scholars who have often been at the forefront of fresh interpretation and creative appropriation of his theology. Study of Barth, both by graduate students and by established scholars, is a significant enterprise; literature on him and conferences devoted to his work abound; the Karl Barth Archive in Switzerland and the Center for Barth Studies at Princeton give institutional profile to these interests. Barth's work is also considered by many to be a significant resource for the intellectual life of the churches.

Drawing from the wide pool of Barth scholarship, and including translations of Barth's works, this series aims to function as a means by which writing on Barth, of the highest scholarly calibre, can find publication. The series builds upon and furthers the interest in Barth's work in the theological academy and the church.

The Resurrection in Karl Barth

R. DALE DAWSON
Tyndale University, Canada

Routledge
Taylor & Francis Group

LONDON AND NEW YORK

First published 2007 by Ashgate Publishing

2 Park Square, Milton Park, Abingdon, Oxon OX14 4RN
711 Third Avenue, New York, NY 10017, USA

Routledge is an imprint of the Taylor & Francis Group, an informa business

First issued in paperback 2017

British Library Cataloguing in Publication Data
Dawson, R. Dale (Robert Dale), 1961–
 The resurrection in Karl Barth. – (Barth studies)
 1. Barth, Karl, 1886–1968 2. Jesus Christ – Resurrection
 I. Title
 232.5

Library of Congress Cataloging-in-Publication Data
Dawson, R. Dale (Robert Dale), 1961-
  The Resurrection in Karl Barth / R. Dale Dawson.
   p. cm.—(Barth studies)
  Includes bibliographical references and index.
  ISBN 0-7546-5555-5 (hardback : alk. paper)
 1. Barth, Karl, 1886-1968. 2. Resurrection. 3. Jesus Christ—Resurrection.
4. Barth, Karl, 1886-1968. Auferstehung der toten. I. Title. II. Series.

  BX4827.B3D39 2006
  232'.5—dc22

                                                                    2005037733

ISBN 978-0-7546-5555-8 (hbk)
ISBN 978-1-138-26508-0 (pbk)

Contents

Foreword

John Webster

Barth regarded the resurrection of Jesus as the material centre of the Christian faith. Pointing back to the life, ministry and death of Jesus, and, beyond that, to his eternal union with the being of God, and pointing ahead to the future of the creation in fellowship with the exalted Son, the resurrection contains within itself the full reach of the gospel. Most particularly, the resurrection is the fulfilment of the covenant between God and humankind which is the ground and goal of creation, and towards the maintenance of which the works of God are directed. Jesus' resurrection is not only the manifestation of his antecedent divine majesty and the indestructibility of his life as the one who has triumphed over sin and death; it is also a movement. As the risen one, he is active in coming to creatures, making himself present and known, demonstrating that the domain of creatures is embraced by his saving rule and so reconciled to God. In this way, Jesus' resurrection is the culmination of the relation between God and creatures: it is itself reconciliation and so revelation; in it, Jesus Christ strides across the divide of broken fellowship and renews creaturely life with God.

Despite their centrality to Barth's portrait of the Christian faith, such claims have rarely been a matter of sustained exposition and analysis in the literature on his theology. The lacuna is curious. It has to do, I suspect, both with the way in which what Barth has to say about the resurrection is very deeply embedded in his theology as a whole (and so is not simply noticeable as a discrete locus of dogmatic teaching), and also with the seriously counter-intuitive character of what Barth has to say when considered against the background of a good deal of modern theology. Dale Dawson's task in this book is to unearth and make visible these deep structures in Barth's thinking. Many, perhaps most, of the major advances in the interpretation of Barth's work have stemmed from close reading of the texts, attending both to their scope and to their details, and alert to their place in the overall shape of Barth's account of the Christian faith. What follows offers just this kind of account: scrupulous in its attention to specifics of what Barth has to say, but also careful to set them in their wider frame. And, further, it is not an exercise in mere reverence, because it considers Barth too important a conversation partner to be granted uncritical agreement.

The book's contribution to the elucidation of Barth's theology of the resurrection is many-sided, but particular attention might be drawn to two points. First, Dawson grasps the significance of an almost entirely neglected early text from Barth, his 1924 exposition of 1 Corinthians, *The Resurrection of the Dead*. Quite apart from its importance for understanding the nature and function of biblical interpretation in Barth's earlier theology, *The Resurrection of the Dead* is a remarkably mature exploration of ideas to which Barth will return throughout his dogmatic work, above all the ontologically constitutive character of the resurrection for a theology of history and human existence. This, in turn, has ramifications for questions about Barth's intellectual development; from the perspective of what Barth has to say there about the resurrection, the continuities of intention and thought are at least as significant as the shifts.

Second, Dawson's book is an invitation to a fresh sense of Barth's remarkable achievement in the 1950s when he produced the several volumes of the doctrine of reconciliation. So much is happening in these texts that the temptation of the interpreter is to reduce Barth to something more manageable, often by making some theme or conceptual pattern into an interpretative key. This Dawson resists: he lets Barth stand in all his complexity, and simply tries to allow the texts to speak for themselves. Yet he does so not simply out of veneration but in order to promote the kind of critical interchange which Barth hoped for but rarely enjoyed.

One of the chief lessons to be learnt in the school of Barth's work is that he uses doctrines to do the jobs often done – for example – by hermeneutics, or by historical or anthropological theory. As he grew older, Barth was increasingly captivated by one single fact, namely that, by virtue of his resurrection, Jesus Christ is utterly alive, utterly real and limitlessly present: 'He is the reality!' This lent an air of cheerfulness, confidence and calm to what he had to say, as well as a pastoral and spiritual helpfulness which no reader ought to miss. Dawson certainly doesn't miss these things, and not the least of the virtues of his study is its pervasive sense that, in the domain of the resurrection, theology is the most joyful of all the sciences.

Acknowledgements

This book has its roots in a doctoral dissertation written under the kind, patient and expert direction of Rev. Prof. John Webster at the Toronto School of Theology. John's uncompromising dedication to excellence and reassuring generosity of spirit have served as a constant source of inspiration and encouragement. I remain deeply grateful. Similarly, thanks are due to David Demson, Joseph Mangina, and Gary Badcock, who read this material in its earlier form, and, in addition to their enduring support and friendship, offered very helpful critical insight.

I am indebted too to a circle of friends and colleagues, who, over the period during which this book has taken shape, have contributed to the process by stimulating thought, engaging in critical discussion, and offering much needed encouragement. I offer my thanks to the members of an emerging Barth reading group in the Toronto area, and particularly to Craig Carter, Hugh Reid, Kurt Richardson, Victor Shepherd and Garth Wilson.

Thanks are due to many others without whose patient understanding this work could not have been completed. This book, written as it was in the context of two succeeding pastorates, demanded that congregants value not only the practical ministry but also the academic pursuits of their pastor. I pay tribute to my friends of Streetsville Baptist Church and City Centre Baptist Church.

Above all, I owe an extraordinary debt of thanks to my wife, Linda, and my children, Joshua, Jeremy, Esther and Sarah. Their love and laughter have afforded me the permission, support and sanity to embark upon this long literary journey and to arrive safely at home once again. To them I happily dedicate this book in much appreciation and love.

Introduction

But if there is no resurrection of the dead, then Christ has not been raised; if Christ has not been raised, then our preaching is in vain and your faith is in vain. ... If Christ has not been raised, your faith is futile and you are still in your sins. Then those also who have fallen asleep in Christ have perished. If for this life only we have hoped in Christ, we are of all men most to be pitied. But in fact Christ has been raised from the dead ... (I Corinthians 15:13–14, 17–20)[1]

The resurrection of Jesus Christ from the dead is indeed the cornerstone of Christian faith. It is not only a central feature of orthodox Christian belief; it is, according to the apostle Paul, the indispensable foundation which undergirds and informs the structure of the whole. Apart from the reality of the resurrection, the truth and power of the gospel of Jesus Christ are nullified.

Karl Barth (1886–1968), widely recognized as one of the greatest theologians of the twentieth century, perhaps more than any other, focused his attention upon this basic conviction of Christian faith. For him, the Christian confession 'Jesus is Risen!' is the definitive opening statement for all Christian theology. The proclamation 'Jesus Christ lives,' he claims, is 'at once the simplest and the most difficult christological statement.'[2] This fundamental confession of the Christian church has in view the inexhaustibly rich origin and spring of all Christian knowledge. It is 'the axiom of all axioms.'[3] In Barth's view, 'While we could imagine a New Testament containing only the history of Easter and its message, we could not possibly imagine a New Testament without it.'[4] And what is more, 'Everything else in the New Testament contains and presupposes the resurrection. It is the key to the whole.'[5] So central is this tenet to Barth's theological understanding that he summarized his position with the claim 'that academic theology was based on the resurrection of Jesus Christ

---

1   The Scripture quotations contained herein are from the *Revised Standard Version of the Bible*, copyrighted 1946, 1952, 1971, by the Division of Christian Education of the National Council of Churches of Christ in the United States of American. All rights reserved.

2   Karl Barth, *Church Dogmatics*, Vol. IV/3.i (Edinburgh: T. & T. Clark, 1961), p. 39. See also Karl Barth, *Church Dogmatics*, 13 vols (Edinburgh: T. & T. Clark, 1936–75). Trans. G.W. Bromiley et al. Hereafter this work shall be cited according to the following pattern: *CD* IV/3.i. See also *The Christian Life* (Edinburgh: T. & T. Clark, 1981). See also *Church Dogmatics: Index Volume* (Edinburgh: T. & T. Clark, 1977).

3   *CD* IV/1, p. 346.

4   *CD* III/2, p. 443.

5   Ibid.

from the dead.'[6] Witness to the resurrection may be given genuine expression by any child, says Barth, yet 'the profoundest meditation cannot master it:'[7]

> It [the doctrine of the resurrection] says something quite formal and yet it also says the most material thing that is to be said of Him. It says something supremely particular, and yet it also says the most embracing thing; something unique, and indeed the one unique thing, and yet also the universally real and valid.[8]

It is essential for any adequate reading of Barth to keep in mind his oft repeated emphasis upon the priority of the doctrine of the resurrection in all his theological thought. Though it does not always receive explicit mention, it is the formative category of reflection for the science of theology. In his *The Resurrection of the Dead*, originally published in 1924, Barth makes the case that the motif of the resurrection of Jesus Christ from the dead is not only the cohesive force and climax of Paul's first letter to the Corinthians, but also the secret nerve and interpretive key of the whole of Paul's theology.[9] It ought not to surprise us then that the doctrine of the resurrection should occupy a similar place of importance in Barth's own thought.

The doctrine of the resurrection of Jesus Christ from the dead remains a theme of axiomatic importance throughout Barth's theological career. This is not to claim that Barth's theology did not undergo significant development. It did. But this development is to be characterized, as Barth himself claimed, as a deepening of his initial insights, which required the various modulations through which his resurrection discourse passed in due course to its latest expression in *CD* IV/1–3. Barth's development of the theme of the resurrection is understood best not as a series of major or minor paradigm shifts, but as variations and extrapolations on a theme. As we shall see, many models of interpretation come up short because too little attention is given to a development of the consistency of Barth's approach, which is consequently overshadowed by a more thoroughly developed, though rarely adequate, delineation of the so-called 'shifts.'

The purpose here is to provide an extended analysis of Barth's understanding of the resurrection of Jesus Christ as it finds expression in substantial and thematically focused tracts of Barth's published material. The prime concern will be to explicate Barth's depiction of the resurrection in both its consistent emphases and its developments (or more significant alterations). I wish then to contend for an interpretation of Barth's resurrection discourse, from beginning to end, as a sustained effort to understand the gospel of Jesus Christ in the light of the decisive movement of the crucified Lord to others. It is well known that from early on in his theological development Barth understood the resurrection of Jesus Christ as the fundamental

---

6   Eberhard Busch, *Karl Barth: His Life From Letters and Autobiographical Texts* (London: SCM, 1976), p. 207.

7   *CD* IV/3, p. 39.

8   Ibid.

9   Karl Barth, *The Resurrection of the Dead* (hereafter *RD*), trans. by H. J. Stenning, (New York: Arno Press, 1977; Fleming H. Revell Company, 1933).

and unique revelatory event in which Jesus of Nazareth was declared and known to be the Son of God. Often overlooked, however, is that fact that along with this Barth held firmly to the conviction that *the resurrection is the event, the way and the power, of the turning of Jesus Christ, in all that he had accomplished for us, to us*. Barth took the resurrection to be the transition of Jesus Christ *in nobis*. That is to say, rather than strictly as a vindicating miracle, a crossing of the boundary between time and eternity, or even as the abstract category 'revelation,' the doctrine of the resurrection for Barth has to do with the movement of Jesus Christ in the fullness of his reconciling work from the christological sphere to the sphere of other human beings.

I will therefore put forward the claim that Barth's theological development is best understood with an eye to his resolute thinking out of the gospel of Jesus Christ from this resurrection perspective. Barth believed it was from and to the foundation of the resurrection of Jesus Christ that all apostolic preaching proceeded, and he believed that responsible theological thinking would follow, with the resurrection of Jesus Christ from the dead as its centre and object. I argue that the various interpretive models put forward to date can be balanced and perhaps sharpened by the critical pressure of a view of Barth's theology as focused upon and governed by a consistent effort to reason from and to the resurrection of Jesus Christ from the dead as the singular event of the turning of the crucified Lord to others.

In broad terms, it was Barth's attention to the resurrection which brought him to an understanding of the revelation of God which could not be conceived as a function of a general relationship of time and eternity, held together in some ubiquitous and overarching continuum which embraces both realities. Rather, the revelation of God was to be understood as the unique and univocal self-revealing act of God at a particular time and place, namely, the resurrection of Jesus Christ from the dead. This meant that God could not be understood by means of universal principles, present always and everywhere, of the relation of God's eternity and human history, but rather God chose to reveal God's self exclusively in the absolutely particular event in human history known as the resurrection of Jesus Christ. It was to the mystery of the revelation of God in the resurrection that Barth continually returned in his theological thought. In it he found both the grounds for the rejection of all other points of departure for theology, and the trinitarian subject matter to which Christian theology looks and on which it stands.

Barth's initial insights can be gathered into four basic themes as regard the resurrection. The first recognizes the resurrection not only as the quintessential, but as the decisive and primordial, *self-revelation of God*. It is the paradigmatic movement of God from silence to speech. In consequence, Barth views the resurrection as *the* theological *a priori* in all his theological thought. It is the bedrock which not only turns back the spade but also constitutes the substance and reference of all that is built upon it. The second theme has to do with *the ineradicable particularity of the resurrection* as the resurrection of Jesus of Nazareth, whose identity as the Son of God is fully disclosed in this unparalleled datable event in human history. God reveals God's self precisely and unsurpassably as Jesus Christ, precisely and unsurpassably in the resurrection event. This christological concentration, together with its essential resurrection concentration, is characteristic of Barth's theological discourse. The third theme reflects Barth's understanding of the resurrection as *the free and unilateral movement of the crucified Lord Jesus Christ to other human beings.* In the 1924 work this takes the form of the miracle of God in raising Jesus from the dead, a creative act which completely transforms the entirety of creation. This act occurs at the point at which the tangent of God's eternity touches the circle of human history, and in so doing transforms the whole. In as much as the resurrection is the miracle of God upon Jesus Christ, it is the miracle of God upon others. The resurrection is ontically and noetically the extension of the divine act upon the crucified Jesus Christ, in and through him, to others. At this early stage, it is because Jesus crosses the boundary from God's eternity to human history in his resurrection that we have the one ineffable act of revelation affecting the whole of creation. By the time of *CD* III, the divide between heaven and earth is seen with more complete christological reference in that the division is now between Jesus Christ in his historical time from Bethlehem to Golgotha and all other times and places. The resurrection in this case speaks of the presence of Christ in the fullness of his fulfilled mission to all times and places. In *CD* IV a still further christological development may be detected in that Barth's concern is now the relation of the completed being and action of Christ to other human beings. The division in this case is depicted in terms of reconciled human being and action over against the as yet untouched anthropological sphere, that is, human being as it is in Christ over against human being as it is apart from Christ. The fourth theme underscores the resurrection as *the establishment and revelation of the relationship of the reality of Jesus Christ to the reality of other human beings.* In Barth's view, the resurrection reveals the particular unity-in-distinction which characterizes the relationship between Jesus Christ and other human beings, that is between Christ's perfect time and all other human time, and between the divine–human action in Christ and the faithful response of other persons. By attending to these early emphases in Barth's discourse on the resurrection we will attempt to discern what remains for him a constant and firm fundamental orientation on the matter. We will inquire as to how the later developments further sharpen, clarify and strengthen, or indeed, reject and replace, his original insights.

Of course, the distinction between the material development of an author's original insights and the contextual development of the same relative to differing problems and themes is without question a problematical and often an indefinite one. Therefore we will at the same time attend to the specific contexts, descriptive language and emphases of his larger tracts of resurrection material, each in its own unique setting, in an effort to elucidate in what contexts and manner Barth raises and discusses the resurrection of Jesus Christ. It is hoped that the two distinct lines of inquiry – the one regarding Barth's more persistent resurrection themes and the other regarding the specific manner in which he develops the matter in each instance – will provide sufficiently offsetting angles of approach so as to provide a balanced and fair representation of the whole. It is hoped that this investigation will provide not only a full and accurate depiction of Barth's understanding of the resurrection of Jesus Christ, but also offer some helpful insights into the manner in which Barth's thinking matured, and perhaps even supply some orientation as to how this theme might have influenced Barth's development of other theological matters had he been granted time and energy to pursue them.

Particularly in his early work Barth has been accused of espousing such a *diastasis* between the Creator and creation that any meeting of the knowledge of the creature with that of the Creator is impossible. His thought has been described variously as 'a deobjectification of theological statements and a surrender of this-worldly reality, into the supraterrestrial and suprahistorical world of transcendence',[10] as an 'ultra-realism' with all the character of *Heilsgechichte*,[11] or even as a form of historical skepticism.[12] Indeed, the view that Barth's understanding differed little from Bultmann's seems almost unshakeable.[13]

Yet the particular divine–human historicality of the resurrection served an important purpose for the early Barth as he attempted to free himself from the psychologism and historicism of Liberal Protestantism. Christian faith was not primarily to be derived from religious feeling as it was for Schleiermacher. Nor could it be reduced to the moral teachings of Jesus as it was for Barth's teacher Wilhelm Hermann. Nor could the Jesus of history be abstracted from the Christ of faith as it was for Ernst Troeltsch. Rather Christianity was founded upon the resurrection of Jesus Christ as the free and real act of God in history and upon history. This decisive and unique action of God in the resurrection of Jesus Christ, breaking into and transforming the sphere of human history and action, was, for Barth, the great offence and stumbling block for liberal theology, as well as the fundamental content of Christian life and witness.

The resurrection of Jesus Christ for Barth in his *The Resurrection of the Dead* has to do with the transition, the crossing of the infinite gulf, from God's eternity to human history – but a transition which involves not merely an entrance into the stream of history (as might be said of the virgin birth) but also a decisive transformation of the whole of historical reality. Whereas the incarnation embraces the particular history of Jesus Christ from Bethlehem to Golgotha, the resurrection is the reality of Jesus Christ which includes and affects all history and every historical moment. The resurrection of Jesus Christ is the event of existential import for every other human being. Apart from this transition there is no sure and reliable revelation of God to humankind. Religion and even the Christian witness is pitilessly nothing more than the dream of human wishes, and the whole of the theological enterprise falls to

---

10   Klaus Bockmuehl, *The Unreal God of Modern Theology*, trans. by Geoffrey W. Bromiley (Colorado Springs: Helmers & Howard, 1988), pp. 78–9. Cf. also pp. 80–106.

11   Richard R. Niebuhr, *Resurrection and Historical Reason* (New York: Scribner's Press, 1957), p. 87.

12   Peter Carnley, *The Structure of Resurrection Belief* (Oxford: Clarendon Press, 1987), p. 100.

13   N.T. Wright, *Jesus and the Victory of God* (Minneapolis: Fortress Press, 1996), pp. 4, 22.

the Feuerbachian critique as being nothing more than a pretence – anthropology in theological guise.

Common among the many interpretations of Karl Barth's later theology is the proper judgment that the defining feature of his massive and manifold discourse, especially as it finds expression in the *Church Dogmatics*, is its 'christological concentration.'[14] That is, the fundamental theme of Barth's theological reflection, even with respect to issues such as history, hermeneutics and theological method, is christology. This christological concentration finds great impetus in his embrace in the mid-1920s of an anhypostatic–enhypostatic christology, and later in his development of the doctrine of election (*CD* II), as Barth works out his more precise understanding of the inclusion of other human beings in the being of Jesus Christ. As his work unfolds he comes to the focal centre of his christocentric theology is his doctrine of reconciliation, which he develops most extensively and explicitly in volume IV of the *Church Dogmatics*. Indeed, Barth himself was not adverse to such a characterization of his work.[15]

But we may specify even further. At the heart of Barth's doctrine of reconciliation is the being and action of Jesus Christ – *extra nos, pro nobis* and *in nobis* – in his crucifixion and resurrection. Distinctive of Barth is his depiction of the supreme ontological weight of the divine–human action of Jesus Christ from Bethlehem to Golgotha. Though this is a theme which takes on increasing definition in the *Church Dogmatics*, it is clearly present in Barth's resurrection material as early as *The Resurrection of the Dead*. So strong is his position on this matter that some have accused him of finally removing the place of other human beings altogether. It is Barth's understanding of the resurrection which begins to address this significant

---

14   For instance, Hans Urs von Balthasar, *The Theology of Karl Barth*, trans. by Edward T. Oakes, S. J. (San Francisco: Ignatius Press, 1992), pp. 37f., 198–200; G. C. Berkouwer, *The Triumph of Grace in the Theology of Karl Barth* (London: The Pasternoster Press, 1956), p. 123; Eberhard Jüngel, *Karl Barth: A Theological Legacy*, trans. by Garrett E. Paul (Philadelphia: The Westminster Press, 1986), p. 50; John Macquarrie, *Jesus Christ in Modern Thought* (Philadelphia: Trinity Press International, 1990), p. 285; Joseph L. Mangina, *Karl Barth: Theologian of Christian Witness* (Louisville: Westminster John Knox Press, 2004), pp. 115–42; Bruce McCormack, *Karl Barth's Critically Realistic Dialectical Theology* (Oxford: Clarendon Press, 1995), p. 22; Alister E. McGrath, *Christian Theology: An Introduction* (Oxford: Blackwell Publishers, 1994, 1997), pp. 265f.; Philip J. Rosato, *The Spirit as Lord* (Edinburgh: T. & T. Clark Ltd., 1981), pp. 3ff.; Stephen W. Sykes, 'Barth on the Centre of Theology' in *Karl Barth: Studies of his Theological Method* (Clarendon Press: Oxford, 1979), pp. 33–42. Thomas F. Torrance, *Karl Barth: Biblical and Evangelical Theologian* (Edinburgh: T & T Clark, 1990), pp. 20–24, 71f.; John Webster, *Barth's Ethics of Reconciliation* (Cambridge: Cambridge University Press, 1995) p. 80; *Barth's Moral Theology: Human Action in Barth's Thought* (Grand Rapids: William B. Eerdmans Publishing Company, 1998), pp. 127, 131; *Karl Barth*, Second Edition (New York: Continuum, 2000, 2004), pp. 114–17.

15   Barth happily acknowledges that 'the christological section' of the second part-volume of his *Doctrine of Reconciliation* 'stands at the head and contains the whole *in nuce*' (*CD* IV/2, p. x.).

question of the reality of other human being and action in face of the all-encompassing reality of the being and action of Jesus Christ.

This is a pivotal point of Barth's theological discourse, for if he fails to account adequately for this turn from the crucified Lord to others, he inexorably falls to the charge of which he is so frequently accused, namely, of espousing such a comprehensive view of the being and action of Jesus Christ that all other genuine human existence is necessarily excluded. Furthermore the whole of his soteriology, pneumatology, harmartiology, ecclesiology, ethics and eschatology collapses, resting as it does upon this essential transition. Barth's doctrine of the resurrection is in large measure an explication of how this transition from Jesus Christ to us is made effectively in his resurrection.

In the resurrection of Jesus Christ from the dead God has elected not to permit the fullness of reconciliation to remain distant and concealed from us, but rather he has revealed himself fully and freely. In his self-revelation, the crucified yet risen Lord has drawn near to us, revealing in himself our own true selves. Included in his self-revelation is his inalienable relatedness to us, into which we are caught up and by which we are transformed. The subjective side of reconciliation is already accomplished and guaranteed in its objective achievement; its noetic aspect rooted and upheld in its ontic aspect. Or better, both are held together in the one eternal existence of the risen Jesus Christ. Barth discovers that the real problem is not the philosophical or external dualities so often cited, but a matter inherent in the reconciling being and action of Jesus Christ. Accordingly, Barth rejects all generally derived schemes and replaces them with the scandal of the gospel, that is, with the ontological depth of the person and work of Jesus Christ for others. Furthermore, it follows that if the real problem of how it stands with God and human beings is to be understood in terms of the reconciling being and action of Jesus Christ, the solution to the problem also lay there. Barth understands the resurrection as the revelation of the reconciling work of Jesus Christ, the drawing near of the One who infinitely distanced and concealed himself from others. The issue is neither the gap of historical or existential distance, nor the separation of the objective and subjective poles of human knowing, nor even the division between divinity and humanity. The real problematic, in Barth's view, is the distance between Jesus Christ in his completed work and others in their contrary and alien anthropological sphere. Hence Barth's understanding of the resurrection of Jesus Christ is to be described not as the solution of a philosophical problem, but as the way of the crucified Lord *pro nobis* in his decisive movement to others.

The resurrection of Jesus Christ is indeed of axiomatic significance in Barth's theological understanding, yet a clear grasp of its nature and scope continues to find little expression in scholarly literature. This book attempts to address this deficiency by providing a sustained analysis of Barth's doctrine of the resurrection of Jesus Christ. For Barth the resurrection of Jesus Christ is the reality, revelation and power of the crucified Lord *in nobis*; it is his free and gracious turning, in the fullness of his completed being and act, to us, to our situation, mediating and guaranteeing our reconciliation, as he renders himself present and known. It constitutes and marks the transition from the objective accomplishment of reconciliation in the incarnation of Jesus Christ to its subjective apprehension in our anthropological sphere. The resurrection is the reality, sign and promise of the movement of the risen Christ from his narrower christological sphere to our anthropological sphere. It is his traversing of the expanse from his remote place, infinitely distant from our existence *hic et nunc*, to this opposed and contradictory human sphere. No longer concealed, he is revealed; no longer historically removed, he is contemporary; no longer absent, he is present; no longer without effect in our sphere, he brings radical and irreversible transformation.

The question of Barth's understanding of the doctrine of the resurrection is a crucial one, not only in and of itself but for its place of importance in Barth's map of the theological field. In consequence our apprehension and appreciation of Barth's doctrine of the resurrection will greatly affect and enhance our understanding of Barth's theological discourse as a whole. Five primary discussions of the resurrection fill out Barth's view as it is developed throughout his academic career. Specifically these are: *The Resurrection of the Dead*; *CD* III/2, §47.1, 'Jesus, Lord of Time'; *CD* IV/1, §59.3, 'The Verdict of the Father'; *CD* IV/2, §64.4, 'The Direction of the Son'; and *CD* IV/3, §69.4, 'The Promise of the Spirit'. In a discussion of each of these focused discourses I will attempt to draw out both the essential and consistent features of Barth's understanding of the resurrection and his development of these in the course of his publishing career.

The exposition proceeds in the following manner. The first chapter provides an analytical survey of much of the important commentary on Barth's doctrine of the resurrection to date. I shall furthermore attempt to demonstrate my claim that the complexity and importance of Barth's doctrine of the resurrection has not been sufficiently appreciated in much of the scholarly literature on the subject.

The second chapter will look at Barth's 1924 work, *The Resurrection of the Dead*, in an effort to isolate both the key concepts of his early understanding and the context in which they are developed. *The Resurrection of the Dead* (written in the summer of 1923) takes up the task of understanding Paul's Corinthian correspondence as primarily a resurrection discourse.

The third chapter moves on to Barth's discussion of the resurrection in *CD* III/2 as the appearance of Jesus of Nazareth in the mode of God. While the resurrection of Jesus Christ from the dead is by no means the only object of Barth's theological vision, it is the event of radical revelation, the act which declares the identity of Jesus as the Son of God, and which with this primordial revelation unveils and illumines the whole of the theological field, and therefore the whole of the history of God and the world. As such it is the *noetic* centre, and, if not the *material* centre, at least the *logical* point of departure and controlling element with which all further theological reflection must be congruent. Barth's exposition takes the form of an explication of Jesus Christ as the Lord of history, who in the power of his resurrection renders himself present and contemporaneous in each and every time and place.

The fourth chapter consists of an analysis of the context of Barth's explicit discussion of the resurrection of Jesus Christ in the fourth volume of the *Church*

Dogmatics. This material looks at the problem of the transition from Christ to others in rather formal terms, focusing primarily on the crucifixion–resurrection relationship. The question of transition for Barth follows upon the *dogmatic* conclusions of his development of the saving work of Jesus Christ *extra nos* and *pro nobis* beginning at Bethlehem and culminating definitively at Golgotha. The pressing question for Barth is, given the supreme ontological weight and inclusiveness of the work of Jesus Christ, how can there be any other human being and action beyond this? Barth's answer is that this is precisely what is secured in the resurrection of Jesus. It is the transition which includes the noetic revelation (with all the force of a divine ontic) of the work of Jesus Christ.

A detailed exposition of the substantial discussion of the resurrection in *CD* IV/1 comprises the fifth chapter. In this chapter we undertake a sustained analysis of Barth's development of the doctrine of the resurrection of Jesus Christ from the dead, understanding it as the 'real' beyond of the crucifixion and death of Jesus Christ. The resurrection of Jesus Christ from the dead is for Barth a supremely real event. Barth accordingly develops his doctrine of the resurrection by taking it, *de facto*, as a given and present reality, a thing of a class all its own, and reading off of it its characteristic features. Barth furthermore underscores the primordiality of resurrection revelation. As a pure act of God it is the primal form and content of revelation. In the resurrection of Jesus Christ the man Jesus is revealed to be the Christ, the Son of the living God; it is the unveiling of the existential unity of Jesus of Nazareth and the second person of the Trinity. As such the resurrection is the scandal of the gospel. More than merely the *datum* of the coincidence of the humiliation and exaltation of Jesus Christ, the resurrection is his self-revelation.

The sixth chapter follows with a detailed exposition of Barth's resurrection material in *CD* IV/2, in which he deals predominantly with the Spirit of the Lord as the power of this transition.[16] Barth develops the doctrine of the resurrection as the inauguration of the radical presence of the new human being in Jesus Christ in the power of the Holy Spirit. That is to say, Jesus Christ in the completed work of reconciliation does not require to be made real and present and pertinent; by virtue of his resurrection he already is this in the most radical way. It is in the power of the Spirit of the Lord that the transition to the free subjective apprehension of the reconciliation already secured in Christ is accomplished. The truth of the reconciling being and action of Jesus Christ presses for subjectivization in other human beings. From this it is to be noted that the problem of the transition has its original form and basis in the triune being of God. The problem of the transition between the existence of the one man Jesus and all other men and women has its antecedent in the relation of the Son to the Father in the Holy Spirit. It is on the basis of the revelation of God in Jesus Christ as the Crucified turns and moves out to others in the power of his

---

16   William Stacy Johnson describes this section as 'one of the most important sections on the Spirit in the whole *CD*', *The Mystery of God: Karl Barth and the Postmodern Foundations of Theology* (Louisville: Westminster John Knox Press, 1997), p. 119.

Holy Spirit that we begin to understand the inner relations of the divine being, says Barth.

The seventh chapter focuses upon Barth's resurrection discourse in IV/3 in which he develops his understanding of the transcending glory of the resurrected one. Barth reiterates his conviction that the resurrection is the first of the three forms of the *parousia*, the one coming again and self-revealing of Jesus Christ. It is then the irrevocable self-declaration of God in Jesus Christ, in which the Father has acknowledged the reconciling being and action of the Son, and hence, has publicly sworn his fidelity, completely and unreservedly, to human persons. It has become a link in the chain of cosmic occurrence, for it is not merely a public proclamation but also a public impartation of reconciliation. Barth also treats of the resurrection as the absolutely new coming of the very one who came before, and with him, the concretely real presence of the future of salvation. He poses the question of the possibility of a post-Easter history, given the rendering present of the world's future in the resurrection. He answers with an explication of the immeasurable power of the glory of the risen one, who chooses to delay his final *parousia* in order to provide opportunity for human beings to engage in free, active and meaningful obedience.

It will be necessary also to bring some critique to Barth's understanding of the resurrection, in an eighth chapter, along a few important lines. Beginning with an explication of the ambiguity resulting from Barth's insufficiently distinct usage of *Auferweckung* and *Auferstehung*, we shall move on to a few corrective proposals regarding the ontological and salvific nature of the resurrection event, and the implications of this for Barth's understanding of the Trinity, of the faith of Jesus in the Father at the time of death, of the nature of the destruction of death, of the once-and-for-all nature of the passage from death to life, and of the essential distinction of the resurrection and the Holy Spirit. We shall now begin with a brief analytical survey of the primary efforts to date to bring Barth's understanding of the resurrection to light.

Chapter One

The Eclipse of the Resurrection

It has long been suggested by commentators that the doctrine of the resurrection held a formative place in Barth's theological understanding. According to T.F. Torrance, Barth spoke of 'the bodily resurrection of Jesus as the starting and controlling point of all his biblical and theological thought.'[1] Torrance claims, 'it was ... an essential element in [Barth's] teaching that our understanding of divine revelation should begin with the resurrection of Jesus Christ from the dead, for it is from that revealing centre that the whole evangelical account of Jesus Christ is to be understood.'[2] Furthermore, '[the resurrection] constituted the absolutely decisive event in space and time on which he took his stand and from which he took his bearings.'[3] With 'the risen Christ' asserts David Ford, we face 'the fundamental challenge of Barth's theology.'[4] Likewise, Eberhard Jüngel asserts that the 'transitional concepts' of the doctrine of reconciliation, which deal with the matter of the resurrection, are 'determinative for the Christology' and they 'open the way to soteriology' in as much as they denote the establishment of an ontological link between the man Jesus and all other men.[5] For Barth, 'true knowledge of God and Christ is rooted in the power of the resurrection and results from being drawn into the eschatological presence of God by the power of the Spirit,' avers Ingolf Dalfert.[6] Similarly John Thompson, following Berthold Klappert, joins the chorus in identifying 'the cross and resurrection' as 'the centre from which Barth starts out to view the whole.'[7] Again, 'The resurrection is supremely important and central to Barth's whole *Church Dogmatics*.'[8]

Despite such a general appreciation of the significance of the doctrine in Barth's overall theological understanding, strikingly little attempt has been made to understand

---

1   T.F. Torrance, *Karl Barth: Biblical and Evangelical Theologian* (Edinburgh: T. & T. Clark, 1990), p. 110. Cf. also pp. 164–7. (Hereafter: *Biblical*).

2   Ibid., p. 106.

3   Ibid., p. 164. Cf. also T.F. Torrance, *Space, Time and Resurrection*, (Edinburgh: The Handsel Press Ltd, 1976), p. x.

4   David Ford, *Barth and God's Story: Biblical Narrative and the Theological Method of Karl Barth in the 'Church Dogmatics'* (Frankfurt am Main: Lang, 1981), p. 84.

5   Eberhard Jüngel, *Karl Barth: A Theological Legacy*, trans. by Paul E. Garrett (Philadelphia: The Westminster Press, 1986), p. 50.

6   Ingolf Dalfert, 'Karl Barth's eschatological realism' in Stephen W. Sykes, ed., *Karl Barth: Centenary Essays* (Cambridge: Cambridge University Press, 1989), p. 22.

7   John Thompson, *The Holy Spirit in the Theology of Karl Barth* (Oxford: Oxford University Press, 1991), p. 72.

8   Ibid., p. 73.

its radical systematic significance. Few interpreters have taken at face value Barth's assertions regarding the centrality of the resurrection of Jesus Christ for his thinking. While the dominant primers routinely indicate the great significance of the doctrine, little is done to unpack its nature and shape or to explicate its place and function in the context of Barth's overall theological contribution. This is particularly true with respect to Barth's early commentary on Paul's First Epistle to the Corinthians, *The Resurrection of the Dead*, to which only a handful of interpreters refer. Likewise the important developments of the resurrection material in *CD* IV/2 and IV/3, remaining largely unknown, have not to date received satisfactory explication. Greater though still inadequate attention has been given to the portions of Barth's writings concerned with the question of the resurrection as an historical event, and hence with the question of the relation of historical science to the object of theology. In this regard commentators generally concentrate upon the earlier writings, the masterful handling of the question in his debate with Bultmann in *CD* III/2 §47.1, and to a limited degree in *CD* IV/1. However, the themes of the later material are crucial for an appropriate appreciation of the pregnant insights of the earlier material. Given the magnitude of the importance of the theme for Barth and the lack of attention given it by many interpreters, the need for clarification concerning the centrality and meaning of Barth's comprehension of the resurrection becomes obvious.

The problem is compounded by the fact that much of the scholarly inquiry into this theme appears to be guided by interests quite foreign to it. Often the line of questioning is limited to historical or hermeneutical issues, which are simply inadequate to the scope and depth of Barth's depiction. As a result Barth is often wrongly classified as a proponent of some form of *Heilsgeschichte*, or as an historical skeptic in the vein of Rudolf Bultmann, from whom Barth clearly distinguished himself. Alternately, some locate Barth among those whose concern it is to address the philosophical problem of existential relevance, or of the separation of subject and object, or of the general theological problem of the infinite qualitative difference of divinity and humanity. Few if any grant sufficient attention to Barth's understanding of the fundamental problem of the gospel – that the same Jesus Christ who has acted definitively as representative and saviour of all men and women is risen and present.

Of equally great concern is the slim account given of the radical systematic significance of the doctrine of the resurrection in Barth's thought. Few acknowledge, let alone expound, the pivotal importance of Barth's understanding of the resurrection as the decisive link between christology and soteriology. Consequently, little effort is made to explore the relevance of the resurrection for Barth's conception of the relation of Jesus Christ to others. No one, it would appear, attempts to develop at length Barth's doctrine of the resurrection as the turning of the crucified Lord to others. Barth's appreciation of the radical severity of the death of human creaturely existence in the death of Jesus Christ and of the astonishing reality of the effective transition of reconciled being and action from Jesus Christ to others in his resurrection is often treated as an odd and inessential digression in Barth's otherwise tight and integrated exposition. The significance which Barth clearly sees in the resurrection for the possibility of other genuine human being and action vis-à-vis the all-determining reality of the history of Jesus Christ is often overlooked, and, hence, allows for the perpetuation of the understanding that Barth's christology has erred on the side of christomonism. Another theological stone left largely unturned has to do with the influence of the resurrection upon Barth's understanding of the incarnation, yet our crucial understanding of the coherence of the divine and human in Jesus Christ comes only as an implication of resurrection revelation. As much can be said also of the import of the resurrection for Barth's development of the doctrine of revelation. Little is written on the importance of the resurrection in Barth's construal of revelation, yet for Barth, the resurrection of Jesus Christ is the primordial form of revelation, in which God reveals himself and in so doing reveals the identity of Jesus Christ, the identity and function of the Holy Spirit, the inner being of the immanent Trinity, as well as the reality and achievement of reconciliation on the cross. Again, it must be noted that the systematic significance of the doctrine of the resurrection for Barth's eschatology has yet to be developed in detail. Barth's construal of the resurrection as the first and proper form of the *parousia* is of immense importance and must not be overlooked. Still further, the relationship of the resurrection reality to the prophetic ministry of Jesus Christ, while a theme of great weight, has gone relatively unnoticed. These shortcomings and others in earlier depictions of Barth's theology of the resurrection can be addressed only in a thorough-going exposition of the rich resurrection materials Barth has supplied us.

A large number of analyses come up short by dwelling upon the historical question, often falsely construing Barth's inversion of the order of the historical enterprise and the resurrection of Jesus as an aspect of his historical skepticism.[9] For Barth the resurrection of Jesus is not a *datum* of the sort to be analyzed and understood, as other data, by means of historical critical science. While a real event within the nexus of space and time the resurrection is also the event of the creation of new time and space. Such an event can only be described as an act of God; that is, an otherwise impossible event. The event of the resurrection of Jesus is that of the creation of the conditions of the possibility for all other events, and as such it cannot be accounted for in terms considered appropriate for all other events. This is not the expression of an historical skeptic, but of one who is convinced of the primordiality of the resurrection as the singular, history-making, yet history-delimiting, act of God.

Among those who see Barth's view of the resurrection as an expression of historical skepticism is Peter Carnley.[10] It is his view that the basic historical presuppositions of Barth (and Bultmann) are in error. That is, according to

---

9　Advocates of the view that Barth sharply distinguishes human history (*Historie*) from divine history (*Geschichte* or *Heils-gechichte*), and offers us no real hope of bringing the two together, are many, but among the more significant are Gerald O'Collins, Daniel Fuller, R.R. Niebuhr, and Peter Carnley.

10　Peter Carnley, *The Structure of Resurrection Belief* (Oxford: Clarendon Press, 1987).

Carnley, the permanent insecurity of all historiographical judgments of the life of the historical Jesus is logically erroneous. And thus the strictures of Barth, which, according to Carnley, suggest that the results of the critical-historical procedures cannot be dogmatically significant, are also erroneous. Carnley understands Barth's development of the resurrection as 'essentially a supra-historical occurrence of eternity which only impinges on history where it is glimpsed in faith by time-bound, historically conditioned people.'[11] Carnley believes that the emphasis of Barth is theologically sterile and unproductive. That is not to say that he sees no redeeming features in Barth's work – he applauds Barth's conception of the resurrection as a revelatory and salvific event – but he gives little attention to Barth's development of these crucial notions. Not only has Carnley overlooked the important differences between Barth and Bultmann, but also he has permitted the historical skepticism of Bultmann to so inform his understanding of Barth that the significant advance Barth has made to this very question has been almost entirely ignored.

Another, more engaging, critique of Barth along these lines is that of Richard R. Niebuhr, who offers an insightful exposition of Barth's view. Niebuhr praises Barth's 'realism' and agrees with his criticism of modern theology for its destruction of 'the natural side of biblical revelation.' He likewise concurs that 'Literary and historical criticism have in fact tended to empty *body, flesh, death* and *resurrection* of their meaning and so purge revelation of all realism.'[12] He demonstrates keen insight in making the claim that the 'univocal relationship between revelation-history and general history, on the one hand, and between Jesus Christ and all other historical agents, on the other, is the determinative influence in Barth's handling of the resurrection texts.'[13] So, too, Niebuhr is justified in asserting that 'The knowledge furnished by revelation transcends all ordinary knowledge of objects or historical events and does not naturally complement the other faculties of created human nature'[14] and that 'the special history of the incarnation of the Word in Christ Jesus is not a part of history in general, but all other history is a predicate of this revelation-history, which is a history constituted wholly and exclusively by the single acting subject, God in Christ,'[15] so long as we understand Barth also to mean, by the incarnation of the Word, a truly historical reality. But because Niebuhr takes Barth to mean the resurrection is not a part of history at all, he wrongly concludes that Barth 'is forced to extrude the resurrection event from the sequence that anchors it in the New Testament, and to say of the "Easter history" that it tells us of the eternal presence of God in time, and therefore it has no eschatological significance.'[16] Quite to the contrary, as we shall see in our discussion of *CD* IV/3,

---

11   Ibid., p. 100

12   Richard R. Niebuhr, *Resurrection and Historical Reason* (New York: Scribner's Press, 1957), p. 45.

13   Ibid., p. 47.

14   Ibid.

15   Ibid.

16   Ibid.

Barth's view of the resurrection implies quite a robust eschatology, which preserves the biblical notions both of the last days and the end of history in which they are consummated. Again, Niebuhr correctly observes that for Barth 'the resurrection event ... raises no questions it cannot answer itself,' but wrongly concludes this to mean 'The resurrection has been construed as the summing-up, the timeless instant of recognition, and so, as the antithesis of the historically real.'[17] Yet, we must note for Barth the resurrection of Jesus is unquestionably an historically real event at the same time as it is the originating and defining historical event. The resurrection is precisely the point at which both history and sacred history and their relation are unequivocally revealed.

Niebuhr further misrepresents Barth by claiming that he rejected the need for a scientific or independent theological method and 'has weakened the reality of the very biblical history he set out to exalt by his emphasis on the unreality of the problems that beset us as we try to accomodate (*sic*) the history of Jesus Christ to our own historical experience.'[18] Such a portrayal obscures Barth's claim that the resurrection itself is the event of revelation in which God fully discloses himself (and our new human being in him) in real, historical and personal encounter and empowers others to embrace their reconciled being in him. In other words Niebuhr appears to reject Barth's claim that the problem of the transition from Christ to others encompasses the problem of the historical and existential distance between Christ and others, and that the resurrection is precisely the answer to this problem. Niebuhr continues to criticize Barth for his 'ultra-realism' as regards the resurrection, seeing it as conforming to the specifications of *Heilsgechichte* even though he acknowledges Barth's rejection of the term.[19]

Evidently taking his cues from selective earlier texts (that is, *CD* III/2) to the exclusion of others, Niebuhr takes the view that Barth treats the resurrection as belonging to a wholly transcendent history without any of the contingency of our time. On Niebuhr's account:

> The inability of Protestant theology to see even a shadow of historicity in the tradition of apostolic resurrection is sufficient comment in itself on the limited insight into its own resources allowed to us by the canons of post-Cartesian reason. As a pure ideal without any content, the resurrection of Christ stands in the realm of sacred history, symbolizing the unattainable limit of human experience, touching 'the old world of the flesh ... as a tangent touches a circle, that is, without touching it.'[20]

Barth's 'monolithic realism'[21] has an inherent 'crippling disadvantage,' avers Niebuhr, namely that 'it can have no content because it belongs to the domain of

---

17   Ibid., p. 48.
18   Ibid., p. 50.
19   Ibid., p. 86.
20   Ibid., p. 88.
21   Ibid., p. 50.

practical reason.'[22] Hence 'contingency' is necessarily ruled out, and we are left with the unsatisfactory conclusion that revelation history permits 'no possibility of noetic response to God.'[23] Niebuhr can summarize Barth's theological discourse on resurrection as an exercise in 'spelling out the inherent limits of practical reason, as it is employed in theology.'[24] He explains:

> The impasse into which Protestant theology has come through its efforts to give significance to the resurrection tradition shows that the dogma of pure reason does not have sufficient resources to give Protestantism that kind of knowledge of Christian origins that its life and doctrine require. The resurrection tradition reveals the inherent incapacity of theoretical and practical reason to provide principles for the interpretation of history. Each of these faculties tries to reduce history to an abstraction, to the status of nature as a self-contained system, or to the rank of Absolute Spirit or Meaning.[25]

Hence Niebuhr concludes:

> Barth's treatment of the resurrection as belonging to a wholly transcendent history or 'perfect time' means that he has to disparage the entire issue of the church's standpoint in the revelation-history of which the resurrection is the center. He solves the problem by severing the connection between revelation and history.[26]

All the while one gets the feeling that while Niebuhr appears to grasp Barth's insistence upon the noetic priority of resurrection revelation, yet he understands this to trade upon the employment of a limit concept devoid of any real historical content. Barth, of course, insists that the resurrection of Jesus is an historical reality at the same time as it is the revelation of the limit of created reality. Yet for Niebuhr this appears to supply insufficient content to satisfy the requirements of a genuine knowledge of Christian origins. It is unlikely that even Barth's later writings, in which the full incarnation reality of Jesus Christ is understood to be taken up and made present to all time in his resurrection, would satisfy Niebuhr's demand for content; content, for Niebuhr it would seem, requires something of continuity between the resurrection reality and the realm of world-history as we know it. This continuity is precisely what Barth's understanding of the resurrection rejects.

Though more cogent than most, Niebuhr's challenge overlooks the dogmatic character of Barth's discourse, and seems not to appreciate Barth's view of the resurrection as precisely that for which he calls:

> The antinomy of the resurrection in particular suggests the need of a critique of historical reason, a reason that will not seek the possibility of biblical history in the conditions

---

22   Ibid., p. 86.
23   Ibid.
24   Ibid.
25   Ibid., pp. 88f.
26   Ibid., p. 96.

of natural science or idealistic metaphysics but rather in the answer to the distinctive question, how do we know historical events.[27]

Barth's doctrine of the resurrection is his specific development of the question of the transition from the perfect reality of Jesus Christ to others. It is this aspect of Barth's understanding of the resurrection that must be brought into full relief and acknowledged if we are to press toward a genuine grasp of Barth's theological thought and development.

Beyond these analyses preoccupied with and at times obscured by historical and hermeneutical questions are the more theological analyses of Barth's doctrine of the resurrection. These, by and large, are more appreciative of the theological implications in their understanding and representation of Barth, though few seem to articulate clearly the fundamental dogmatic issue Barth addresses in his development of the doctrine. Once again, this is true throughout, but especially of the later tracts of resurrection material in the *Church Dogmatics*.[28]

G.C. Berkouwer refers to Barth's doctrine of resurrection in the context of a discussion of the relationship of the doctrine of the two states. Berkouwer correctly understands Barth to say that the deity of Christ is the noetic principle for understanding the identity of God.[29] According to Berkouwer 'Barth's fundamental idea in his doctrine of reconciliation is that God's glory is revealed *in* the humiliation, His power *in* weakness, His life *in* death.'[30] However, Berkouwer disagrees claiming that the revealed glory of the incarnate Word 'nowhere in the New Testament leads to an obscuring of the decisive transition from humiliation to exaltation which took place at the resurrection.'[31] Berkouwer's rejection of Barth here is based upon his understanding that the temporal aspect of the transition from humiliation to exaltation is disregarded.[32] For Berkouwer the transition from crucifixion to resurrection can be nothing other than the temporal transition from humiliation to glorification:

27　Ibid., p. 89.

28　Perhaps one of the more theologically stimulating accounts of the resurrection is that in Walter Künneth's *The Theology of the Resurrection*. Künneth's book is a major work of a strongly theological character. But because it attends to the dialectical tensions in the early Barth to the near exclusion of the notion of the resurrection as the real crossing of this boundary, it likewise can claim comprehensive understanding neither of his early nor his mature thought.

29　G.C. Berkouwer, *The Triumph of Grace in the Theology of Karl Barth* (London: The Paternoster Press, 1956), p. 314.

30　Ibid.

31　Ibid., p. 315.

32　T.F. Torrance, in *Space, Time and Resurrection* (Edinburgh: Handsel Press, 1976) and Douglas Farrow (*Ascension and Ecclesia: On the Significance of the Doctrine of the Ascension for Ecclesiology and Christian Cosmology* (Edinburgh: T. & T. Clark, 1999), each in their own way, criticize Barth along similar lines. For a thorough and helpful account see Andrew Burgess, *The Ascension in Karl Barth* (Aldershot: Ashgate Publishing Limited, 2004).

When this transition is obscured all that we can still speak of on the score of Christ's exaltation is the 'unveiling' of the *previously existing* divine glory. Thinking consistently in this line would require that we see already in the time of His humiliation the presence of His unlimited power and life. This would mean losing from sight, however, the full emphasis which the New Testament places on the *temporal* aspect involved in the progression from humiliation to exaltation. It is precisely this emphasis which Barth's intertwining of Christ's natures with states is not able fully to honor.[33]

Berkouwer proceeds to challenge Barth on exegetical grounds from the Gospel of Luke, from the letter to the Philippians and from Peter's first epistle. His account, however, does not do justice to Barth's thought. First, on a strictly exegetical level, given the strong New Testament, particularly Johannine, emphasis upon the glorification of Jesus Christ on the cross, Berkouwer's exegetical challenge to the simultaneity of the humiliation and exaltation of Jesus Christ is at best tenuous.[34] And what is more, Barth more than adequately honours the temporal aspect of the transition from crucifixion to resurrection with his understanding of the resurrection as the new and gracious act of God which follows the crucifixion in chronological sequence. One wishes at this point that Berkouwer had developed in greater detail his earlier, seemingly more sympathetic, understanding of Barth's doctrine of the resurrection: 'Justification may not be seen exclusively as an action that is related to the cross, of whose meaning the resurrection is only a sign. The resurrection is, rather, a *new* deed of God, 'and therefore not merely the noetic reverse side of justification. (*KD* p. 335)'[35] And again: 'Our concern is not only with Christ who was crucified in the past, but with the Crucified One and the Risen One who now lives.'[36] Second, on a theological level, Berkouwer discounts the seriousness with which Barth takes the radical severity of the death of Jesus Christ as the representative of all human persons, and hence he undervalues the temporal transition from crucifixion to resurrection, fully honoured by Barth in the transition from Jesus Christ to others. The matter which Barth sees resolved in the resurrection is not primarily that of the temporal transition of Jesus Christ from the state of humiliation to exaltation, but of the possibility of any future whatsoever in light of the supremely determinative reality of the death of Jesus Christ for us and us in him. The theological contribution of Barth's doctrine of the resurrection can neither be understood nor overturned simply

---

33   Berkouwer, *The Triumph of Grace in the Theology of Karl Barth*, p. 315.

34   I agree with Berkouwer that there is a challenge to be made to Barth on this point, but it is not so much a challenge to the simultaneity of the humiliation and exaltation of Jesus Christ, but to the co-termination of the humiliation and exaltation of Jesus Christ in his crucifixion and death. I wish to argue that the fact that the humiliation of God comes to its culmination at the cross does not necessarily imply that the exaltation of the new human being in Jesus Christ shares the same *terminus*. Even with the Johannine focus on the glorification of Christ at his cross, Barth speaks far more consistently from the view of the glorification of Christ in his resurrection. We will take this up again in our final chapter.

35   Ibid., p. 137.

36   Ibid., p. 139.

on the basis of a discussion of the (non-)sequential relationship of the humiliation and exaltation of Jesus Christ.

John Macquarrie locates the theology of Karl Barth amidst the 'theological renaissance' of the early 20th-century.[37] He rightly understands Barth's objection to the humanistic approach in theology epitomized by Schleiermacher:

> It was mistaken in basing itself on human experience, because this was to overlook the fact that human nature is flawed by sin and cannot find the way to God; and it was further mistaken in its attempts to represent Jesus Christ as virtually a natural development in the history of humanity. In Barth's view, religion never gets out of human subjectivity; it is a search for God which leads only to idols fabricated by our own minds. Also, in Barth's view, Jesus Christ is so far from being the culmination of human development that he stands over against humanity in judgment as one who has been sent by God.[38]

But what Macquarrie does not appear to recognize is that Barth's rejection of Schleiermacher draws its force from his conviction of the ontological significance of the crucifixion of Jesus Christ. Jesus' death is so pervasive and final that it brings all human creatureliness – objective and subjective – to an end. Macquarrie mistakenly locates the problem in Barth's dialectical opposition of 'the otherness of God' and 'the incarnation,'[39] rather than in the wrestling to death of all human possibilities in the crucifixion of Jesus, the man for all others.

In a similar manner, while Macquarrie appreciates the importance of the theme of eschatology for Barth, he still understands it as somewhat distinct from the judgment, end and new creation of the cosmos brought about in the death and resurrection of Jesus. Says Macquarrie: 'Like Weiss and Schweitzer before him, Barth, even at his most radical, felt unable to take eschatology in quite the literal way that we suppose Jesus and Paul took it.'[40] Macquarrie incorrectly surmises that Barth meant by eschatology a message of 'crisis', but not a 'real' end of history.

Macquarrie agrees with Alister McGrath, adding that the comment is a particularly suitable description of volume IV of the *Dogmatics:* 'It is perhaps significant that Barth appears to be most at home in his dialogue with the Christology of the sixteenth and seventeenth centuries, rather than with that of the modern period.'[41] By this Macquarrie reveals that he, like McGrath, fails to appreciate Barth's trenchant theological decisions as a radical engagement with the tenets of modernity.

One rather dominant theological view of Barth's doctrine of the resurrection is that it is heavily overshadowed if not totally eclipsed by his doctrine of the incarnation. According to this view it is his doctrine of the Trinity that is understood to form the

---

37   John Macquarrie, *Jesus Christ In Modern Thought* (Philadelphia: Trinity Press International, 1990), p. 267.

38   Ibid., p. 279.

39   Ibid., p. 280.

40   Ibid.

41   Alister E. McGrath, *The Making of Modern German Christology: From the Enlightenment to Pannenberg* (Oxford: Basil Blackwell, 1986), p. 115.

fundamental assumption and structure of Barth's thought. This, too, leads if not to a skewed view, at least to an underdeveloped view of his doctrine of the resurrection, which in turn leads to other significant misunderstandings.

Wolfhart Pannenberg appears to hold this view. He depicts Barth's as a 'Christology from above' in which 'the doctrine of the trinity is presupposed.'[42] With it, says Pannenberg, goes the presupposition of the divinity of Jesus, which slights the 'most important task of christology' which is 'to present the reasons for the confession of Jesus' divinity.'[43] Pannenberg further claims that a christology which takes its point of departure 'in the concept of the incarnation' is less able to grapple with 'the determinative significance inherent in the decisive features of the real, historical man, Jesus of Nazareth.'[44] Finally Pannenberg argues that since one cannot 'stand in the position of God himself in order to follow the way of God's Son into the world' we must begin with the question about the man Jesus for 'only in this way can we ask about his divinity.'[45]

It is difficult, however, to square this account of Barth's theology with Pannenberg's later portrayal which understands the doctrine of the Trinity not as the presupposition but as the logical inference of revelation. According to Pannenberg, Barth deduces God's eternal essence from revelation.[46] 'The identity of the essence of Jesus with God claimed in the concept of God's self-revelation through Jesus has been worked out especially by Karl Barth and has been made the basis of his theology.'[47] This 'demonstration of the connection of Jesus' divinity with the concept of revelation' is, in Pannenberg's view, fundamentally right. God's eternal essence is properly deduced from the manner in which God appears in his revelation. 'Barth quite rightly has built the doctrine of Jesus' divinity and the doctrine of the Trinity on the concept of God's revelation in Jesus.'[48] Pannenberg describes this insight as 'one of Barth's greatest theological contributions.'[49] He laments, however, that, in his view, this insight 'has not affected the methodology of [Barth's] Christology.'[50]

Pannenberg's analysis would be clarified by greater attention to Barth's development of the doctrine of the resurrection, for it is there, he asserts, that primal revelation of the identity of Jesus of Nazareth and the Son of God occurs. The doctrine of the divinity of Christ and the doctrine of the Trinity are secured in the resurrection revelation. Yet as Pannenberg understands Barth, 'Jesus' resurrection is not a completely new event with its own decisive importance, but still only the

---

42   Wolfhart Pannenberg, *Jesus – God and Man*, trans. by Lewis L. Wilkins and Duane A. Priebe (Philadelphia: Westminster Press, 1964, 1968), p. 34.

43   Ibid.

44   Ibid.

45   Ibid., p. 35.

46   Ibid., p. 130.

47   Ibid.

48   Ibid.

49   Ibid.

50   Ibid.

"revelation" of Jesus' history consummated on the cross.[51] But just the opposite is the case. Barth does see the resurrection as a novel act of God, in and upon history, and with ontic force. While Pannenberg appreciates the significance of Barth's understanding of revelation as the self-revelation of God in Jesus Christ,[52] he underplays the importance of Barth's notion of the resurrection as the primordial and effective form of this revelation. Because he sees Barth's doctrine of revelation in abstraction from his doctrine of resurrection he has mistaken Barth's resurrection christology for a christology from above. A firmer grasp of Barth's treatment of the resurrection as the primordial self-revelation of God would show that Barth's christology is neither a christology from above (that is, rooted in the doctrine of the incarnation) nor a christology from below (that is, rooted in human history) but a resurrection christology in which Jesus Christ discloses himself and in so doing discloses both divine and human realities from the point of the union of the two.

Hans Urs von Balthasar's comments on Barth's theology are especially insightful and illuminating.[53] Von Balthasar identifies Barth's first and perduring flash of insight as 'his desire to create a theology, not of being but of "happening,"'[54] an insight which captivated Barth from his second *Romans* commentary on:

> If we try to generalize Barth's position and to express it in more abstract terms, we can say a few things. There is such a thing as being, and such a thing as nature; but both become valid and authentic only at the point of supreme reality. At their core, being and nature are happenings in history, so they are not being and nature in the typical sense. Reality is more happening than being, and the being of God is one with his creative willing. ... In Christ, who is the supreme happening, the being and nature and continuity of all creation finds its origin, support, and guarantee.[55]

In speaking of the overall cast of Barth's thought von Balthasar notes that 'the happening of Revelation is the most concrete reality for man.'[56]

In addition to the great importance of the *historicity* of revelation in Barth's account is the matter of the *encounter* of revelation with human persons. According to von Balthasar, the 'critical point' which 'sets the whole theological train of thought in motion' for Barth is 'man's encounter with the Word of God.'[57] Whereas a theology of being locates the prime matter of reconciliation in the event of the

---

51   Ibid., p. 127.

52   Ibid.

53   Hans Urs von Balthasar, *The Theology of Karl Barth*, translated by John Drury (New York: Holt, Rinehart and Winston, 1971).

54   Ibid., p. 47. Incidentally, von Balthasar rarely gets credit for his perceptive acknowledgment of Barth's enduring early insight, being predominantly characterized as one who played off Barth's earlier dialectical method with his later, materially distinct, analogical orientation. But closer attention to von Balthasar's emphasis on revelation as event in Barth can help in our understanding of Barth's consistency.

55   Ibid., p. 196.

56   Ibid., p. 165.

57   Ibid., p. 172.

incarnation, and a theology of happening places greatest stress upon the history of the life and crucifixion of Jesus Christ, a theology of encounter includes weighty emphasis upon the resurrection of Jesus Christ from the dead and the outpouring of his Holy Spirit. Perceptively, von Balthasar identifies the trend of Barth's thought as toward the latter. We must look then to the events of the crucifixion and resurrection for the supreme moment of the human person's encounter with God's eternal Word. According to von Balthasar:

> The point of absolute intensity essentially lies beyond the knowledge of human reason, even though it is the ground of all reasoning. It is Kant's transcendental apperception, Fichte's protoground of the ego, Schleiermacher's primeval actuality of religiously toned feeling, Hermann's personal decision of faith, and Barth's divine gift of faith to man. If our line of thought does not proceed from this absolute point and move back towards it, then it is a meaningless and empty reflection.[58]

In order to press further into what is to be understood as this 'divine gift of faith to man' we must turn once again to the themes of crucifixion and resurrection. Once again von Balthasar brings the issue into sharp focus: 'Where the German Idealists posit identity at the source point, Barth posits an encounter between two radically opposed beings: the God of grace and sinful, self-centered man.'[59]

With this perception, von Balthasar assists us greatly in approaching an understanding of the significance of Barth's doctrine of the resurrection. But von Balthasar's insight here has been overshadowed by attention to his comments on Barth's movement from dialectical to analogical theology. Sadly, even von Balthasar himself does not provide a sustained analysis demonstrating how Barth's doctrine of the resurrection addresses this fundamental question, especially as regards Barth's depiction of the particular encounter of the risen God-man Jesus with the as yet unaffected wider anthropological sphere.

Philip J. Rosato picks up this theme and develops an understanding of Barth's theology as 'pneumatocentric.'[60] Once again, Rosato is able to take the argument to such an extreme only at the cost of a balanced understanding of Barth's doctrine of the resurrection. It is Barth's understanding of the resurrection in relation to the life, crucifixion and death of Jesus that ensures the christological ground of his grasp of the Holy Spirit. Careful analysis of Barth's understanding of the resurrection will demonstrate that Barth's doctrine of the reconciliation is in no way a veiled pneumatology.[61] Barth's pneumatology, rather, is thoroughly grounded in his christology.

In his *Karl Barth: Biblical and Evangelical Theologian* Thomas F. Torrance offers an insightful and well-rounded introduction to Barth's theological thought

---

58   Ibid.
59   Ibid., p. 174.
60   Rosato, *The Spirit as Lord*, pp. 3ff.
61   Rosato's critique of Barth will be given greater attention in our discussion of Barth's pneumatology.

and legacy. In the *Church Dogmatics*, asserts Torrance, 'evangelical and reformed theology of the Word is given its fullest and most rigorous expression within the context of the development of all Christian theology in ancient and modern times.'[62] Torrance believes the distinctive character of Barth's doctrine of the Trinity is owing to his emphasis upon 'the consubstantiality of the Word and activity of God.' He takes Barth's recasting of traditional Chalcedonian christology in dynamic as well as ontological terms – resulting in an understanding of God in which God has his 'being-in-his-act and his act-in-his-being' – to be one of Barth's 'most important contributions to Christian theology.'[63] Equally highly appreciated is Barth's reclamation of the Reformation emphasis upon the Word of God as the revelation of the 'very *being* and *Person* of God.'[64] Barth's achievement lay in his unprecedented integration of 'the Reformation emphasis upon the consubstantiality of the Word with the Nicene emphasis on the consubstantiality of the Son.'[65]

> It was the genius of Karl Barth that he should combine in one both forms of this evangelical principle, thus bringing together the Greek Patristic emphasis upon the *being* of God in his saving acts and the Reformation emphasis upon the *act* of God in his being revealed to us through Christ and in the Spirit.[66]

It is interesting that despite his numerous recollections of Barth's repeated emphasis upon the bodily resurrection of Jesus Christ from the dead as the starting point for scientific theology, Torrance seems to make little of Barth's doctrine of the resurrection in connection with these momentous theological achievements. Instead, Torrance traces Barth's trenchant insight to his doctrine of the Trinity,[67] leaving us to wonder if Barth's emphasis is simply misleading or whether there may be more to Barth's resurrection perspective in these connections than has been supposed.

The analysis offered by Eberhard Jüngel notes the importance of the ontic and noetic moments in Barth's theology:

> In express opposition to the modern philosophical and theological turn to the subject and to consciousness, Barth presupposes an ontic necessity and rationality which is ontologically prior to the corresponding noetic necessity and rationality. Furthermore, he firmly anchors this ontological priority in a truth which is identical with God.[68]

Jüngel, too, has a clear grasp of the centrality and significance of Barth's understanding of the doctrine of reconciliation:

---

62   Torrance, *Biblical*, p. 163.
63   Ibid., p. 172.
64   Ibid., p. 173.
65   Ibid.
66   Ibid., p. 175.
67   Thomas F. Torrance, *Biblical*, p. 163.
68   Eberhard Jüngel, *Karl Barth, A Theological Legacy*, p. 42.

Finally, with the doctrine of reconcilation [*sic*] the *Church Dogmatics* arrived at the 'center of all Christian knowledge.' [*CD* IV/1, p. ix.] This doctrine was both a massive recapitulation and a thorough revision of Barth's entire dogmatics, broken off in the midst of the section on the ethics of the Christian life. Barth undertook this exposition of the doctrine of reconciliation as part of 'a broad and intensive ... debate with Rudolf Bultmann' [*CD* IV/1, p. ix.] and as 'an attempted Evangelical answer to the Marian dogma of Romanism.' [*CD* IV/2, p. ix.][69]

In addition, Jüngel rightly judges that for Barth: 'The resurrection of Jesus Christ is the quintessence of the time of revelation.'[70] He, furthermore, acknowledges the crucial importance of Barth's treatment of the resurrection:

The transitional concepts (judgment of the Father, direction of the Son, and the promise of the Holy Spirit) are determinative for the Christology and also open the way to the soteriology. These concepts ordain an 'ontological connection between the man Jesus on the one side and all other men on the other,' so that his work, accomplished *extra nos* and *pro nobis*, makes all human beings into 'virtual' (and not anonymous) Christians. [*CD* IV/2, p. 275][71]

However, despite Jüngel's awareness of the pivotal importance of Barth's doctrine of the resurrection, he nowhere develops this theme in detail.

Further admirable treatments are to be found in the work of David Mueller[72] and the German source upon which he is so heavily dependent. Mueller bases much of his analysis on both Bertold Klappert's more general 1967 work, *Diskussion um Kreuz und Auferstehung*[73] (which when discussing Barth focuses on his *Resurrection of the Dead* and *CD* IV/1, making little reference to Barth's later part-volumes) and his 1971 work, *Die Auferweckung des Gekreuzigten*[74] (a much more focused, subtle, and extended analysis of Barth's understanding of the cross and resurrection, though still concentrating largely upon the text of *CD* IV/1). Klappert's excellent work is, to be sure, insightful and detailed, though, in his zeal to identify the 'differentiated relationship' of the cross and resurrection as the interpretive centre of the doctrine of reconciliation, his account of the resurrection is incomplete, and consequently inaccurate, in at least two important ways. The first is his insufficient appreciation of the place and significance of the doctrine of the resurrection in relation to the whole

---

69   Ibid., p. 46.

70   Ibid., p. 44.

71   Ibid., p. 50.

72   David Mueller, *Foundation of Karl Barth's Doctrine of Reconciliation: Jesus Christ Crucified and Risen*, Vol. 54 of Toronto Studies in Theology (Lewiston/Queenston/ Lampeter: The Edwin Mellen Press, 1990).

73   Berthold Klappert, *Diskussion um Kreuz und Auferstehung*. Zur gegenwärtigen Auseinandersetzung in Theologie und Gemeinde (Wuppertal: Aussaat, 1967).

74   Berthold Klappert, *Die Auferweckung des Gekreuzigten. Der Ansatz der Christologie Karl Barths im Zusammenhang der Christologie der Gegenwart*, (Neukirchen-Vluyn: Neukirchener Verlag, 1971).

of the fourth volume of the *Church Dogmatics*. Greater attention here would help to bring out further aspects of the disjunction between the cross and the resurrection in Barth's understanding, and particularly of the resurrection as a unique event, and not merely as another in a series of salvific events. The second is the relation of the resurrection to the prophetic ministry of Christ in which the scandal of the gospel, the message of the radical presence of the crucified yet risen One, is brought forward and elucidated. Further attention to this second matter will bring out the distinction of the resurrection as the way of the crucified Reconciler to others, and the consequent implications for the doctrines of soteriology, pneumatology and ecclesiology.

In addition to these more strictly theological assessments of Barth's work, a great deal of effort has been expended in the task of delineating a construal of the crucial theological turns made by Barth in the course of the maturation of his thought. Many such construals have now been advanced, each in some way identifying a particular shift or series of shifts as the dominant interpretive key to Barth's development and indirectly to Barth's overall theological perspective. Yet again, none of these reflects a significant appreciation of the role of doctrine of the resurrection of Jesus Christ in the shaping of Barth's theological understanding and expression, a deficiency which again leads to less than satisfactory results. We will now consider the dominant such construal in greater detail.

Bruce McCormack's outstanding contribution to our understanding of Barth's theological development has done much to disabuse interpretation of Barth in the English-speaking world of falsely imposed schema and to reorient Barth's readers along lines much more in keeping with the actual texts.[75] Though the significance of McCormack's achievement can hardly be overstated, it nevertheless requires some refinement in the light of the central role of the doctrine of the resurrection in Barth's thought.

According to McCormack, the theory outlining Barth's development as having undergone a dramatic shift from dialectical theology to analogy (*analogia fidei*), taking place largely with the writing of the Anselm book in 1931, was first advocated by Hans Urs von Balthasar.[76] This view until 1995 has prevailed as the dominant interpretation of Barth's theological development. Other perhaps uneasy advocates of this view are T.F. Torrance, Hans Frei, and Eberhard Jüngel.[77] McCormack disputes this formulation, arguing instead that Barth's development 'did not entail the abandonment or even the weakening of his early commitment to 'dialectical theology'.'[78] Rather Barth's mature theology is better understood as a 'critically realistic dialectical theology.' Where this distinctive form of dialectical theology has

---

75   Bruce L. McCormack, *Karl Barth's Critically Realistic Dialectical Theology: its Genesis and Development 1909–1936* (Oxford: Clarendon Press, 1995).

76   Ibid., pp. 1–28.

77   Ibid., p. 4.

78   Ibid., p. ix.

not been perceived, claims McCormack, 'virtually the whole of Barth's theology has been read in the wrong light.'[79]

McCormack refers to Hans Urs von Balthasar's 1951 book, *Karl Barth: Darstellung und Deutung seiner Theologie*, and the thesis advanced there that Barth's development passed through two significant breaks, the first referring to his break with Protestant Liberalism and the second to Barth's turn from dialectical to analogical theology. According to von Balthasar it was Barth's study of Anselm which made it necessary for him to leave aside his prolegomena to dogmatics, *Christliche Dogmatik im Entwurf* (1927), in order to begin again with his *Church Dogmatics*, in the first volume of which was to be found the classical expression of Barth's *anologia fidei*. On this view the Anselm work marks a radical shift.[80] However, McCormack points out that von Balthasar is not entirely consistent in this conviction, in as much as he is also able to speak of a gradual transition from dialectic to analogy.[81]

In distinction to the von Balthasarian thesis is the theory advanced by Eberhard Jüngel in 1982 claiming there was only one break in Barth's theology, namely the break with Liberal theology. Jüngel preferred to describe Barth's as a theology of the Word of God.[82] Jüngel made reference to a dialectical phase in Barth, but on the basis of Barth's own admission of his desire to penetrate through the Bible to the 'inner dialectic of the *Sache*'.[83] Jüngel then suggested the dialectical phase came to an end when 'Barth abandoned the thought that the being to be known was itself dialectically structured.'[84] McCormack recounts Jüngel's argument that Barth rejected the false inference attributed to his theology – that the object of revelation is itself dialectical or paradoxical – and spoke of a notion of dialectic which functions in theology only as 'a dialectic of human knowing'.[85] From this point on Barth altered his descriptive style and began to develop his doctrine of the *analogia fidei*. Thus for Jüngel Barth's dialectical phase moves from 1921 to 1925, with the turn to analogy occurring gradually between 1927 and 1931. McCormack agrees with Jüngel's analysis that 'a significant development had occurred sometime around 1925'[86], but contends that Jüngel's explanation for this was deficient, arguing that Barth's understanding of revelation was never 'simply "undialectical"',[87] even in the *Church Dogmatics*.

McCormack details favourably further developments along these lines in the work of Ingrid Spiekermann and Michael Beintker. These scholars advocated for 'a more or less continuous unfolding of a single material insight or intention', namely

---

79   Ibid., p. x.
80   Ibid., p. 2.
81   Ibid., p. 3.
82   Ibid., p. 6.
83   Ibid.
84   Ibid.
85   Ibid., p. 7.
86   Ibid.
87   Ibid.

'to ground theology in the objectively real Self-speaking of God in revelation.'[88] Along with this was advocated the occurrence of analogy even as early as *Romans* II and the persistence of a form of dialectic well into the *Church Dogmatics*.[89] McCormack acknowledges Beintker's advances over Spiekermann's depiction by virtue of his isolation of four distinguishable types of dialectic at work in *Romans* II, an observation which makes it impossible to speak any longer of a simple turn from dialectic to analogy.[90] Especially noteworthy is the fact that Beintker identifies two forms of *Realdialektik* ('a dialectic in objectively real relations'[91]) in *Romans* II, which found conceptual expression as forms of a 'dialectic of time and eternity', but which served to witness to their underlying 'soteriological theme'.[92] Though McCormack passes rather lightly over this, it is important to see that the time–eternity dialectic is not entirely 'dispensed with' as a result of Barth's 'eschatological reservation' having been '*built into the very structure of his [anhypostatic–enhypostatic] Christology*,'[93] but rather an aspect of the time-eternity dialectic persists (as a soteriological theme) throughout Barth's thought as integral to his understanding of the resurrection revelation. The significance of this will become more apparent in due course.

McCormack proceeds to challenge the formulations of both Spiekermann and Beintker with being unnecessarily bound to the von Balthasarian thesis of a definite shift from dialectic to analogy. McCormack then argues for no less than a completely new way of understanding Barth's theological development. Building upon the Jüngel–Spiekermann–Beintker thesis with further devaluation of the developmental importance of the book on Anselm – 'marking a modest shift from the predominance (thought not exclusivity) of a dialectical "thought-form" to the

---

88   Ibid., p. 9. The conviction of the presence of a consistent single material intention in Barth goes at least as far back as von Balthasar and persists in most of Barth's major interpreters. While many approaches to reading Barth have their particular merit – George Hunsinger, a synchronic and rather philosophical thematic approach, *How to Read Karl Barth: The Shape of His Theology* (New York: Oxford University Press, 1991); Bruce McCormack, a genetic-historical approach, *Karl Barth's Critically Realistic Dialectical Theology*; Kurt Anders Richardson, a privileging of Barth's latest work (especially *CD* IV) for interpreting and correcting his earlier work, *Reading Karl Barth: New Directions for North American Theology* (Grand Rapids: Baker Academic, 2004); Philip Rosato, an identification and extrapolation of Barth's increasingly pneumatocentric orientation, *The Spirit as Lord* – Barth's own hermeneutical principle of immersing oneself in the thought of an author, straining to see what she sees, and perhaps to express even more adequately the object in view, offers a promising approach. That is, to read Barth with a view to his persisting single material intention, in the harmonies and dissonances of its thematic movements and diachronic developments, in the tension and cohesion of its mutually illuminating parts, and throughout his many efforts to go back to the beginning and 'start again', and to submit it all to the critique of theology's enduring object, constitutes, I suggest, an approach of which Barth himself would approve.

89   Ibid., pp. 9ff.

90   Ibid., p. 12.

91   Ibid., p. 11.

92   Ibid., p. 12.

93   Ibid., p. 328, emphasis as in the original.

predominance (though not exclusivity) of an analogical "thought-form"[94] – and with added emphasis upon the significance of Barth's new anhypostatic–enhypostatic christological understanding. McCormack prefers to understand Barth's development in four successive stages of dialectical theology in which new insights are combined with the deepening and refining of earlier insights. The four stages are: i) 'process eschatology,' describing the period of *Romans* I (1915–20) in which Barth conceived of the coming of the kingdom of God as the gradual arrival of this world's history; ii) 'consistent eschatology,' describing the period of *Romans* II (1920–24) in which Barth understood the kingdom of God as absolute future; iii) anhypostatic–enhypostatic christology with a pneumatocentric focus, describing the period from 1924 to 1936 in which Barth was able to take up the doctrine of incarnation in a coherent way without undoing his consistent eschatology, the present actualization of revelation accomplished by the Holy Spirit in this stage; and iv) anhypostatic–enhypostatic christology with a christocentric focus, describing the period from 1936 on, in which Barth took up and developed the doctrine of the election of Christ as Mediator and of human beings in him.

What is of significant interest to us here is the fact that McCormack acknowledges the possibility of tracing back to 1924 (notably proximate to the time of Barth's first publishing on the resurrection) the transition from dialectical method to analogy. While this may contain a measure of truth, he says, certain insurmountable conceptual problems remain: 'Periodization alone is not the problem. The problem is that the formula itself is inadequate for describing Barth's development.'[95] While McCormack appears to be willing to see a significant advance in 1924, he accounts for this not as a shift from dialectical to analogical theology, but from an undifferentiated hypostatic christology to an anhypostatic–enhypostatic christology. The human nature of the man Jesus subsists not in itself but in the divine Word. Jesus exists as a man only in union with the Son of God. Thus the Son of God takes into union with himself not 'a man' but the *humanum* of all human beings. McCormack appears to believe this settles the matter not only of the *diastasis* between divine and human being, but also of the *diastasis* between Jesus Christ and all other human beings – the Son of God is united to others by virtue of his participation in their common *humanum*. The anhypostatic–enhypostatic christology then encompasses and renders superfluous the extra-christological time-eternity dialectic Barth had previously employed to under gird his 'consistent eschatology'. McCormack then concludes that the dialectic which persists throughout the remainder of Barth's corpus must be that based upon the *Realdialektik* of the veiling and unveiling of Jesus Christ in his self-revelation.

But, helpful as it is, does this construal account for all that McCormack claims? Surely McCormack is correct to claim that Barth's embrace of an anhypostatic–enhypostatic christology explains the persistence of a divine–human dialectic throughout his writings, but in what sense does it secure a 'consistent' over against a

---

94   Ibid., p. 14.
95   Ibid., p. 16.

'process eschatology'? Similarly, what is the relationship between Barth's apparently concurrent discovery of an anhypostatic–enhypostatic christology and a doctrine of the *analogia fidei*? McCormack follows Beintker in seeing the *analogia fidei* as first expressed in the *Christliche Dogmatik* of 1927 where it describes 'an analogical relation between God's speech (*Deus dixit*)' and the 'human knowing of it.'[96] But can the dialectic of the *analogia fidei* be identified without remainder with that of an anhypostatic-enhypostatic christology? Might it not be the case that the resurrection of Jesus Christ provides a more solid theological basis for the *analogia fidei*, seeing as both divine self-revelation and the human response of faith find their primordial form there?[97]

Strangely absent from McCormack's depiction of Barth's theological development is any substantial reference to the role and significance of the doctrine of the resurrection. Yet precisely in this time of crucial discovery Barth has given significant attention to the theme. Barth's commentary on Paul's First Epistle to the Corinthians, entitled *Die Auferstehung der Toten*, was published in 1924. Can such a matter be wisely overlooked, given Barth's emphasis of the importance of the theme for his own theological understanding? McCormack rightly stresses that Barth's *analogia fidei* is not an *analogia entis*, that is, the suggestion of a real continuum between the being of the Creator and the being of the creature. Rather, the focus here 'is not being but rather a highly concrete event: the event of revelation.'[98] McCormack continues, observing that the *analogia fidei* has an '*inherently dialectical* character',[99] which explains, he suggests, the ongoing presence of dialectic even into Barth's *Church Dogmatics*. He accounts for the dialectical character of the *analogia fidei* by grounding it in the *Realdialektik* of the divine veiling and unveiling in the revelation-event. This he claims is 'the motor which drives Barth's doctrine of analogy and makes it possible.'[100] The revelation-event of which McCormack speaks is of course the whole life history of Jesus Christ, an understanding which is now possible for Barth by virtue of his adoption of an anhypostatic–enhypostatic christology. But does McCormack sufficiently account for the highly nuanced event of revelation as Barth conceives of it? While he took the whole of the history of Jesus Christ to be revelation, more particularly Barth understood the divine being of Jesus Christ to be veiled in his incarnation from Bethlehem to Golgotha, but gloriously unveiled in his resurrection. Barth's anhypostatic–enhypostatic christology does

---

96   McCormack, p. 10. Interestingly, McCormack here notes that had the Göttingen Prolegomena come into Beintker's hands earlier, he would have placed the first occurrence of the *analogia fidei* in 1924, shortly after Barth had completed his *The Resurrection of the Dead*.

97   At issue in the *analogia fidei* is 'an analogical relation between divine speaking in the act of revelation and human knowing in the act of faith' (ibid., p. 11, fn. 33). On this account the *analogia fidei* reflects remarkably the theme which Barth develops consistently under the rubric of the resurrection.

98   Ibid., p. 17.

99   Ibid., p. 18.

100   Ibid.

not fully account for his notion of the dialectic of veiling and unveiling in God's self-revelation. It is rather firstly in his resurrection – and only on that basis and in that light in his incarnation – that his self-revelation has the dialectical character of unveiling and veiling. One wonders at this point whether McCormack's conception of what is at issue here is too heavily invested in the incarnation as the union of the divine and human natures, eclipsing the significant role of the resurrection of Jesus Christ for Barth. What seems to slip McCormack's attention at this point is the fact that Barth at a very early stage saw the event of the resurrection of Jesus Christ as the primordial revelation-event, a perception which he carried with him throughout his career. Attention to Barth's understanding of the resurrection reveals that it is not a matter of significance secondary to his incarnation christology, but rather is foundational to his theology.

Clarification here as to the role of Barth's resurrection thought assists us with some necessary refinements of McCormack's scheme. For instance, according to McCormack the first phase of Barth's development was controlled by a 'process eschatology' which preserved a 'tension between present realization and future fulfilment in its conception of the Kingdom of God'[101], whereas his second phase (1920–24) identifies a 'consistent eschatology' in which 'very little present realization' was conceived.[102] However, a recognition of the complete realization of eschatology in the resurrection continues to find expression in the 1924 work on 1 Corinthians 15, and indeed, throughout the later *Church Dogmatics* material. The kingdom of God is fully present in the risen Jesus Christ, but present only in hope for others. Discrepancies of this sort are significant, but the real problem lies deeper in the systematic structure of Barth's thought. McCormack rightly recognizes that 'shifts in Barth's models of explication had their roots in material decisions in dogmatic theology'.[103] Yet for the supposed shift from a process to a consistent eschatology he offers no substantial dogmatic explanation. What McCormack neglects to take into account here is that Barth's eschatology is an implicate of his resurrection theology. That is the eternity–time dialectic (to be distinguished from the divine–human dialectic), whether finding expression in a process or a consistent, or, as developed in *CD* III/2 and IV/3, a more complex threefold eschatology, is not firstly one of a loosely connected eschatology, nor one correlated to a preconceived notion of the time–eternity relationship, but one of a unique tension inherent and preserved already in the resurrection reality. The persistence of both 'process' and 'consistent' aspects of Barth's eschatology can be explained only in light of those tensions which obtain in the resurrection. That is to say, there emerges very early on in Barth a tendency to develop his eschatology in terms of the relationship of the Christ reality to that of other human beings, rather than in terms of the union of divine and human natures or of an absolute distinction of eternity and time. As early

---

101 Ibid., p. 21.
102 Ibid.
103 Ibid., p. 20.

as *The Resurrection of the Dead* Barth is working with a discernable distinction between the God-man dialectic and the Christ-others dialectic.

McCormack's third phase brings in Barth's new commitment to an anhypostatic–enhypostatic christology, 'which enabled him to conceptualize how revelation can be fully present *in* history without becoming a predicate *of* history.'[104] But while Barth's anhypostatic–enhypostatic christology surely does this, it is not yet the revelation and impartation of that reality. It denotes an ontic, but not yet a noetic christology. It affirms the incarnation and the crucifixion but not the resurrection of the God-man. Yet these are clear and distinct emphases Barth wishes to sustain. According to McCormack, it was in May 1924 that Barth came upon the anhypostatic–enhypostatic christological formulation, in which he saw 'an understanding of the incarnate being of the Mediator which preserved that infinite qualitative distinction between God and humankind which had been at the forefront of his concerns throughout the previous phase.'[105] In McCormack's view Barth here safeguards two of his earlier insights. First, the time–eternity dialectic was no longer necessary, for the eschatological reservation it safeguarded was now structurally incorporated into his anhypostatic–enhypostatic christology, which by this remained 'as much a *critically* realistic theology as the previous theology in the shadow of a consistent eschatology had been.'[106] And second, the incarnation could be afforded its full significance, for there was no longer a need to restrict the occurrence of revelation to the 'mathematical point' of the cross. McCormack explains: 'Now, the dialectic of veiling and unveiling on its objective side could comprehend the whole of the incarnate existence of the Mediator.'[107]

Yet, while McCormack's explanation helps to clarify our understanding of the 'objective side' of revelation for Barth, it does not adequately account for Barth's understanding of the 'subjective side' of revelation as it were, which he saw as concentrated specifically in the resurrection event, a conviction which figures prominently in Barth's thought throughout. Left unexcavated in McCormack's account is Barth's soteriological use for the time–eternity dialectic. For just as the time–eternity dialectic safeguarded Barth's earlier eschatological reservation, ensuring the infinite qualitative distinction between God and humanity, so too it safeguarded a soteriological reservation, which ensured the distinction between what is true and actual in Jesus Christ and what is true and actual in other human beings. While the former is incorporated into Barth's anhypostatic–enhypostatic christology, the latter is preserved by a notion of the resurrection movement of Jesus Christ to other human beings, i.e., his crossing from eternity to time. Only on the basis of the latter can we understand Barth's need to develop his accounts of i) the contemporaneity of Jesus' time (his time from Bethlehem to Golgotha) to all other human times, ii) the resurrection as the turn of the crucified Lord to others, and iii) the threefold

---

104   Ibid., p. 21.
105   Ibid., p. 327.
106   Ibid., p. 328.
107   Ibid.

parousia of the Redeemer, which has its primordial form in the resurrection. In each of these ways the time–eternity dialectic continues to serve Barth's soteriological reservation. Thus, the time–eternity dialectic is not incorporated unproblematically into Barth's new christology. His anhypostatic–enhypostatic christology, as important and integral an insight as it is, is not a sufficiently broad category to account for all that Barth envisions here. It is rather Barth's constant return to the resurrection event which allows for all of these facets of the Christ reality to come to light.

On McCormack's account, the final phase in Barth's theological development is to be identified with the publication of the *CD* II/1, where the christocentric focus intensifies as Barth develops the election of Christ as Mediator and of individuals in him, 'rather than the election of individuals as the effect of a revelation-event in the present.'[108] This he takes as a christocentric concentration as shifted from a pneumatocentric concentration. But again this distinction does not hold in our examination of Barth's resurrection material. In fact, Barth later on (in *CD* IV/2 and IV/3) argues for a form of inclusion of individuals into the sphere of reconciled human being as a result of their encounter with the *Spirit* of the risen Lord. Apart from this encounter, it is as though the work of Christ is of no effect. And furthermore, many leading Barth interpreters believe that Barth's projected fifth volume of the *Church Dogmatics* would have been characterized by pneumatocentric discourse.

We conclude then that Barth's developing thought is not comprehensively represented by the notion that his anhypostatic–enhypostatic christology takes priority of place, relegating, even inadvertently, the resurrection revelation-event to a place of secondary importance. Barth's anhypostatic–enhypostatic christology, isolated from the resurrection revelation-event, along with the supposed shift from pneumatocentrism to christocentrism, cannot fully account for the shape of Barth's thinking here.

At this point it must suffice simply to assert that Barth's understanding of the resurrection of Jesus Christ from the dead as it is discussed throughout his academic career does not fit neatly into the expectations established even by the best of the models of interpretation proposed to date. From this stems the call for yet further refinement in our understanding of Barth's development, refinement which at minimum undertakes a tracing Barth's theological development along the lines of a deepening and expanding of his initial insights, with particular attention to his understanding of the resurrection. If, as Barth himself claimed, the resurrection of Jesus Christ remained the focal centre of his theological vision, any effort to grapple with Barth's thought must first attempt to comprehend it, in all its complexity and profundity. To this end, let us now turn our attention to Barth's discussion of the resurrection of Jesus Christ as the decisive movement of Jesus Christ to others.

---

108   Ibid., p. 22. McCormack later specifies that 'the election or rejection of the individual' is for Barth no longer 'decided moment by moment in the revelation-event' but 'has already been decided in Jesus Christ' (ibid., p. 459). What is decided in the revelation-event is whether the elect individual will respond 'in faith and obedience' to her election.

Chapter Two

The Resurrection of the Dead

On the terms of the von Balthasarian thesis, Barth's 1924 work *The Resurrection of the Dead* should be essentially a work of dialectical theology in which the otherness of God precludes any direct human knowledge of him. The infinite qualitative distinction of the Creator and his creation renders knowledge of the Creator from the side of the creature absolutely impossible. Yet, Barth insists, we do know God, but only on the basis of divine revelation. Whereas human beings could in no way apprehend the divine, God has revealed himself in truth in the resurrection of Jesus Christ. According to T.F. Torrance, *The Resurrection of the Dead*, together with the revised *Romans*,[1] emphasizes this dialectical tension in terms of an eschatological distinction of time and eternity.[2] We are prompted to observe a shift from a 'timeless eschatology' (an understanding of eternity strongly influenced by a notion of the absence of the features of time) to a 'realistic eschatology' (an understanding of eternity shaped largely by the notion of eternity as primordial and originative *reality*). On the terms of the thesis advanced by McCormack, the transition from dialectical to analogical theology is a matter of emphasis, with the recognition that a dialectical element persists throughout. We should find then in *The Resurrection of the Dead* clear examples of a time–eternity dialectic which is not yet grounded in an anhypostatic–enhypostatic christological formulation. Somewhat distinct from Torrance, McCormack puts us on the alert for traces of a noticeable shift from the 'process eschatology' of the *Romans I* period, in which the Kingdom of God gradually arrives in the unfolding of human history, to a 'consistent eschatology' in which the eternity of God remains the absolute future of all of human time.

Though McCormack's thesis represents an important advance – for he correctly sees in Barth's thought, as do the others, a 'continuous unfolding of a single material insight or intention,'[3] – he does not explicate further the matter of that insight. And though the eschatological observations of both Torrance and McCormack are helpful and offer some light, they do not sufficiently account for the importance of the resurrection for Barth's eschatology. What I wish to contend for is an understanding Barth's characteristic thought here as neither purely dialectical nor a function of

---

1   Karl Barth, *The Epistle to the Romans* (hereafter, *Romans*), trans. from sixth edition by Edwyn C. Hoskyns (London: Oxford University Press, 1933).

2   Cf. Thomas F. Torrance, *Karl Barth: An Introduction to His Early Theology, 1910–1931* (hereafter, *Introduction*), (London: SCM Press Ltd, 1962), pp. 74ff for a helpful discussion of the rediscovery of an eschatological understanding of the New Testament.

3   McCormack, *Karl Barth's Critically Realistic Dialectical Theology*, p. 9.

a shifting eschatology, but as a consistent unfolding of the resurrection of Jesus of Nazareth as a single material *terminus a quo* and *terminus ad quem* for all his theological thought. Thus, while we find in *The Resurrection of the Dead* a form of dialectical argumentation, it is better described as an explication of the crisis of all human knowing and action in light of the revelation of God in the resurrection of Jesus Christ. What we find is not strictly dialectics at all, for it is not a *dialectical method of argumentation* originating in disparate and competing sources of truth and moving toward without ever arriving at a singular comprehensive resolution. What we have here rather is a highly refined *dialectical method of witness* which originates in the revelation-event of a singular cohesive and coherent object and moves outward from its own centre toward human beings.

For Barth the revelation of God in the resurrection of Jesus Christ has at the same time both the most critical and the most positive function. In the light of resurrection revelation it can be seen that all things this side of the resurrection are of death, that is, of the dead and dying. In the same light it can be seen that all things dead and dying are what they are not and cannot possibly be, that is, truly alive. For Barth, what confronts us in the resurrection is precisely the revelation of the negation of what we are (of sin and death) and the proclamation of what we are not (of righteousness and life). This inescapably dialectical structure of witness, based in the utterly coherent reality which underlies it, remains a fundamental aspect of Barth's resurrection discourse throughout his career. It is crucial to understand that this dialectical tension is not one which he derives generally from the observable realities and processes of the created order. It stems rather from the resurrection revelation. It is not that one begins with knowledge from utterly distinct sources which must then be integrated as much as possible. It is rather that both a critical and a constructive form of knowledge stem from a singular and simple, that is, already wholly integrated and cohesive, source.

Similarly, the key to Barth's already highly sophisticated and nuanced depiction of eschatological themes is to be found in his understanding of the resurrection. I propose here that rather than as a resurrection treatise infused with a preconceived or shifting eschatology, it is more accurate to view this work as Barth's discovery of the Apostle's theological method – a kind of real eschatological pro- and retro-spection, which has the resurrection of Jesus Christ as its focal point. That is, Barth understands the chief object of focus to be at the same time the real object and the authenticating source of the apostolic witness. The eschatological reality of the resurrection of Jesus Christ is the reality to which all things attest and from which all things draw their relative meaning. Barth himself says that he conceives of this more as an understanding of the method of the Apostle's preaching than as strict eschatology.[4]

Our purpose in this chapter is to examine Barth's *The Resurrection of the Dead* in an effort to draw out Barth's earlier thought on the resurrection and to explicate

---

4   Karl Barth, *The Resurrection of the Dead* (hereafter *RD*), trans. by H.J. Stenning, (New York: Arno Press, 1977; Fleming H. Revell Company, 1933) p. 109.

the resurrection as that 'single material insight' which remains the focus and driving force of his discourse. To achieve this it will be necessary to examine three fundamental characteristics of Barth's conception of the resurrection. The first of these characteristics is what I shall call the *primordiality* of the resurrection. By this term I mean to speak of the important ways in which Barth believes the resurrection to be of axiomatic significance in Paul. The second deals with the character of the resurrection as *revelation*. The third deals with Barth's understanding of the resurrection as *reality*. Let us begin with a general overview of Barth's view of the resurrection as it is developed in this work.

The Resurrection as Last and First Word

That Karl Barth believes the resurrection of the dead to be the centre and basis of Paul's preaching is indisputable. 1 Corinthians 15, he claims, deals with 'the most positive subject that can be imagined' and is the 'very peak and crown of this ... Epistle.'[5] In this chapter Paul's fundamental orientation is finally disclosed: 'The Resurrection of the Dead is the point from which Paul is speaking and to which he points.'[6] In Barth's view, the word of the resurrection is the *last* word – the resurrection of the dead is the great answer which calls into question all of the great, yet penultimate questions of life. And because this great answer is given there 'exactly on the threshold of death'[7] it firstly poses the problem all of the questions of life *en masse*. Thus Paul, in Barth's view, in pointing to and from the resurrection of the dead, effectively relativizes the significance of every other question.[8] It is in this sense that Barth understands Paul to be speaking of last things.

Barth does not deny the importance of thought about the end times, that is, the times at the so-called end of history, whether they be in the near or distant future, cataclysmic or benign. It is rather a good thing that we be reminded of the possibility of things passing away. If the extinguishing of a star reminds us of the possibility of our own end then it is good and instructive. Thus, Barth's eschatology preserves here a 'processive' element. But, according to Barth, 1 Corinthians 15 does not speak of last things in this sense, and neither, for that matter, does the New Testament generally. The concern of the New Testament is not such final possibilities within the same nexus of cause and effect. These last things can only be last things in a world where the fundamental structures remain the same. Last things in a biblical sense, according to Barth, have to do with the end of all things:

---

5   *RD*, p. 101.

6   Ibid.

7   Ibid.

8   Christoph Schwöbel correctly notes that for Barth 'theologians are not called to answer the many questions of human existence, but the one question which *is* human existence and which points beyond human existence to God.' 'Theology' in *The Cambridge Companion to Karl Barth*, ed. John Webster (Cambridge: Cambridge University Press, 2000), p. 22. Cf. also pp. 23–4.

He only speaks of *last* things who would speak of the *end* of all things, of their end understood plainly and fundamentally, of a reality so radically superior to all things, that the existence of all things would be utterly and entirely *based* upon it alone, and thus, in speaking of their end, he would in truth be speaking of nothing else than their beginning.[9]

Barth understands Paul to be speaking of the 'finiteness of history' and the 'finiteness of time' as a function of speaking about 'that upon which all time and all happenning is *based*.'[10] In understanding last things as the limits of time, Barth understands the 'end of history' to be synonymous with the 'pre-history', that is, with 'the *origin* of time.'[11] While Barth concedes that the Bible does at places lay emphasis upon last things or events at the end of history, it does this only on the basis of a distinct idea of eternity, which is the 'real end at last, the absorption of all this and that, all here and there, all once and now into the solemn peace of the One'[12] and this end of history has a definite place of occurrence:

Somehow and somewhere the infinite series is apt to come to a stop in a thought somehow determined by the Bible, the infinite series thus becoming a finite one, in view of the insurmountable wall which is placed against it by the eternity where God is all in all.[13]

Hence, biblical eschatology is not about the extension of the world of time into its beyond, but rather about the fundamental finiteness of the world of time, as it is bounded by the eternity of God.

What is more, the word of the resurrection is also the *first* word. Barth is concerned that we do not go only half-way and lose the positive side of what is revealed in the resurrection. It is not merely that God's eternity sets a limit upon the endlessness of the world-history, but rather that this last word is also to be understood at the same time as the first word of a new history. The history of the end is also the history of the beginning. Hence God's eternity is to be understood as both the last word which closes history and the first word which establishes history anew. Thus, God's eternity delimits time but in so doing heals time, giving new meaning and wholeness to time. And hence though it may be said that 'the *real* end-of-history' may be said to be near at any time, this does not mean the annihilation, but rather the fulfilment, of history.

In Barth's view Paul's doctrine of the resurrection does not provide an account of something which perdures through death but rather a doctrine of the '"End," which is at the same time the beginning, of the last things, which are, at the same time, the first.'[14] He seeks to bring all things into the light of this single recollection: that all things come to death. And having argued that all things assuredly come to death,

---

9   *RD*, p. 104.
10   Ibid.
11   Ibid.
12   Ibid., p. 105.
13   Ibid.
14   Ibid., p. 107.

Paul then speaks of the *resurrection* of the dead. To speak of death on its own, to speak of the limiting of time and its universe of possibilities on its own, *that is*, from within the world-time order, is nothing more than a veiled extension of the conditions and potentialities of the same continuum – it is not an end at all, but merely (and as a matter of deep despair) a cosmic narcissism, quite unaware of its origin and end. Barth understands Paul's emphasis upon the resurrection of Jesus Christ as that which reveals the real limits of world-history and thus grants meaningfulness to our knowledge of these limits. Paul refers to the resurrection only as that which is uttered at the end of all that can be said humanly:

> With the word 'resurrection,' however, the apostolic preaching puts in this empty place against all that exists for us, all that is known to us, all that can be possessed by us, all things of all time – what? not the non-being, the unknown, the not-to-be-possessed, nor yet a second being, a further thing to become known, a higher future possession, but the source and the truth of all that exists, that is known, that can belong to us, the reality of all *res*, of all things, the eternity of time, the *resurrection* of the dead.[15]

What Barth takes from Paul is that the resurrection is spoken of exactly in this place, exactly in the place where nothing can be said, precisely in the place where it seems that all we have is an inconceivable nothingness. Barth underscores the failure of all merely human reason to deal adequately with the end just at this point. Instead of recognizing the end as real end indeed, as the last word beyond which nothing can be spoken, another merely human word is posited, a new being (or non-being) derived unwittingly from the pre-End reality is put in that place. But it is nothing more than an image fashioned of this-worldly matter (wood and stones) by human hands. In stark contrast, Paul, precisely in this place, speaks of the resurrection. It is in the place where death would seem to have the last word that Paul, in speaking of the resurrection, is able to speak of a meaningful beyond and at the same time maintain the real end character of the last human word.

In Barth's view, Paul's use of resurrection indicates that what is claimed is the great contradiction: we who are dead are in fact truly alive. To speak of the impossible possibility of the resurrection is to speak of 'the dead living, time eternity, the being truth, things real.'[16] Thus, what lies behind the recollection of the fact that we all must die is the fact that the resurrection of the dead is already complete in God, in God's eternity:

> The recollection of death is so important, so urgent, so disturbing, so actual because it is in fact the tidings of the resurrection behind it, the recollection of the *life*, of our life that we are not living and that yet is our life.[17]

It is this continual returning to the great recollection of death and the meaning and significance placed upon that final word in the word of the resurrection, which allows

---

15   Ibid., p. 108.
16   Ibid.
17   Ibid., p. 109.

Paul to proclaim with integrity a genuine end, which brings all penultimate things into crisis, but which itself owes its force and power to the humanly unspeakable word spoken from beyond.

The ideas developed in 1 Corinthians 15 then are better described as 'the *methodology of the apostle's preaching*, rather than eschatology, because it is really concerned not with this and that special thing, but with the meaning and nerve of its whole, with the whence? and the whither? of the human way as such and in itself.'[18] With this procedure, Barth claims, Paul is attempting to utter the impossible utterance, hoping despite his certain failure to draw attention to that which only can be heard from the other side of the limitations of world-history. Barth marvels at the daring exhibited by the apostle Paul 'to make this impossible attempt in such detail, and offering so many weak points.'[19] This chapter stands alone in all of Pauline literature as 'the connected exposition of this truth.'[20] Says Barth:

> it must be said that the impossible attempt to say *that*, the word of all words, is nothing else than the essence of the apostolic preaching generally. All the time, the question in the *background* is concerning *this* God, *this* Christ, *this* Holy [Spirit], *this* last word.[21]

It is important to observe that Barth believes it is the reality of the resurrection that informs Paul's theological method, which accordingly takes the form of a battle for the Christian theological perspective. His purpose is to bring to recollection *the exclusive* theological perspective which has as its origin, object and end nothing other than the resurrection of Jesus Christ. What Barth says of the resurrection in his *Romans* II holds here as well:

> Within history, Jesus as the Christ can be understood only as Problem or Myth. As the Christ, He brings the world of the Father. But we who stand in this concrete world know nothing, and are incapable of knowing anything, of that other world. The Resurrection from the dead is, however, the transformation: the establishing or *declaration* of that point from above, and the corresponding discerning of it from below. The Resurrection is the revelation: the disclosing of Jesus as the Christ, the appearing of God, and the apprehending of God in Jesus. The Resurrection is the emergence of the necessity of giving glory to God: the reckoning with what is unknown and unobservable in Jesus, the recognition of Him as Paradox, Victor, and Primal History.[22]

This impossible attempt is always what is in the background of Paul's manner of preaching.

---

18   Ibid.
19   Ibid., p. 111.
20   Ibid.
21   Ibid.
22   *Romans*, p. 30.

The Primordiality of the Resurrection

This understanding of the priority of the resurrection for Paul opens up the question of the significance of the resurrection for the establishment of the Christian church. Unlike those who want to understand resurrection language as a symbolic expression of prior human needs and predispositions, Barth sees the resurrection as altogether primary, comprising the origin, reality and end of the church's faith. Three observations will assist us here. First, Barth sees the resurrection of Jesus Christ from the dead as the secret theme of Paul's apostolic witness. Second, he exposes Paul's concern to root the origin and existence of the Corinthian church in the apostolic witness to the resurrection reality. And third, he underscores the prime significance of the resurrection of the dead by marking Paul's insistence upon it as the sum and substance of the gospel message.

The Resurrection as the Secret Theme of the Epistle

Intriguingly Barth dedicates almost one half of the book to a demonstration of the resurrection of the dead as the unifying theme of the epistle. Our comments must however be confined to a few summary descriptions. Barth begins with an explanation of the usual understanding of 1 Corinthians 15 as 'the last fragment in the great conglomerate of exhortations, rebukes, and doctrinal pronouncements … arranged externally according to the needs and inspirations of the moment,'[23] and acknowledges the apparently 'haphazard character of the series of *subjects* dealt with in 1 Cor. i.–xiv.', as well as 'the lack of connexion by which 1 Cor. xv., with its new theme, is at first joined to this series.'[24] But he is not persuaded by the common interpretation that these are without connection. Rather, he proposes that there is a thread which binds into a whole these apparently disparate subjects, and further, that this thread becomes visible in 1 Corinthians 15 in such a way that its theme cannot be seen as simply another subject in a parade of unrelated issues, but rather is the subject of the entire epistle. In this way chapter 15 forms 'the close and crown' of the whole epistle and 'provides the clue to its meaning.'[25]

He believes that in the First Epistle to the Corinthians, Paul, with greater specificity than evidenced elsewhere, manifests his central focus and chief assumptions. As he works through the first 14 chapters of First Corinthians, Barth notices in Paul a kind of *via negativa*: a tendency to apply the critical pressure of the reality of God to each and every consideration. Barth begins with what he believes to be the fundamental Pauline assumption that there is no genuine knowledge of God as object among women and men (cf. 1 Cor. 1:20; 2:9, 11, 16). The point is not merely that this is not, but that this *cannot* be by virtue of the transcendence of God. Human knowledge is at its best 'indirect knowledge,' that is, 'a dialectical knowledge, the two halves

---

23   *RD*, p. 6.
24   *RD*, p. 6.
25   *RD*, p. 5.

of the truth, which we cannot unite, sharply perceptible as such, but allowing none to perceive directly the Whole, that which is meant by the two sides.'[26] It is simply impossible for eternity to be captured and contained within the strictures of time. As Barth cites time and again: '*finitum non capax infiniti.*' He insists that the 'testimony of Christ' is 'shrouded in complete obscurity,' eluding every human attempt to apprehend or comprehend it.[27] As in the *Romans* so here: 'the assumption that Jesus is the Christ (i. 4) is, in the strictest sense of the word, an assumption, void of any content that can be comprehended by us.'[28]

Bultmann is correct: the main theme of Barth's *The Resurrection of the Dead* is that the underlying unifying force of Paul's First Epistle to the Corinthians can be detected in the Apostle's manner of understanding all things in light of the eschatological reality of the resurrection of Jesus Christ from the dead.[29] 1 Corinthians 15, far from being just another new theme, is rather the chapter containing *the unifying theme* of the epistle – it is through the subject matter of 1 Corinthians 15, according to Barth, that the illumination with which Paul views the other subjects achieves its greatest brilliance.[30] It is the critical point to which Paul seeks to draw attention, and the critical point from which all things are granted new meaning – in Barth's view, their 'real' meaning, their specifically Christian meaning.

Barth depicts the negative polemical element of the first fourteen chapters of the epistle in this way:

> There stands Paul, and behind him a mountain-high, marvellous secret, and he points his finger to what passes under the name of Christianity in Corinth: and then he stands again by the side of the Corinthian Christians, and once more points his finger, but now back to the place whence he was speaking a moment before. *In this thence and thither consists the critical and polemical element of the First Epistle to the Corinthians.*[31]

And again:

> The essential unity of the First Epistle to the Corinthians is a quite specific criticism which Paul applies to the Christian Church. He reproaches it with the fact that the human ... elements, which are mixed up in its Christianity, are in process of ... becoming an end in themselves.[32]

We cannot then be satisfied with the notion that Barth, quite indifferent to the subtleties of the biblical text, carries on with his own critical and polemical agenda, when it is clear that he perceives this criticism to be a fundamental component,

---

26   *RD*, p. 91.
27   *RD*, p. 20.
28   Karl Barth, *Romans*, p. 36.
29   Rudolf Bultmann, *Faith and Understanding*, trans. by Louise Pettibone Smith (New York: Harper & Row, Publishers, 1966), sixth edition, pp. 66f.
30   *RD*, p. 6.
31   *RD*, pp. 98f. Emphasis mine.
32   *RD*, p. 97.

not of Paul's style, but of and requisite to Paul's theological perspective! Paul's method of criticism, in Barth's view, is not an arbitrary choice. On the contrary, it is a language apposite to the critical character of the resurrection reality. Likewise Barth's dialectical method results from his effort, following Paul, to give expression to the critical force of the eschatological reality of the resurrection. As Barth sees it, even in Paul the resurrection reality prompted both a negative (critical) and positive (constructive) account. What remains normative is that Barth, following Paul, consistently understands the 'Resurrection of the Dead' to be the incomparable reality to which Christian theology points and from which it speaks.[33]

The Gospel of the Resurrection as the Origin of the Church

The Corinthian error, in Barth's view, was to claim there was no resurrection of the dead, which they saw as an unnecessary Pauline accretion to the fundamental truth of the Christian gospel. The resurrection of the body was thought unnecessary because the eternal blessing of the soul was considered guaranteed, once the soul was freed from its bodily imprisonment. The Corinthians, then, preferred to think of the teaching of the resurrection of the dead as a curious, but wholly peripheral oddity of Paul's message, a rather embarrassing 'Paulinism' which would be better left behind.[34] They did not understand the resurrection of the dead to be the bedrock and surety upon which they stood as Christian believers.[35]

Against this Corinthian threat of rejection of the primary matter, Paul, in Barth's view, argues the impossibility of escaping the embarrassment of this 'extreme paradox.'[36] The attempt to get behind Paul to a more original and pure expression of the message is a wholly impossible attempt. Paul, though among the witnesses to the risen Christ, does not originate the testimony. He passes on that same testimony which he also has received. Paul cannot own it as an idiosyncrasy of his distinct understanding. The gospel of the other witnesses has no other meaning than the gospel Paul has preached since the beginning.[37] As Barth sees it, Paul recounts the list of witnesses as demonstration that they all, without exception, testify to the same reality to which Paul testifies.[38] Hence Barth understands the force of Paul's appeal to Peter, the Twelve, the more than five hundred, James and even finally himself, not as an apologetic argument for the reality of the resurrection, but as a statement of fact that all of these founding members of the church without exception preach as the substance of the gospel that the Crucified appeared. The focus of the witness is not on the awakening of Jesus Christ from the dead, but on the resurrection appearances which reveal the Crucified as risen. The apostolic witness then is not to an historical

---

33 *RD*, p. 101.
34 *RD*, p. 126.
35 *RD*, p. 143.
36 *RD*, p. 127.
37 *RD*, p. 132.
38 *RD*, p. 139.

fact of any ordinary sort. It is certainly not a witness to the empty tomb. Nevertheless the apostolic witness is to a datable event in which the same Jesus of Nazareth who was crucified revealed himself to them as God. There is no way of getting behind the apostolic witness to something more original or substantive. The witness is only to be accepted or rejected as a serious and faithful witness. But that this particular witness of the apostles is the foundation of the church is undeniable.

Barth notes in Paul a thoroughgoing dependence upon revelation:

> For this reason Paul fought, for his apostolic method, of which he cannot even concede that it was perhaps only *his* method, and for this reason he now conjures up the cloud of witnesses, *not* to confirm the fact of the resurrection of Jesus, not for that purpose at all, but to confirm that the foundation of the church, so far as the eye can see, can be traced back to nothing else than appearances of the risen Christ ... [and therefore] the origin of Christianity along the whole line is revelation, and only revelation.[39]

Barth insists that Christ's appearances must be understood as revelation. What Peter, the other disciples, and the five hundred saw with their physical eyes was one thing, but the fundamental testimony could be traced back to nothing other than revelation of the risen Christ as the one who was dead but now is alive:[40]

> What Paul wants to call the attention of the Corinthians to in verses 3–7 is that if they seek to push themselves behind or past him, Paul, back to the gospel of the primitive Church, they come up against the *same* testimony, the *same* 'appeared' comprised in its whole incomprehensibility; that, however much they may turn and tack about, they must trip over this stumbling-block: Christ lives![41]

This testimony is not to be understood as a witness to a human experience somewhat like all other human experiences, only of a higher and purer kind, however real and verifiable those experiences may be. It is rather a witness to God's revelation precisely as the event of the resurrection. The Corinthian Christians could not escape the fact that the initial and perpetual foundation of the Church in which they stood was the witness to the self-revelation of God in the resurrection of Jesus Christ from the dead.

Barth understands the apostolic witness as a witness to revelation. That is, it is a witness to something beyond, yet inclusive and determinative of, world-historical reality. The only proper approach to this witness is to believe what the apostles averred: He who was dead now lives. And therefore the appropriate question to ask is not 'How is one to understand this witness in historical or theological terms?' but rather 'How are history and historical science and theology and theological science

---

39   *RD*, p. 143.
40   *RD*, p. 137.
41   *RD*, p. 139.

to be understood in terms of this witness?' Only in this way is the witness faithfully heard and the subject matter of the text preserved.[42]

Thus, as Barth expounds Paul, the church at Corinth could not dismiss the resurrection of the dead as an unwarranted and unnecessary accretion to the true gospel. The testimony of the early witnesses to the risen Christ is the foundational testimony of the church.

The Resurrection of the Dead as the Meaning of Faith

By resurrection the Corinthians understood the bodily resurrection of Jesus, but, explains Barth, only as a peculiar anomaly.[43] For them death was just an inevitable moment in the stream of human existence, which included the existence of the soul after the death of the body. According to Barth, 'for them the overcoming of *sins* is not inseparably connected with a victory over death, they do not perceive why this victory should be *the* victory.'[44]

Against the Corinthian objection that the resurrection of the dead had no fundamental significance for them, Paul intends to demonstrate that the miracle of the revelation of God in the resurrection of Jesus Christ was the sum and substance of the gospel. Any other purported significance of the Christian message was nonsense. According to Barth, Paul argues *probare negatum per negatum* ('to prove a negative by a negative'): Christian faith, cut off from the radical and comprehensive significance of the resurrection of the dead, is in fact nothing more than 'the dream of human wishes.'[45] And, if that is the case, Feuerbach's critique of Christianity was correct. Paul, in opposition, wages an all out war against Christianity without resurrection. According to Barth, Paul says as strongly as he can that a Christianity

---

42   Gerald O'Collins is mistaken in his charge that Barth would be on much surer ground 'if he had invoked the divine initiative which effected these decisive encounters [with the risen Christ].' Fr. Gerald O'Collins, S. J., 'Karl Barth on Christ's Resurrection,' in *The Scottish Journal of Theology*, Vol. 26 (1973) p. 92. The same article is reprinted later in O'Collins's *Jesus Risen: An Historical, Fundamental and Systematic Examination of Christ's Resurrection* (New York: Paulist Press, 1987). Barth's point is that the resurrection is precisely the supreme initiative of God and therefore the supreme revelation of God (Cf. *RD*, pp. 127f). And, that it is fatal 'to allege that the objectivity of the Easter appearances stands or falls with an ordinary sense–perception of the risen Christ' (O'Collins, 'Karl Barth on Christ's Resurrection,' p. 40.) is precisely Barth's contention, despite O'Collins's belief that Barth claims the contrary.

43   In this respect Barth's early thought is in keeping with the conclusions of recent leading New Testament scholarship as represented by N.T. Wright in *The Resurrection of the Son of God*, Minneapolis: Fortress Press, 2003.

44   *RD*, p. 116.

45   *RD*, p. 157.

without resurrection 'is a lie and a deceit, not because it is still without this article of faith, but because it is in itself an illusion, a fiction.'[46]

One cannot deny the resurrection of the dead if the substance of the gospel of Christ is that Christ rose from the dead.[47] To deny it is to deny the gospel:

> What is involved is the *substance*, the *whole* of the Christian revelation. It was *not a theological doubt*, to be corrected incidentally or even overlooked, but an attack upon what made Christianity to be Christianity in the case of those who said 'there is no resurrection of the dead'.[48]

And furthermore:

> The meaning of a Christianity without resurrection, this remarkable assertion, faith, confession, hope, and struggle, the meaning of this in affirmation and negation, in action, speech, and experience, in outward and inward appearance an equally extravagant situation, is nonsense itself, if the resurrection of the dead is not the very central point to which all this relates, if God is not just God.[49]

Barth argues that regardless of what one may think of Paul and Paul's gospel, it must be granted at the very beginning that Paul is firmly convinced that what is at stake is the essence of the gospel.[50] With this belief or unbelief the testimony to Christ in Corinth lives or dies.[51]

The notion of the resurrection as the primal reality is of crucial importance for Barth's understanding of the significance of Paul's resurrection theology. Barth is taken by the fact that Paul deduces from the reality of the resurrection of Jesus Christ necessary implications for the reality of the Corinthian believers. He traces out the Pauline argument for the *general* resurrection of the dead – that is, the resurrection of all the dead – from the particular yet all-encompassing reality of the resurrection of Jesus Christ. Barth contends: 'The whole meaning of verses 12–28 is, indeed, this – that this historical fact, the resurrection of Jesus, stands and falls with the resurrection of the dead, generally.'[52] If the resurrection of the dead generally is denied, there can be no special meaning to the resurrection of Jesus. In that case

---

46   *RD*, p. 153. T.F. Torrance correctly asserts that Barth consistently understood the resurrection as foundational to the gospel message as a whole: 'The truth that Barth was so concerned to stress here is this: it was in the resurrection of Jesus from the dead that divine revelation in Jesus Christ became recognised by the disciples as identical with God himself. That is what actually governed the composition of the Gospels, for the understanding of Jesus Christ by the Evangelists, including their identification of him as the Son of God, flows directly from the resurrection.' Torrance, *Biblical*, p. 107. Cf. also *CD* III/2, p. 443.

47   *RD*, p. 150.

48   *RD*, p. 112f.

49   *RD*, p. 162.

50   *RD*, pp. 139, 141.

51   *RD*, p. 119.

52   *RD*, p. 133.

the resurrection of Jesus has no revelatory value. It offers nothing new. It reveals nothing of the relation of history as a whole to God's eternity. It is not God's decisive act toward the sphere of human history. It can be accounted for as simply an oddity of human experience, which witnesses to the ongoing life of the immortal soul. It does not bring into question the facile monism of the Greeks, but rather Jesus' resurrection itself becomes relative to the ideal monist system. Barth says 'it is just here that Christian monism dashes itself in vain against the discontinuity, against the dialectic of Pauline thought, against the No, which in its gospel of their hope in Christ they set against this life.'[53] Barth reasons:

> If my life and all our lives do not stand in the light of that divine horizon, then I must accordingly interpret otherwise my beginning in Christ and, consequently, that of the primitive Church: then the divine horizon of all things has by no means appeared there, then that which happened there may be interpreted as a miracle, myth, or inward experience, in this way or that; it then belongs, in any case, to the sea of life, among the many shapes and events, which may be explained in this way or that. ... What is referred to even there cannot be anything that is qualitatively new and different. If God is not God in *our* life, then He is also not that in the life of *Christ*. ... Either God is known and recognized as the Lord and Creator and Origin, because He has revealed Himself as such, or there is no revelation in history, no miracle, no special category 'Christ.'[54]

Barth sets out the options very clearly. Either this is the singular event in which God reveals himself fully and finally, once and for all, to the whole of human history, *or* this is nothing but an event like any other, having nothing to do with questions of *the* origin and *the* end at all.

On Barth's reading, the Corinthians did not understand the range of the truth in which they believed: Paul's understanding of the resurrection of Jesus is such that it demands the general resurrection. Regarding the ontological and existential significance of the resurrection of Jesus Barth says:

> [T]he conclusion from Christ to us others is based upon the far deeper-lying assumption that the resurrection of Christ, in that 'appeared,' to which Paul appealed in the name of the primitive Church and in his own name, was a question of the revelation of God. If that be true, if the end of history set by God is here, if the new eternal beginning placed by God appears here, than that which has appeared from God applies to the whole of history within the scope of this horizon, then the miracle of God to Christ is immediately and simultaneously the miracle of God *to us*, and not a miracle about which it may, at any rate, still be asked: what has it to do with us? If we see God at work there, then what is true there is also serious for us here and now, then our life, too, it goes without saying, is placed in the light which proceeds from that horizon of all we call life. ... We are living the life limited by that horizon, we are living in time for eternity, we are living in the hope of the resurrection, it is that which cannot be denied, if Christ's resurrection is to be understood,

---

53   *RD*, pp. 116–17.
54   *RD*, pp. 153f.

not as miracle or myth or psychic experience (which all come to the same thing), but as God's revelation.[55]

Precisely because this resurrection is God's self-revelation the conclusion from Christ to all others is necessitated. Because God is revealed in the resurrection of Jesus Christ, it must affect the whole of history and not just a part of it. Otherwise it would not be the crossing of the boundary between the eternity of God and the whole of creaturely existence. It therefore affects every human being and all of creation. The grounds for Barth's understanding of the universal effectuality of Jesus Christ for humankind here lay not in Barth's adoption of an anhypostatic-enhypostatic christology – this had not yet occurred – but in the event of Jesus Christ's crossing the boundary between eternity and time, that is, in his resurrection from death to life. This early notion of the movement of Christ in God's eternity to others in their own time remains a persistent theme in Barth's resurrection understanding throughout his career. Significantly, Barth does not make reference here to the agency of the Holy Spirit – a theme which figures much more prominently in *CD* IV/2. The transition from Christ to Christians appears in this description almost mechanical, almost as if by the laws of physics set in motion by God's act upon Christ. The act of God upon Jesus Christ amounts directly to the act of God upon creation as a whole.

Paul argues that the implications of what is believed by the Corinthians entails something strange to them, something which was neither anticipated nor admitted by them, namely, the general resurrection of the dead. This implicate of their faith takes them by surprise. For Barth if there is no resurrection then there are no last things, no crisis which puts this whole into question:

> If the world and the life that we know is endless, then the belief in the beyond is also only an expression in idealism, with which we affirm the endless progress of this man; then what applies to the remoter spheres, unknown to the majority of men, of the life beyond, and to the stages and stations which man may reach there, may also be said of his life this side of death: judgment and destruction also rule there. ... Dying is pitilessly nothing but dying, only the expression of the corruptibility of all finite things, if there be no *end* of the finite, no *perishing* of the corruptible, no *death* of death.[56]

Barth argues that the meaning of the resurrection of Jesus consists in the fact that the resurrection is the divine horizon of our existence also and not only that of Jesus. As he refers to 1 Corinthians 15:22 ('as in Adam all die so in Christ shall all be made alive,') he claims 'the former indicates our condition with which we have to reckon; the latter is the promise in which we may hope.'[57] With regard to the 'all', which Barth says is obvious from the start, those who belong to Christ are representative but not exclusive, and he says, 'the resurrection, like death, concerns *all*.'[58]

---

55   *RD*, pp. 151–2.
56   *RD*, pp. 158–9.
57   *RD*, p. 166.
58   Ibid.

Barth sees in Paul an understanding of the resurrection of Jesus Christ as the most concrete reality which under girds all other reality. Its influence is exerted fundamentally and comprehensively upon the whole of contingent reality. The resurrection is primordial, and thus, it alone affects the whole of the rest of reality, necessitating the resurrection of that whole. In Barth's clear summary: 'That is our hope; the meaning of the resurrection of Jesus consists in this, that the resurrection is the divine horizon also of our existence. Life and the world are finite. God is the end. Hence He is also the beginning.'[59]

The Resurrection as the Substance of Hope

In his exegesis of vv. 20–28 Barth begins to disclose his understanding of Pauline eschatology. Far from an 'eschatological mythology' Paul has here developed clear and distinct ideas expressed in 'impetuous crowding metaphorical language:'[60]

> Christ as the second Adam is the beginning of the resurrection of the dead. Perfection is the resurrection also of His own, and therefore the very fundamental thing that was denied in Corinth. This perfection is, as the abolition of death generally, His highest and at the same time His last act of sovereignty. As yet He is not fulfilled (*vollzogen*), His power is still in conflict with the other penultimate powers, and to that extent we are now standing in His Kingdom, awaiting that last, but only just awaiting. When He is fulfilled, then His Kingdom, as a special Kingdom beside the Kingdom of God (His Kingdom as the period of the merely 'adjacent' Kingdom of God, the period of hope, which is indeed hope but no more than Hope), is at an end. To this end has the Kingdom in fact been given [H]im, that God should be all in all. Therefore this 'God all in all,' and hence the general resurrection of the dead, is the meaning, misconceived in Corinth, of the resurrection of Christ, the meaning of the Christian faith.[61]

With verse 20 Barth sees Paul turn from the untenable presupposition, assumed in verses 12–19, that the desperation of the human condition belies the resurrection of Jesus. Rather Paul claims the resurrection is the solution, the ray of hope which falls upon this condition. The reference to the Old Testament metaphor of first fruits indicates that God claims the first portion of the harvest for himself, signifying thereby that the other part, the whole, belongs to him. 'That is our hope; the meaning of the resurrection of Jesus consists in this, that the resurrection is the divine horizon also of our existence.'[62]

In verses 21–2 Barth sees the contrast between the old man, Adam, with whom death begins, and the new man, Christ, with whom life begins. But all this is to be placed under the heading of a 'not yet.' To apprehend the revelation of God in Jesus Christ involves laying hold of its promise. Christ's *parousia* is not another thing following his resurrection. It is 'only the definite coming-to-the-surface of the

---

59   *RD*, p. 165.
60   *RD*, p. 164.
61   *RD*, pp. 164f.
62   *RD*, p. 165.

same subterranean stream which in revelation for the first time became perceptible in time.'[63] Christ's *parousia*, the fulfilment of his resurrection, can only be grasped in time as a promise. The resurrection announces the general victory of Christ which 'although never and nowhere present, is yet always and everywhere to be conceived of as the crisis of every human temporal thing.'[64]

In verses 24–8 Paul emphasizes that the world in its present form and also our present relationship to God is a provisional state in the midst of transition. In this state we are standing in the kingdom of Christ under the rubric of revelation and faith. The Corinthians were mistaken to understand the resurrection of Christ 'as something finished and satisfying in itself.' Christ is come to deliver the kingdom to the Father and hence Christ is in conflict with all powers that are hostile to God. The kingdom of God is not already established but is in the process of coming. The kingdom of God arrives when the final enemy, death, is defeated. 'Peace cannot and must not be concluded just here in such a way as to establish a spiritual–religious–moral Kingdom of God on earth, the while forgetting the enemy.'[65] The kingdom of Christ, the kingdom of transition and struggle, involves the prospect of peace in the overcoming of the final enemy. In as much as the resurrection is not yet present in its fullness the kingdom of God has not yet arrived, 'not even in what the Christian Church has and is in its faith.'[66] The kingdom of Christ:

> is rather in its essence a hope and expectation of what at all times is only coming, only promised, the Kingdom of God, of the Father, in which there are no longer any princedoms, powers, and authorities, no greatness and splendour that would be secondary to the grandeur and splendour of God, in which therefore also the last enemy, death, is thus abolished.[67]

Christianity for Barth is nonsense if it does not mean the abolition of death.

Barth is firmly convinced that the resurrection of the dead is of absolutely primary importance for the Apostle Paul. The testimony to the risen Christ is the testimony foundational to the church. The resurrection of the dead is the sum and substance of the gospel message. Without it there is no gospel.

The Resurrection as Revelation

For Barth that which is human, while valued as human can never lay claim to being anything more than human. Even religion without revelation has no advantage over anything else in human experience:

---

63   *RD*, p. 167.
64   *RD*, pp. 167f. Barth's early notion of the integral unity of the resurrection and the *parousia* remains constant even, as we shall see later, into *CD* IV/3.
65   *RD*, p. 169.
66   *RD*, p. 171.
67   Ibid.

> Even the faith, without reference to revelation, will be a substitute faith, not addressed to God, but to the human something in Christ, whose divine resemblance is there asserted. ... Then, Feuerbach is right. Then [human religion, and in particular Christianity] is to be explained as no more than the dream of human wishes.[68]

Of utmost significance for Barth, and clearly the fundamental matter for Paul, is the understanding of the resurrection of Jesus Christ as *the* unsurpassable miracle of the self-revelation of God.[69]

The Resurrection of the Dead as the Revelation 'of God'

According to Barth, the absolute origin and foundation of all things is necessarily fundamentally different from all things which come from it, otherwise it would not be *the* origin. God as he is in himself is qualitatively distinct from his creation. There can be no continuity between God and the contingent world of human reality, and hence no unbroken line of being or conceptuality from the created realm to the Creator. An *analogia entis* of any expression is quite impossible.

Likewise, God is utterly free. He cannot be co-opted within a human movement or program. God's revelation therefore must originate and remain within his own divine freedom:

> The truth and the worth of the testimony of Christ lie in what in them *happens* to the man, happens from God; not what he is as man, nor what he makes of it, not in the word or the 'gnosis' in man's acceptance of it. 'The Kingdom of God is not in word' (generally understood: not in the subjective constitution of man) 'but in power' (I interpret: to be and abide in the freedom of God the Lord) (iv. 20). ... God always remains the *subject* in the relationship created by this testimony. He is not transformed into the object, into man's having the right to the last word: otherwise it is no longer *this* testimony, *this* relationship.[70]

God, in his revelation, remains God, and therefore remains subject of his self-revelation. Revelation therefore cannot be recalled, repeated or rehearsed, or otherwise objectified by human effort. According to Torrance, 'Barth held with increasing vigour that revelation is *act* of God, dynamic *event* impinging upon us in our historical existence and actuality.'[71] Hence, real knowledge of revelation must remain God's knowledge. That is, only God can know God's self objectively, only

---

68   *RD*, p. 156f.

69   Cf. Trevor Hart's 'Revelation' in *The Cambridge Companion to Karl Barth* (Cambridge: Cambridge University Press, 2000), pp. 41–4 for more on revelation as miracle in Barth. Hart rightly parallels the 'impossibility of humans knowing God' with the 'impossibility of resurrection from the dead' in the logic of Christian faith (p. 43).

70   *RD*, p. 16.

71   Torrance, *Biblical*, pp. 41f.

he can know the knowledge of God.[72] Human knowledge of God must be knowledge that is more akin to love than to cognitive apprehension:

> In this connexion love must at any rate mean devotion of the subject of knowledge to its object ... This love (in knowledge) edifies, says Paul ... *God* is then true in this *cogitor*, this 'being thought-of' (by God), and all men with their *cogitare*, with their *self*-thinking, are liars.[73]

Knowledge of God then is and remains a deep reverence for and appreciation of God in his sovereign freedom.

The overwhelming theological problem for Paul, and in turn for Barth, is how to speak of God as he is in himself. Is he not as Creator, as Absolute Origin, entirely different from any other thing? How can we then speak of him? Paul is, according to Barth, concerned with 'the testimony of God's self-revelation'[74] – it is God himself in his own being who is the object of Christian faith and knowledge. The question is not of something that is like God, for in as much as it is something like God, but not truly God himself, it is knowledge of something other than God, and, therefore, something radically other than God. To know *something* about God is an impossibility. Since God is unlike any *thing*, *things* have no likeness to God. There is nothing that can serve as an adequate analogy for God. Knowledge of God must be direct knowledge of God as he is in himself or it is no knowledge at all. For this reason Barth sets at odds 'specific human experiences, convictions, trends of thought and theories' or 'special human content' and 'belief in God.'[75] He opposes 'the testimony of Christ' with 'an object of energetic human activity, a vehicle of real human needs.'[76] Barth insists that: 'Either God is known and recognized as the Lord and Creator and Origin, because He has revealed himself as such, or there is no revelation in history, no miracle, no special category "Christ."'[77]

Barth is convinced that the biblical text deals with something weighty, something quite unlike anything other, something which validates it as a book admired, studied, preached, and reflected upon within the worshipping community for the purpose of knowing God. Barth follows Paul in insisting that the chief concern of Christianity is 'Christian knowledge,' not of the variegated multiplicity of things, nor their unity, but of the final source and origin of all things.[78] God reveals himself as he is in himself:

> The sole, or at any rate vital, assumption which I make, is that when Paul spoke of God (from the side of God, from God, to God's glory), he really meant *God*, and that it is permissible, even imperative, and from this standpoint, to interpret all his ideas, however

---

72   *RD*, p. 25.
73   *RD*, pp. 45f.
74   *RD*, p. 26.
75   *RD*, p. 15.
76   *RD*, p. 15.
77   *RD*, p. 154.
78   *RD*, pp. 16ff.

they may otherwise be historically and psychologically determined, to take him at his word, calculating that all his utterances, however ambiguous they may be regarded within the realm of history, relate, beyond the realm of history, unequivocally to God, and that this relationship gives to everything its peculiar concrete meaning, however little we are able to ascertain this everywhere with equal distinctness.[79]

Once the question is developed to this point Barth can respond with the great message of the Christian gospel – the gospel of the resurrection, the gospel of revelation. The message of the gospel is this: though we as humans can in no way act towards God, God can and does act toward us. God's great act is the resurrection of Jesus Christ from the dead. In this God is revealed for who he truly is. Thus Barth, following Paul, speaks of the resurrection as revelation.[80]

The Resurrection as the Revelation of the Infinite Gulf Between Heaven and Earth

In his original attempt to speak of this fundamental distinction between God and humanity Barth employed metaphors of spatial separation and boundaries.[81] While separation language of this sort in *The Resurrection of the Dead* is less pronounced than in his earlier work, Barth continues to use it, as he does even in his most mature work. Though Berkouwer believes in the *Romans* it was possible to confuse the form and content of Barth's discussion (the content being 'affected by the philosophic mold in which it was cast'[82]), this does not hold for *The Resurrection of the Dead*. In fact, Barth does not resort to separation language at all in the first half of the book. He merely draws out the very Pauline notion of the distinction between that which is 'of God' (*apo tou theou*) and everything else. Only when he breaks off from his running commentary in chapter II to combat the contemporary misunderstanding regarding the reality of the distinction between human history and God's eternity does he employ boundary language.[83] In doing this he does not import philosophical ideas into the text but illumines other notions of the time–eternity relation for what they are – systems that do not take seriously the infinite soteriological gulf between God and humanity – in order that Paul's most extreme message can be heard. Barth's

---

79   *RD*, p. 97.

80   One might be tempted to think that Barth so radicalizes the distinction between God and his creation that God own freedom is violated – God has become imprisoned by his otherness, in much the same way as Barth speaks of Allah as being imprisoned in his transcendence. But this is just to miss the point of Barth's whole development of the resurrection as the exercise of God's freedom to reveal himself in human history, all the while maintaining his utter and inalienable distinction as Creator.

81   Barth appropriately denied having a 'system,' but did emphasize the infinite qualitative distinction between God and humanity (*Romans*, p. 10).

82   Berkouwer, *The Triumph of Grace*, p. 32.

83   Thus Berkouwer is correct in understanding the boundary language to be still important in *The Resurrection of the Dead*, but Berkouwer does not make clear the fact that Barth has left the philosophical 'form' of his message – largely carried in boundary language – behind. Cf. Berkouwer, *The Triumph of Grace*, p. 328ff.

use of boundary language serves largely as a framework with which to understand the even greater, genuinely *biblical*, antitheses – what he calls the greater 'tension of faith'[84] – such as Condemnation vs. Justification, Death vs. Life, and Crucifixion vs. Resurrection. While some of the images of spatial separation used in the *Romans* remain – the notion of frontier (*Romans*, pp. 231f/*RD*, pp. 70, 134) and the notion of distinct worlds or realities (*Romans*, p. 30/*RD*, pp. 68, 119, 191) – other images having to do with a more general notion of revelation – such as 'every impress of revelation' acting as 'a sign-post to Revelation' (*Romans*, p. 79), the crater formed by the explosion of a shell no longer accessible (p. 65), or the empty canal through which the life-giving water no longer flows (pp. 65f, 72) –are clearly left behind. While in the *Romans* Barth employs rather extensive use of the notion of 'Krisis' (e.g. pp. 106, 114, 118) and the 'wholly Other' (e.g. pp. 49, 107, 115), these are not easily found, if at all, in *The Resurrection of the Dead*. In *The Resurrection of the Dead* the self-revelation of God is much more closely allied to the resurrection of Jesus Christ. The images from the *Romans* which perdure in *The Resurrection of the Dead* with greater distinctness are: God as Primal Origin (e.g. *RD*, pp. 77, 94, 154), the notion of history and the frontier of history (e.g. *RD*, pp. 134, 139, 151, 154), the contrast of the old and the new (e.g. *RD*, pp. 82, 87, 166, 170, 196), and revelation as personal encounter with the risen Christ (e.g. *RD*, pp. 72, 136f, 143, 146f).

Berkouwer's essentially correct, though somewhat over-stated, critique of the *Römerbrief* applies less adequately to *The Resurrection of the Dead*:

> Undoubtedly some philosophic, especially Platonic, thoughts have placed their stamp on Barth's *Römerbrief* and this has not infrequently created the impression that he was more concerned with the crisis of 'eternity' over time than with the judgment of the living God. Biblical thoughts are constantly obscured by a transcendental *boundary*-idea, which reminds one more of philosophical idealism than of the gospel.[85]

It is more accurate to claim the 1 Corinthians 15 commentary represents a shift in focus to a more biblical 'eschatologically realist' position, a correction to what Berkouwer calls the 'over-accentuation of the divine future as a boundary.'[86]

Similarly, T.F. Torrance's depiction of Barth's earlier work, as employing a dialectical expression as a result of his own intention to destroy the grounds for belief in an accessible continuity between God and humanity, requires modification. According to Torrance:

> In this essentially polemical period when the ground had to be cleared of false conceptions, and the positive relation between man and God had yet to be worked out dogmatically, it was inevitable that the two poles should be held together only in a dialectical relationship, and that in that dialectical relationship the No should sound louder than the Yes. Until the No had done its work, until the whole root of pantheism was pulled up and cast aside, there could be no fruitful or positive affirmation of the union of God and man and of man

---

84   *RD*, p. 212.
85   Berkouwer, *The Triumph of Grace*, p. 31.
86   Ibid., p. 32.

and God, for it would no sooner be said than the acids of immanentism would start to eat it all away. Dialectical theology is therefore the attempt to affirm both God and man in their utter difference, that God may be God and man may be man, and at the same time to suspend (at least, full) positive account of their relation to one another.[87]

However, as we have seen here, Barth's rejection of any notion of continuity between God and humanity derives precisely from the proclamation of the resurrection. It is the resurrection reality (the 'Yes' of God) which discloses the extent and severity of the death (the 'No' of God) which is the end of all things. Only in the resurrection light, the light of new beginning, can the end be seen as radical end. Barth asserts the radical discontinuity of heaven and earth, not from an independent characterization of each, but from the reality of the appearance of the kingdom of heaven on earth in the resurrection of Jesus. Far from the employment of a dialectical construct from a neutral vantage point, Barth argues from the dogmatic perspective that God's incontrovertible 'Yes', as sounded in the resurrection of Jesus, includes within it already the revelation of the destruction in the death of Christ of any other common ground between God and humanity. It is not that the 'No' has to be sounded in order to prepare a hearing for God's 'Yes'. It is that God's 'Yes', which at the same time grounds and surpasses his 'No', has been irrevocably enacted.

The Resurrection as the Revelation of the Radical Severity of Death

In Barth's view, to understand Paul in 1 Corinthians 15 is to understand the radical severity of what he meant by the 'resurrection of the dead.' That means comprehension not only of the incomprehensible resurrection but also of the severity of death and dying. Of greatest importance is the recognition that death receives its full and final meaning in the light of the resurrection. Barth understands Paul's conception of 'the dead' to mean 'everything that comes under the rule of death,' that is, not only the death of every human individual, but the entirety of life that falls under the shadow of death, tending toward death and ending in death. It is this threshold of death that Barth understands to be the 'question of all questions,' 'the last severity,' 'the last hope,' and these together are the theme of 1 Corinthians 15, 'the *last things*'.[88] The tendency of Barth's thought here is towards, not a death and dying in general, abstracted from the judgment of God, but a death and dying as that which is effected in the death of Jesus Christ and revealed in his resurrection. Barth has effectively demonstrated this critical mode of the 'of God' throughout the first 14 chapters of the epistle. Paul attempts to correct the Corinthian tendency to celebrate this-worldly realities by reminding them that all things fall under the shadow of the eschatological reality of God to which they point.

Barth understands Paul to speak of the doctrine of the resurrection of the dead as a recollection that 'All those things which the Corinthian Christians were previously

---

87   Torrance, *Introduction*, pp. 84–5.
88   *RD*, p. 101.

bidden to lay to heart appear here in the pale light of the fact that they must die.'[89] Recollection of death cannot be arrived at generally, independently of revelation, but rather confronts us precisely in the light of the resurrection. Death, for Paul, is the only visible, humanly knowable final reality of all things, even things religious. The apostle intends to remind all of the only final conceivability: death. Barth comments that Paul is surprised by the fact that those who have seen the risen Lord have died.[90] They saw God's power overturn the death of Jesus, but they did not see their own deaths overturned. At the time of Paul's writing they were indeed dead. If it is to be understood that they had just fallen asleep, as would be explained apart from any notion of the resurrection of Jesus, then their experience of the appearance of the risen Lord was a common experience like any other in the continuum of this worldly experiences, and thus was not revelation. But, Barth argues:

> If the resurrection of Jesus were only an isolated miracle and not the revelation *of the* miracle that God worked on men, if it is only to mean 'Christ rose again' but not the 'Resurrection of the Dead,' then even this miracle is not true, then Christ is not risen, and those whom we now so amiably call 'those that have fallen asleep' are perished (verse 18). For then life and death are equally meaningless.[91]

Barth insists that the essence of Paul's argument is that it is the *dead* who are being raised, 'the dead' signifying those who have forfeited completely all human possibilities of life and meaningfulness. What is meant by the resurrection from the dead is not merely an extension of the immortal life of the soul as the body is cast off, but the most complete and utter ending followed by a miraculous and unexplainable 'repredication'[92] of the same body. There is nothing else to anticipate; apart from the resurrection miracle of God, the dead remain entirely and unalterably, the dead.

The Corinthians did not perceive the severity of the reality of death because they did not perceive the grandeur of the reality of life as revealed in the resurrection of Jesus. The resurrection of the dead means that what we are not, that is, risen, is equivalent with what we are, that is, dead. Berkouwer has captured it well:

> That the crisis is not simply the form in which a reigning sense of catastrophe is cast appears especially from the fact that the absolute No of God is not the *last* and *only* Word of God. The crisis stands rather – regarded from God's point of view – in direct connection with the *Yes* of God, with *redemption*, with *grace*, the great *miracle* of God. This divine Yes does not arise from the heart of man, nor is it heard and understood by means of a logical dialectic which can turn the No into a Yes. It comes to us *exclusively* from God Himself and is heard at *that* point where, in the acknowledgment of the judgment that is pronounced over all human righteousness, the divine forgiveness and justification by faith are appropriated.[93]

---

89   *RD*, p. 107.
90   *RD*, p. 144.
91   *RD*, pp. 144–5.
92   *RD*, pp. 190f.
93   Berkouwer, *The Triumph of Grace*, p. 30.

For Barth 'the recollection of death is so important, so urgent, so disturbing, so actual because it is in fact really the tidings of the resurrection behind it, the recollection of the *life*, of our life that we are not living and that yet is our life.'[94] The chasm which separates the impossible from the possible is not abolished, but is crossed in hope, that is, the now dead and the risen are already one in God. Barth declares: 'Behind the impenetrable walls of impenetrable reality in front of which we stand, and whose unmistakable sign is death, stands and awaits the new real life, which has appeared in Christ, but is the very life of all of us.'[95]

The Resurrection as the Revelation of the Frontier of History

Barth's repudiation of the hermeneutics of historicism, psychologism and immanentism (that is, the search for a subject matter exclusively in scientifically verifiable history or its psychological causes or in human consciousness) results from his clear perception that Paul does not speak in the first instance of a history which satisfies the criteria of historical-critical inquiry. To insist otherwise is to deny God's revelation as self-revelation, to limit the freedom of God and to profane the singular revelation of the resurrection, and therefore to misconstrue the entire meaning and orientation of the Apostle Paul.

Because of his strong statements on the matter, Barth's understanding of the historicity of the resurrection has been sorely misunderstood, and in part Barth's polemic is to blame. Some of Barth's statements are clearly polemical, and expressed with characteristic rhetorical force:[96] the emptiness of the tomb of Jesus 'is really a matter of indifference;'[97] 'time and place are a matter of perfect indifference;'[98] and 'the *last* word that can be said on the basis of historical observation: a fact as doubtful as all earthly facts are: he might, in fact, have been stolen, he might only have appeared to be dead.'[99] Such statements are to be understood as combating an inadequate historicist interpretation of Paul's main point, not as a devaluation of history. Accordingly, Ronald H. Nash is incorrect to assume that the '*early*'

---

94   *RD*, p. 109.

95   *RD*, p. 166.

96   Rudolf Bultmann, *Faith and Understanding*, p. 83, and Hans Conzelmann, *1 Corinthians: A Commentary on the First Epistle to the Corinthians*, trans. by James W. Leitch (Philadelphia: Fortress Press, 1975), pp. 257f., have both contended from textual evidence that Paul is actually adducing proof of the resurrection in some historical sense. Barth has deliberately underplayed the importance of the observable, objectifiable side of the resurrection so as to underscore the significance of the eschatological character of the resurrection. Barth does eventually speak of the objective historical component but only in the new context of the primordial reality of the resurrection. Cf. *CD* III/2, section 47.1, pp. 448f. Barth's prime emphasis remains unscathed – the unobservable, unobjectifiable act of God's self-revelation continues to be the chief matter in the miracle of the resurrection.

97   *RD*, p. 135.

98   *RD*, p. 135.

99   *RD*, p. 136.

Barth 'denigrated history in favor of some type of superhistory.'[100] On the contrary, Barth wanted to understand history as significant but established and framed by the essentially eschatological reality of the resurrection. Nash also errs in his understanding that the later Barth's attitude toward history has changed, explaining the elements of understanding common to the earlier and later Barth as 'occasional lapses that appear to be reversions to his earlier position.'[101] It would be more accurate to understand these common elements as the central perduring elements with which Barth concerned himself consistently as primary issues. Like other critics, Nash fails to appreciate Barth's attempt to contextualize history within the larger theatre of eschatological reality as revealed in the resurrection.

John Wenham, too, misses the point. He speaks of the resurrection narratives as 'an intriguing puzzle,'[102] and confidently claims he 'gradually found many of the pieces of the jigsaw coming together.'[103] The issue, however, of the possibility of a harmonization of the resurrection accounts is secondary. Even if such a harmonization were produced, the adequacy of that purely historical account to depict the foundational reality of the resurrection is called into question. Barth believes the resurrection reality cannot be adequately depicted by purely historical accounts. Because the resurrection reality is the source and ground of history, marking the beginning and ending of history, the impartial, objective eye of the historian cannot observe it.

Daniel P. Fuller misreads Barth along similar lines. Fuller concludes: 'there remains in Barth an unreconciled tension between faith and the historical method.'[104] The error arises from Fuller's perception that Barth understands the testimony of the Apostles to be an 'independent control of our knowledge of the resurrection.'[105] Fuller seizes upon one sentence which accounts for Barth's unreserved dependence upon the witness of the Apostles, but ignores its context. Barth asserts 'the inexplicable and inconceivable nature' of the miracle of 'the revelation of God in the flesh'[106]

---

100   Ronald H. Nash, *Christian Faith And Historical Understanding* (Grand Rapids: Zondervan, 1984), p. 120.

101   Ibid. Likewise, S. Paul Schilling understands Barth's 'Encounter with Reality' as a later development 'result[ing] in several important modifications of his earlier thought.' Cf. Schilling, *Contemporary Continental Theologians* (New York: Abingdon Press, 1966), p. 26. Among these modifications Schilling notes a moderation in the 'dialectical character' of Barth's later theology, a minimized stress on the infinite qualitative distinction between time and eternity, and an abandonment of 'the attempt to interpret theology in existentialist terms' (p. 26f.). Schilling, along with a number of others who make this same observation, is undoubtedly incorrect.

102   John Wenham, *Easter Enigma: Are the Resurrection Accounts in Conflict?* (Grand Rapids: Academie Books, 1984), p. 9.

103   Ibid., p. 11.

104   Daniel P. Fuller, *Easter Faith and History* (Grand Rapids: William B. Eerdmans Publishing Company, 1965), p. 150.

105   Ibid., p. 149.

106   *CD* IV/ii, p. 147.

which is 'bound' and 'conditioned' only by Christ.[107] According to Barth, the manner in which the 'decisive' knowledge of Christ is ordered by the apostolic witness is as love (which 'does not know neutrally and with complete objectivity') is 'ordered' by the 'objective knowledge' which forms its 'presupposition.'[108] It is evident that Barth is speaking of two very different orders of knowledge. The one has to do with the apostolic witness which is provisional and preparatory. The other has to do with unconditional knowledge (love) which is gained only as the risen Christ personally engages the one who would know him. Fuller does not seem to appreciate the possibility of a manner of knowing which is of a higher order than the knowing of objective historical facts.

The view of Walter Künneth at this point is much more in keeping with Barth:

> No matter how important the historical relationships may be in detail, when the resurrection message is looked at in its essential character it does not exhaust itself in history but points decisively beyond the sphere of history. The whole weight and extraordinary character of the witness to the resurrection of Jesus simply does not depend at all on its historicality. What makes the witness to the resurrection different from other statements lies beyond the historic plane.[109]

However, when Künneth describes Barth's view of the resurrection as the mythical concept of 'proto-history *as opposed to history* [emphasis mine]'[110] he is incorrect. Künneth depends largely on a citation from the *Römerbrief*, but he does not seem to take note that Barth uses the term 'myth' very loosely, often in association with terms such as 'Problem' and 'Paradox.'[111] What is more, only a few lines later Barth insists: 'The Resurrection is therefore an occurrence in history.'[112] Barth would heartily agree with Künneth that '*The application of the concept of myth to the resurrection of Jesus means a levelling down of the particular to the universal, the changing of the* "revelatio specialis" *into a general revelation*, the confusing of the accidental with the essential.'[113] Barth's desire is to assert the reality of the relatedness of God's history with human history, but not merely as a natural state of affairs, discernable within human experience. It is rather a relationship established, guaranteed and revealed in the resurrection of Jesus Christ. This means the resurrection is the act of God which establishes, guarantees and reveals the truth of history. This order is irreversible.

Barth's interest in *The Resurrection of the Dead* is not to deny the historicity of the resurrection of Jesus Christ from the dead (he, rather, emphatically affirms it),

---

107   Ibid., p. 149.

108   Ibid.

109   Walter Künneth, *The Theology of the Resurrection* (St Louis: Concordia Publishing House, 1965), p. 30.

110   Ibid., p. 54.

111   Barth, *Romans*, p. 30.

112   Ibid.

113   Künneth, p. 57.

but to insist that at heart the resurrection is more than merely historical. In fact that which makes the resurrection the object of Christian faith, that which distinguishes it from all historical things as *the* resurrection, is precisely the fact that it is a reality greater than historical reality. Barth does not intend to say that history, as perceived in the science of historical-critical inquiry, has no place; however, he does intend to say emphatically that it is entirely and utterly subordinate to the question of the resurrection as the saving revelation of the reality of God. He claims explicitly that Paul intends to speak of revelation as he speaks of the resurrection and thus Paul cannot be speaking of a resurrection narrative or an historical proof of the resurrection. According to Barth, what Paul meant by these verses has the effect 'not of disconnecting the *historical position of the question as such*, but of *relativizing it*.'[114] The crucial question has not to do so much with the objectifiable historical details, as with the sum and significance of these things vis-à-vis God. The question has to do with the relation of the whole of history to its Creator, a relation which is foundational to history. The question which concerns Barth – and, in as much as Barth has his finger on the pulse of the epistle, Paul – has to do not with the realm of time and space, the realm thoroughly characterized by death. It has to do, rather, with the divine action, the post-mortem miracle of the resurrection, which ever and always remains beyond the range of human comprehension. Just as God remains supremely beyond human apprehension so the act of God which is genuinely revelatory of God as he is in himself remains supremely beyond. It is that which is supremely beyond which is the ultimate concern of Paul.

It is in this light that we are to understand Barth as he asserts that the substance of the testimony of the primitive church was the testimony to the appearances of Christ and in these appearances the boundary has been seen. The boundary has been seen in history, but in history the boundary of the frontier of history has been seen.[115] The witnesses to these appearances are spoken of by Barth in this manner: 'time and place are a matter of perfect indifference' and 'Of what these eyes see it can really be equally well said that it was, is, and will be, never and no where, as that it was, is, and will be, always everywhere possible.'[116] Barth would distinguish between what the witnesses saw and Christ who appeared to them; this appearing and their seeing must be two different things if we are to understand the category of revelation.[117] And in this he insists that the appearances were of the risen Christ.[118] This is why, according to Barth the resurrection of Jesus cannot be asserted in a 'positive' manner:

> [We must understand] the resurrection as the deed *of God*, whom no eye has seen nor ear heard, who has entered no human heart, neither outwardly nor inwardly, not subjective and not objective, not mystical nor spiritistic and not flatly objective, but as a historical

---

114   *RD*, p. 131.
115   *RD*, p. 134.
116   *RD*, p. 135.
117   *RD*, p. 137.
118   *RD*, p. 137.

divine fact, which as such is only to be grasped in the category of revelation and in none other.[119]

Barth insists that all that can be testified is that the Lord appeared: 'all ideas as to the way in which this appearance was *seen* are incapable of being completed; they can only converge upon a denial of the appearance.'[120]

For Barth, Paul's knowledge of the resurrection or of the appearances of the risen Christ does not consist in the end of the apprehension of a purely objectifiable historical actuality. It consists rather of the knowledge of the relatedness of God to the entire scope of history, a knowledge which apprehends the *ending* of history, and therefore, a knowledge dependent entirely upon revelation.

As Barth understands Paul, it is precisely the resurrection of Jesus Christ from the dead that accomplishes the revelation of God himself in the fullness of his eternal glory, the undoing of the kingdom of death, and the crossing of the gulf between heaven and earth. In Barth's view, the resurrection of Jesus Christ from the dead is at the heart of Pauline theology. What remains to be understood is the utter reality of this resurrection. It is not merely history, story, hope, myth, or dream. It is God's primordial and definitive *reality*.

The Resurrection as Reality

For Barth the resurrection of Jesus Christ *is* the revelation of the reality of God and at the same time it casts interpretive light over the whole of contingent reality. On the one hand he appears to understand the resurrection purely as the 'impossible' self-revelation of God (which is different than any other kind of knowledge or experience), while on the other hand he unfolds the meaning of the resurrection as it touches the world of contingent reality in a retrospective reading, that is, he understands the central truths of resurrection reality to be the inner structure of contingent reality. The resurrection miracle has no likeness with anything within contingent reality, yet it reveals the deepest truth of contingent reality:

> Paul is not philosophizing, he is preaching. He is not exhibiting the truth, that is to say, merely the conceivability of an idea, but he is showing how we ought to think from the standpoint of Christ, of revealed truth. Beyond the whole argument there is already the other thing, which is no longer argument, but only intimation: The resurrection as reality ...[121]

Barth rigorously denounces the identification of God and God's action with any element of contingent reality. The relationship of God's reality and human reality, as established and revealed in the resurrection, remains miraculous and ineffable in nature. And thus, the grounds for the meaningfulness of the resurrection as primal

---

119   *RD*, p. 138.
120   *RD*, p. 139.
121   *RD*, p. 184.

history remain miraculous and ineffable. Ingolf Dalferth offers a helpful explanation when he claims that theologians are required to work with models of thought which satisfy two distinct criteria of adequacy:

> On the one hand they have to be true to the eschatological reality confessed and proclaimed by the Church. On the other hand, they have to preserve the unity of reality and the coherence of truth by enabling us to relate intelligibly the truth-claims of the Christian faith to what we know to be true by experience and reflection. This is precisely what Barth's theology has attempted to do. ... [Barth] unfolds in a painstaking and detailed way a theological perspective of universal inclusiveness which incorporates and reconstructs the shared and public reality of our world within theology; and he achieves this by interpreting it theologically within the frame of reference provided by the christological exposition of the eschatological reality described.[122]

Barth makes no effort to disclose the rationale for the companionability of these two strands of discourse. He simply grasps the resurrection of Jesus Christ as the concrete reality which participates in both the reality of God and the world of contingent reality. The reality of the resurrection is the miracle of the relatedness of these two otherwise vastly divergent realities. Thus, Barth follows Paul in arguing from the resurrection of Christ, not as a pattern to be emulated in the religious world, but as an established and irrefutable reality that has definite and inevitable consequences upon the world.

The Actuality of the Resurrection

Earlier we noted that Barth claimed the resurrection could not be captured in positive terms. Yet, at the same time Barth affirms that I Corinthians 15 deals with 'the most positive subject that can be imagined'.[123] The resurrection reality stands on its own, uncaused, unconditioned and unaffected by this-worldly forces. It alone is the final determinative reality. Barth is deeply struck by the fact that Paul simply proceeds from the resurrection as reality, and he testifies to it for what it is. He observes that in chapter 16 Paul follows with 'perfectly human objectivity,' almost in a business-like manner, and from this Barth concludes: 'This, then, is the way in which we can talk to each other, touching lightly upon the most difficult 'uprooting' errors and misunderstandings, when we are really talking about the *resurrection of the dead*.'[124] That is, for Barth the matter which underlies everything that we speak of and do as Christians is the resurrection of the dead.

It is precisely this utter actuality of the resurrection which eludes the grasp of the Corinthian believers. Paul desires to bring them to the recollection that all of

---

122   'Karl Barth's eschatological realism' Ingolf Dalferth, 'Karl Barth's eschatological realism,' in Stephen W. Sykes, ed., *Karl Barth: Centenary Essays* (Cambridge: Cambridge University Press, 1989), p. 30.

123   *RD*, p. 101.

124   *RD*, p. 205

their religious activity and knowledge have significance only by virtue of their relationship to the prior and all-determining act of God in the resurrection of Jesus Christ. According to Barth:

> [The Corinthians] must realize the relativity of their Christian religion. Relativity means relationship. The object of relationship is God, who speaks His decisive word in the resurrection of the dead, and upon the existence or non-existence of this relationship hinges the question whether your Christianity is full of real meaning or is utter nonsense.[125]

Nothing of the whole relationship between God and humanity can be properly understood without an account of the reality of the resurrection. The entire First Epistle to the Corinthians is written from the standpoint of this relativity, or as Barth refers to it, 'the most positive thing that exists, which looms behind and that is the very Resurrection of the Dead with which this chapter [15] deals.'[126]

It is difficult then to comprehend Walter Künneth's charge of 'theological formalism' in Barth which does not do justice to the 'concreteness of the primal miracle of the resurrection of Jesus.'[127] He accuses Barth of using terms such as 'righteousness,' 'kingdom,' 'eternity,' and 'the impossible possibility' in a manner synonymous with 'resurrection,' concluding that, for Barth, 'the resurrection becomes an epitome of general Christian statements and "values".'[128] Künneth goes on to imply that this insight leads Barth to 'a diffuse and ambiguous description which is in danger of failing to see the essential feature of the resurrection witness.'[129] However, the statement Künneth makes as a corrective to Barth appears to say precisely what Barth himself would want to say:

> The decisive thing for the understanding of the reality of the resurrection is its concrete and personalistic character. That is to say that God has not everywhere or in many places revealed the reality of his life, but has bound it to one, single point. ... *The risen Christ is the life, the primal life, the true everlasting life*; he is the authentic reality beyond death, the existence which alone can be meaningfully described as real.[130]

Barth repudiates all reductionistic views of the resurrection which would place that event in the context of a greater, more comprehensive reality. For Barth the resurrection of Jesus Christ from the dead is the all-comprehensive reality, and at the same time it is supremely concrete reality. That is, it exists in and for itself. It is not an abstraction of or function of or symbol for some other thing. This all-comprehensive yet particular and concrete character of the resurrection is its uniqueness.

---

125   *RD*, p. 181.
126   *RD*, p. 124.
127   Künneth, p. 76.
128   Ibid.
129   Ibid.
130   Ibid.

The Doctrine of Synchronism (Simultaneity)

For Barth the mystery that Paul discloses is the mystery of the *synchronism* or the *simultaneity* of the living and the dead in the resurrection. In the resurrection both the living and the dead are changed: 'The resurrection, the crisis which concerns all men in all ages, means, as surely as it is God's decisive word to mankind: "In Him they *all* live."'[131] Barth insists that if we confess the revelation of God in Christ we place ourselves in its promise, not proleptically, but in the *reality* of the relationship. The mystery is that though we are all presently dead, we are also all alive. The past is no more certain reality than is the present or the future. The reality which determines all other reality is not divided up into past, present and future. The resurrection reality is the relationship of God to all time and space. What is known to us now only in hope is equally real and certain as what we know in present experience. We are thus, at the same time, the dead and the risen.

Barth insists that the resurrection of the body is the resurrection of the same body that we plainly see perishing, therefore, involving the notion not of a duality of life of the present life and the life yet to come, but an identity of these two lives, an identity not now present but to be hoped for and believed in:[132]

> Between us and Christ exists no continuity. Only the relationship of hope. But the relationship of hope *exists*: 'We *shall* bear.' ... We thus stand in the connexion of *salvation history*, which is a real history: the perishing of an old, the becoming of a new, a path and a step on this path, no mere relationship, but history which is not enacted in time, but between time and eternity – *the* history, in which the creation, the resurrection of Christ, and the End, as verse 48 indicates, are one day.[133]

It is only with these victorious tidings that Paul is able to say death is swallowed up in victory. In speaking about this resurrection as reality, Barth draws attention to the present tense in Paul's statement that God gives us the victory, and says that the reality of the resurrection is:

> a valid word spoken to us, not to be forgotten, not to be dragged down into the dialectic of *our* existence, not to be restricted, not to be weakened, not to be doubted. But just for this reason everything depends upon this 'victory' being and remaining God's gift 'through our Lord Jesus Christ' present in *hope*.[134]

The relationship between God and the world of contingent reality, though indubitably real and evidenced to be so in the resurrection revelation, is from the perspective of the contingent world, a reality present in hope. It is not demonstrable in terms of other things. It is to be received in faith from God, to be believed and to be preached. Because the resurrection of Jesus Christ from the dead is a reality for

---

131   *RD*, p. 207.
132   *RD*, p. 117.
133   *RD*, pp. 202f.
134   *RD*, p. 211.

all time, determining all time, the resurrection of human history is *really* present, though from within history this reality is one we relate to in terms of hope.

The significance of the resurrection of Christ cannot be exhausted in historical terms. It is not merely a past event with present historical implications. It is rather an event on the horizon of history, creating and sustaining history. It draws into itself the world of contingent reality, granting it new life and meaning. The resurrection is dealt with adequately, not when it is *explained*, but when it is *testified* and *believed*.[135] The nature of the resurrection is such that cannot become an object of human judgment and predication. It does not fall within the realm of human scrutiny. Rather humans and human history fall under its rubric. Human history is judged, redefined and established anew in the resurrection. Thus the only appropriate human response to the resurrection is vibrant hope.

Conclusion

Karl Barth's *The Resurrection of the Dead* is a commentary on 1 Corinthians 15 which focuses upon Paul's witness to the resurrection reality of the risen Christ as the key by which to understand the whole. Barth is convinced that Paul's theological perspective rests upon his foundational commitment to the priority of the resurrection of Jesus Christ from the dead. As Barth reads Paul, he discovers at least three crucial aspects to Paul's understanding of the resurrection. First, the resurrection is of singular priority in Paul's witness. It is not an accretion to a more primitive, more pristine, more essential, or more real gospel. The only gospel of the apostolic witness is exclusively the gospel of the resurrection of the dead. Second, the resurrection of Jesus Christ must be understood as the supreme revelation of God. Against the radical skepticism of all things divine reached in the exhaustion of all human possibilities is preached the miracle of God's revelation in the resurrection. Third, Barth sees in Paul's conception of the resurrection an understanding of its *reality*, that is, of the resurrection as profoundly actual. It is and guarantees its own reality. Barth sees in Paul no apologetic attempt to explain, prove or otherwise support the reality of the resurrection. Rather Paul preaches and reasons only from the resurrection reality outward to other matters. The resurrection reality is thus both the starting point and the critical force of all theological reflection.

---

135 *RD*, p. 135.

Chapter Three

The Resurrection as the Contemporaneity of Jesus Christ

We now turn our attention to the first extended treatment of the resurrection of Jesus Christ in the *Church Dogmatics*. Analysis of the second part of the third volume, on the doctrine of creation,[1] reveals both important developments and significant consistencies in Barth's understanding of the resurrection. The differences, however, as well shall see, have more the character of implications and extrapolations of his previously declared orientation rather than of fundamental alterations. That in the resurrection the life history of Jesus Christ from Bethlehem to Golgotha is taken up and made contemporaneous with all times is Barth's dominant theme at this point.

The specific context of Barth's resurrection discourse here is that of the doctrine of creation, and more pointedly, that of the conditions of the reality and being of the human in the created order. In *CD* III/2, §47.1, entitled 'Jesus, Lord of Time,'[2] Barth comes to the theme of the resurrection of Jesus Christ in the context of a set of theological questions regarding the constitutive structure of human creaturely existence.

Human beings are soul and body 'in indissoluble differentiation, inseparable unity and indestructible order.'[3] Human beings, Barth adds, are creatures of time: 'Time is the *conditio sine qua non* of [human] life.'[4] Having time is a necessary condition if one is to fulfil one's nature as the soul of one's body. A further observation of the

---

1   *The Doctrine of Creation* was written in four parts in the months closing the Second World War and several years following. *CD* III/2, which contains our second extended development of the doctrine of the resurrection, was published in the Spring of 1948, while Barth was in Basel.

2   Of note is Barth's intimation in the preface to the volume (p. ix) that he is straying significantly from the received dogmatic tradition, even more so, he suggests, than he did in the doctrine of predestination (*CD* II/2). Because of this he has found it necessary on this occasion to adduce a very large number of biblical texts to prove his basic points. He also acknowledges that it may be argued he has strayed from his prime expertise especially 'in the first sub-section of §47' (p. ix), which is the section that we take as our point of departure. Careful scrutiny of his exegesis of Scripture and his dogmatic moves here may be particularly useful. The point is simply that Barth acknowledges significant differences from the dogmatic tradition, and makes the open admission that his extraordinarily distinctive biblical exegetical work invites testing at this point.

3   *CD* III/2, p. 437.

4   Ibid.

fundamental nature of human being is that one has one's being in one's action. True human being cannot be abstracted from individual human historical activity. One has one's being in a very real sense in the totality of one's historical action. This stems from an understanding of the time of the human being as *finite* time, that is, as having a beginning and an ending, a birth and a death. But human time, which Barth describes as the totality of the succession of past, present and future, must be clearly distinguished from God's eternity – 'the simultaneity of present, past and future.'[5] Eberhard Busch correctly asserts that time and eternity are not to be equated, yet neither are they to be set in antithesis. Rather 'God's eternity conditions all time' and 'stands in a positive relation to it.'[6]

George Hunsinger characterizes Barth's view of eternity as fitting neatly neither into the category of eternity as 'the abiding present of unitary consciousness' nor as 'the flowing present of successive instants', but rather as overlapping aspects of each while transcending both.[7] He seeks to understand God's eternity in thoroughgoing trinitarian terms: 'Eternity for Barth is not the container in which God lives. It is a predicate of God's triune being. For that reason eternity exemplifies and guarantees God's full and sovereign freedom.'[8] Hunsinger rightly perceives 'the mystery of eternity' for Barth as 'a subtopic in the mystery of the Trinity'[9] and offers the important observation that Barth's distinction between God's being in itself and God's being in relation to the world is not always carefully distinguished:

> Barth presupposes, but does not always make sufficiently clear that God's trinitarian life includes a form of beginning, middle, and end peculiar to itself. The beginning, middle, and end that God possesses simultaneously and totally are, first of all, peculiar to the trinitarian perichoresis, to the eternal process of becoming, in which God moves from perfection to perfection in and for himself. This eternal becoming, in which his own absolute beginning, succession, and end are all present to God simultaneously – that is, his own eternal self-positing of himself as Father, Son, and Holy Spirit – in turn serves as

---

5   Ibid., p. 438.

6   Eberhard Busch, *The Great Passion: An Introduction to Karl Barth's Theology*, trans. by Geoffrey W. Bromiley (Grand Rapids: William B. Eerdmans Publishing Company, 2004), p. 269. Busch's chapter entitled 'Limited Time – Time and Eternity, Eschatology' (pp. 264–88) provides a broad based and sensitive guide to a wide range of issues concerning Barth's understanding of the relation of time and eternity.

7   George Hunsinger, '*Mysterium Trinitatis*: Karl Barth's Conception of Eternity', pp. 186–209 in *Disruptive Grace: Studies in the Theology of Karl Barth* (Grand Rapids: William B. Eerdmans Publishing Company, 2000), pp. 187f. We do well to take into account Hunsinger's observation of Barth's multifarious and often 'ambiguous' use of the word 'time' (p. 189). Cf. also Brian Leftow's helpful response to this essay in *For the Sake of the World: Karl Barth and the Future of Ecclesial Theology*, ed. by George Hunsinger (Grand Rapids: William B. Eerdmans Publishing Company, 2004), pp. 191–201.

8   Ibid., pp. 188f.

9   Ibid., p. 189.

the basis on which all creaturely time can be and is taken up by God and made present to himself in its totality simultaneously.[10]

Hunsinger explains that it is the prior simultaneity of God's unique time which makes the simultaneity of all creaturely time in God possible and intelligible. Furthermore, Hunsinger writes: 'As the Mediator between God and humankind, between heaven and earth, Jesus Christ is also the Mediator between eternity and time. Eternity and time find their unity and their distinction in him.'[11] This is correct, yet it is important to add the further differentiation that while this description holds for the distinction between divine and human time as they cohere in the life-history of Jesus Christ, so too we must attend to the relation of the life-history of Jesus Christ to the time of all other human beings. That is to say, we must also account for Barth's view of resurrection time, in which, in the risen one, eternity and time find their unity and distinction *in extension* to all other times. As regards the resurrection, it is not only a matter of the relation of divine and human temporality, but of the relation of the time of the God-man to every other human time. It is not only that all time (past, present and future) co-inheres without the loss of differentiation in a perfect simultaneous unity in God's present, but that the time of the God-man becomes present (in its own perfectly co-inhering and simultaneous past, present and future) to every man. This too accounts for some of the complexity in Barth's conception of God's triune being in itself and in relation to the world. That is, not only the Trinity and the incarnation, but also the resurrection, forms the basis of Barth's understanding of the nature and relation of eternity and time.[12] In addition to the downward and upward vectors of the relation of eternity and time in the incarnate Christ there is also the outward vector, the movement of the risen Lord in his time to all other time.

Central to Barth's discussion of the resurrection in this context is an inquiry into the relation of the 'perfect time' of Christ and the time of every other human being. While Jesus in his own time lives as all other human beings with a definite closed totality of past, present and future,[13] it must also be said that he lives for all others as their representative before God. This makes his life 'at once the centre and the beginning and the end of all the times of all the lifetimes of all men.'[14] In this way the man Jesus has his own time but also more than his own time. His time acquires in relation to the time of all other human beings 'the character of God's time, of eternity, in which present, past and future are simultaneous.'[15] It is in this sense that Barth describes Jesus as 'the Contemporary of all men.'[16] According to Barth it is necessary that we hold together the form of Jesus' lifetime as a time bounded by his

---

10   Ibid., p. 200.

11   Ibid., p. 202.

12   Cf. ibid., p. 203.

13   Barth here warns against the heresy of Docetism, which he characterizes as the failure to respect the truly historical character of the action of Christ. Cf. *CD* III/2, p. 440.

14   Ibid., p. 440.

15   Ibid.

16   Ibid.

birth and his death together with the 'eternal content' of his life, which he describes as the 'presence of God' and 'the life of God with that of man.'[17] With this Barth clearly echoes the New Testament assertion of the ἅπαξ or the ἐφάπαξ, that is, the 'once for all', nature of the life of Jesus.

It becomes clear then that the whole history of Jesus Christ from Bethlehem to Golgotha and its relation to the remainder of human history is now the object of concern. Barth does not abandon the distinction between divine and human time, but chooses now to take into account the significance of the life history of Jesus from his birth to his death.[18] The time–eternity dialectic has not been displaced by Barth's adoption of an anhypostatic–enhypostatic christology,[19] but it has taken on an importantly different character. Barth's anhypostatic–enhypostatic christology does not in itself overcome the distance between Jesus Christ and his own. The time–eternity dialectic remains the boundary between God's time and human time, but now God's time is understood to include the lifetime of Jesus. The dialectic now takes the form of a christo-anthropological *diastasis*, which is overcome only in the power of the resurrection. Hence Barth discusses the relationship of the life history of the God-man Jesus Christ (His being in act from Bethlehem to Golgotha) and the life history of all other human beings (past, present and future) in terms of the resurrection. It is not now, as it might be said to have been in *The Resurrection of the Dead*, merely the movement of Jesus Christ as the resurrected one, more or less abstracted from his earthly life, in the reverse crossing of the threshold of death from the eternity of God to the created realm. It is rather a matter of the immediate presence of Jesus' in the totality of his earthly history to the remainder of human history. Without relinquishing the true humanity of Jesus, inclusive of his life-act in time, Barth seeks to work out the implications of the life of Jesus, with its unique beginning, duration and end, in light of the resurrection of this life, subsequent to its close, as the powerful demonstration of the presence of God (in this life!) to every other human being of every other time.

Why, we may ask, does Barth not see the universal reach of the life history of Jesus Christ as already effected by virtue of the fact that he is the *God*-man, that is, by virtue of the fact that he already has both *divine* and human time? If indeed he already has divine time, for he is God, why is it not already the case that the limits

---

17   Ibid.

18   Torrance explains how this principle, which Barth consistently maintains, is worked out constructively in the *Church Dogmatics*: 'While the birth of the Son of God into the human race meant the veiling of revelation, the resurrection of Jesus meant the unveiling or revealing of his divine-human reality as the Son of God. Thus far from cutting our understanding of Jesus off from his concrete historical and earthly existence before the cross, the resurrection has the effect of gathering it all up and confirming its concrete factuality by allowing the historical Jesus to come to his own within the dimension of the risen Jesus, and the risen Jesus is discerned to have no other fabric than that in the life and mission of the historical Jesus.' Thomas F. Torrance, *Biblical*, pp. 108f.

19   *Contra* McCormack, *Karl Barth's Critically Realistic Dialectical Theology*, pp. 16ff.

of normal human life are removed by virtue of the fact that his is also God's time? Does Barth overlook the force of the divine nature of Christ somewhat here? Why is it necessary for Barth that this universal reach of the life-history of Jesus Christ eventuates in the resurrection and not by simple virtue of the divine nature of the Lord? Though he does not explicitly answer the question in this section, it is perhaps best to see the issue as a temporal corollary of the *extra Calvinisticum*, which Barth embraced though within very narrow limits.

The problem overcome in the resurrection then is the historical distance between the time of Jesus in AD 1–30 and all other times, but is this the full extent of the problem? It is true that Barth saw the problem of historical distance as a significant one. He raises the issue on a few occasions with reference to Lessing's great ugly ditch, impassable except by a leap of faith, between the necessary truths of reason and the contingent truths of history. While this is somewhat distinct from the problem of historical distance, it is a problem of the same basic kind, which Barth often refers to *via* Lessing as the problem of the uncertainty of the truth of events which fall outside of direct experience. In such instances one must rely on the testimony of others as they bear witness to their own experience. But, Lessing objected, is such knowledge a sufficient basis on which to establish the weighty matters of faith? These matters are not explicit in Barth's discussion here, but that they are part of the sub-text we can surely glean from his earlier[20] and later[21] explicit references to the theme in the context of his reflections on the resurrection.

At first glance Barth appears to be concerned with the problem of the historical skeptic, that is, the problem of the relative uncertainty of all historical knowledge. The historical and experiential distance between the life history of Jesus and the life history of every other human being seems to suggest that human knowledge of the life of Jesus can be at best only relatively certain. But does this amount to more than merely a problem of historical and experiential distance? Is this the problem of mediated historical knowledge or is it the problem of the time–eternity boundary, the precise borders of which have now been re-envisioned to align with the soteriological distance between the life-history of Jesus Christ and that of all others? A closer look reveals that this is the boundary having to do with the presence of Jesus Christ in the fullness of his life-act to all others, that is, the boundary which is at root that of the real soteriological appropriation in others of their reconciled human being and action in Christ. Barth is concerned with a continuing form of the time–eternity dialectic which has to do with the separation of the 'perfect time' of God in Jesus Christ from Bethlehem to Golgotha and the time of every other human being. This is to be distinguished clearly from the divine-human dialectic in terms of the absolute qualitative distinction between divine and human natures, which is a dialectic

---

20   Karl Barth, *Protestant Theology in the Nineteenth Century: Its Background and History* (Grand Rapids: William B. Eerdmans Publishing Company, 2002), pp. 220–51. First published in German as *Die protestantische Theologie im 19. Jahrhundert*, (Theologischer Verlag Zürich, 1947, 1952).

21   *CD* IV/1, pp. 287ff.

addressed in the anhypostatic–enhypostatic union of the two history-natures in the one person of Jesus Christ himself. The latter has to do with the *diastasis* of human and divine natures while the former has to do with the *diastasis* of the God-man and other human beings. While it is correct to claim that the resurrection overcomes the historical and experiential barrier between the history of Jesus and the histories of all others, we must go further and affirm that it does more. The resurrection overcomes the soteriological distance between the One who was crucified effectively for all and those others (all) for whom he was crucified. The distinction is that it is not enough to claim that God had been present to the disciples in the life-history of Jesus Christ, but one must go on to declare that God *is* immediately (and, so to speak, soteriologically) present, and is revealed as such in the risen Jesus.

It is at this point that Barth underscores the biblical witness to the fact that this Jesus who, like every other human being has his time as the definite and completed whole of his beginning, duration and end, also has a further history beginning on the third day after his death. This is a history that Barth calls 'the fragments of a second history,'[22] that is, the Easter-history comprised of the forty days between Jesus resurrection and his ascension.

The Reality of the Resurrection

Barth presses the point that it is indeed the witness of the New Testament that Jesus really did have this second history. Once again Barth asserts the centrality of the resurrection:

> It is impossible to read any text of the New Testament in the sense intended by its authors … without an awareness that they either explicitly assert or at least tacitly assume that the Jesus of whom they speak and to whom they refer in some way is the One who appeared to His disciples at this particular time as the Resurrected from the dead. All the other things they know of Him, His words and acts, are regarded in the light of this particular event and are as it were irradiated by its light. Whatever they proclaim in His name, the power of their message, derives from the fact that it was conveyed and entrusted to them by the man Jesus after He was raised from the dead.[23]

According to Barth it was through the prism of the event of Easter that his apostles and their communities saw the man Jesus as the One who 'was, and is, and is to come (Rev. 4:8).'[24] The Easter history must be taken as absolutely essential and indispensable to the New Testament depiction of Jesus:

> The Easter history is the starting-point for the Evangelists' portraits of the man Jesus. It is the real word with which they approached the outside world, whether Jewish or pagan,

---

22   *CD* III/2, p. 441.
23   Ibid., p. 442.
24   Ibid.

whenever they spoke of this man. It is the axiom which controls all their thinking about this man in His time.[25]

Barth takes the occasion to explicitly disavow the hermeneutical program of Rudolph Bultmann, who 'demythologizes' the Easter event. Barth says plainly, 'This will not do.'[26] He rejects the interpretation of the resurrection of Jesus as the rise of faith in the first disciples, and takes what he claims to be a directly opposite view, namely, that the statement 'Jesus is risen' is valid in its 'simplest sense' and only in this sense is it 'the central affirmation of the whole of the New Testament.'[27] For Barth, 'Jesus Himself did rise again and appear to His disciples. This is the content of the Easter history, the Easter time, the Christian faith and Christian proclamation, both then and at all times.'[28]

Jesus Appeared in the Mode of God

Barth describes the significance of the resurrection as the revelation that the same Jesus of Nazareth was indeed God of God. Inquiring about the implication of the fact that having completed the span of his own time from birth to death, Jesus also had a second, subsequent time, Barth concludes: 'The answer is that the particular content of the particular recollection of this particular time [the forty days] of the apostolic community consisted in the fact that in this time the *man* Jesus was manifested among them in the mode of *God*.'[29] We can arrive at a true understanding, says Barth, only when we keep in view both his humanity and his deity: 'During this period they [the first disciples] came to see that He had always been present among

---

25   Ibid., p. 443.

26   Ibid.

27   Ibid., p. 445.

28   Ibid. Barth lists five explicit reasons why he must differ from Bultmann. First, he rejects the view that a theological statement can be valid only if it can be proved a genuine element in the Christian understanding of human existence (ibid.). He also rejects the notion that an event can be regarded as historical only if it is open to the methods of verification endorsed by modern historical scholarship (ibid., p. 446). Barth furthermore rejects the assertion that acceptance of the historicity of an event which is inaccessible to historical critical verification is intellectual dishonesty (ibid.). And in addition he challenges the sufficiency of modern thought as capable in all regards to deal with the matter of the resurrection of Jesus Christ from the dead (ibid., p. 447). And Barth finally rejects the idea that simply because a statement was compatible with a past mythical worldview does not imply that it is to be rejected as untrue. He argues that Christians have always participated in other worldviews in order to communicate what transcended all worldviews (ibid.). He summarizes: 'These are the decisive reasons why, in spite of Bultmann, we must still accept the resurrection of Jesus, and His subsequent appearances to His disciples, as genuine history in its own particular time' (ibid.).

29   Ibid., p. 448.

them in His deity, though hitherto this deity had been veiled.'[30] It was during this time that they 'actually beheld His glory' such that 'the presence of God in the presence of the man Jesus was no longer a paradox.'[31] It is in the resurrection that the unparadoxical reality of God in Christ – which otherwise can only be witnessed to in paradoxical terms – is fully revealed: '"God was in Christ" (2 Cor. 5:19) – this was the truth which dawned upon the disciples during the forty days. ... He had been veiled, but He was now wholly and unequivocally and irrevocably manifest.'[32] What occurred for the apostles was 'the total, final, irrevocable and eternal manifestation of God Himself ... as the man Jesus.'[33] Says Barth:

> This, the Revealer of His hidden glory as God's eternal Word incarnate, is what Jesus was in His real and therefore physical resurrection from the dead, in His appearances as the one who was really and therefore physically resurrected. This is the way in which He was 'manifested in the mode of God' to His disciples.[34]

In the Easter history the eyes of the apostles were opened to the hidden reality of the man Jesus and his history. The 'previously concealed character of this history as salvation history,' the fact that it had happened 'once and for all' and that 'the "once" of this event differed absolutely from that of their own history and all history, and indeed from every other "once"' – this is what was made manifest to the apostolic witnesses during the forty days.[35] The whole history of the man Jesus in his time had been illuminated and interpreted for them in the light of the fact that 'God the Creator had not merely been present to them in the man Jesus, but He had actually appeared in this post-history.'[36] We insist that Jesus is the Lord of time for the reason that 'in the resurrection His appearance has proved to be that of the eternal God.'[37]

The fact that in the resurrection revelation the apparent paradox of the presence of God in the man Jesus is removed, however, does not mean that the paradoxical nature of subsequent human witness to this revelation is similarly removed. Barth explains the chronological contradictions of the resurrection accounts as the result of the effort to describe 'an event beyond the reach of historical research or depiction.'[38] Nonetheless, Barth asserts that these events are not to be read as myth: 'The Easter story is differentiated from myth, both formally and materially, by the fact that it is all about a real man of flesh and blood,' however, 'the stories are couched in

---

30   Ibid.

31   Ibid., p. 449. This is a significant expression for Barth, for it recalls his much earlier usage of the language of paradox, and in a form of inter-textual interpretation, excludes the notion of paradox from a proper description of the wholly coherent resurrection reality.

32   Ibid.

33   Ibid.

34   Ibid., p. 451.

35   Ibid., p. 454.

36   Ibid.

37   Ibid., p. 465.

38   Ibid., p. 452.

the imaginative, poetic style of historical saga, and are therefore marked by the corresponding obscurity.'[39] Yet, Barth insists, all these narratives do hold together in as much as they have the same singular event in view. About this they are in agreement in substance, intention and interpretation:

> Any idea of a harmony of the Gospels is quite foreign to the Early Church. That we should have Gospels 'according to St. Matthew,' 'according to St Mark,' etc., with all their parallels, their overlappings, and contradictions, is supremely in keeping with the theme recorded, with the figure of the past who in the forty days appeared to so many different people in so many different ways. All that matters was that they should all go back directly and indirectly to this source, the revelation of the event of Easter.[40]

According to Barth (and contrary to his statement in *The Resurrection of the Dead*, cf. pp. 135f.) the stories of the empty tomb and the ascension are 'indispensable' to the understanding of the New Testament proclamation of the Easter message. They mark the beginning and ending of the Easter period.[41] Barth does not give a lot of time to the ascension, taking his cues from the New Testament witness. He claims that in the strict sense the ascension does not find mention in the genuine Markan ending, but occurs only in Acts 1:9–10. Furthermore, it is only implied Matthew's reference to Jesus and the power given him in heaven and on earth. But there are reasons for this, assures Barth:

> The content of the Easter witness ... was not that the disciples found the tomb empty or that they saw Him go up to heaven, but that when they had lost Him through death they were sought and found by Him as the Resurrected. The empty tomb and the ascension are merely signs of the Easter event, just as the Virgin Birth is merely the sign of the nativity, namely, of the human generation and birth of the eternal Son of God.[42]

Barth does not deny that the tomb was empty but simply claims that the tomb being empty is not the same thing as the resurrection. It is not the appearance of the One who is now living again. It is only the presupposition; it is only a sign, however indispensable.[43]

Barth claims the same thoughts apply with regard to the ascension. It too is a sign, but it differs from the sign of the tomb in that it points 'forwards and upwards' while the tomb pointed 'downwards'.[44] Barth identifies Acts 1:9 as the most important verse in relation to the ascension story, in which the cloud receives Jesus out of the sight of the disciples. Barth notes that in the imagery of the Bible the cloud signifies the hiddenness of God; yet not merely this, but also his hidden presence; and,

---

39   Ibid.
40   Ibid., p. 473.
41   Ibid., p. 452.
42   Ibid., p. 453.
43   Ibid.
44   Ibid.

furthermore, the coming revelation which penetrates this hiddenness.[45] For Barth 'The ascension is the proleptic sign of the *parousia*, pointing to the Son of Man who will finally and visibly emerge from the confinement of His heavenly existence and come on the clouds of heaven (Matt. 24:30).'[46]

Jesus as the 'Contemporary of All Men'

While the time of Jesus retains the common character of a time with a beginning, duration and end, Barth understands the Easter time of Jesus to entail the removal of the limitations of sequential time: 'The removal of the limitations of its yesterday, to-day and to-morrow, of its once, now and then, is the distinctive feature of the time of the man Jesus.'[47]

Barth draws the conclusion that Jesus is the Lord of time from the basis that in his resurrection his appearance was demonstrated to be that of God.[48] The reason the Apostles find their beginning point in the resurrection of Jesus, in Barth's view, is that they see in the resurrection light 'the real meaning of Jesus' previous existence in time, and because they regard it as axiomatic that all their thinking and speaking about His whole being in time should start at this point.'[49]

For Scriptural support Barth turns to Revelation 1:8, which he takes to teach the overcoming of the confines of chronological time:

> The all-inclusive 'I am' rules out any notion that the three dimensions, present, past and future, simply follow one another in succession. The very fact that [Revelation] 1:8 puts the "I am" and the 'which is' first is a plain warning. It means: 'I am all this simultaneously. I, the same, am; I was as the same; and I will come again as the same. My time is always simultaneously present, past and future. That is why I am the Alpha and Omega, the beginning and the ending, the first and the last. Since my present includes the past and future it is both the first and the last of all other times.'[50]

Barth adduces Hebrews 13:8 as evidence that 'Jesus Christ belongs not only to yesterday, or to-day, or an indefinite future. He belongs to all times simultaneously. ...He is really the Lord of time.'[51] That is to say, '[Jesus'] time acquires in relation to their [other persons] times the character of God's time, of eternity, in which present, past and future are simultaneous.'[52] This does not imply that other human beings experience themselves as the contemporaries of Jesus. Barth asserts that others do not become the contemporaries of Jesus but that Jesus 'becomes and is their

---

45   Ibid., p. 454.
46   Ibid.
47   Ibid., p. 464.
48   Ibid., p. 465.
49   Ibid.
50   Ibid., p. 465.
51   Ibid., p. 466.
52   Ibid., p. 450.

Contemporary' with the result that 'His past life, death and resurrection can and must and actually do have at all times the significance and force of an event which has taken place in time but is decisive for their present existence.'[53] For Barth this is a wholly unilateral relationship, which, though it does not pass over into the experience of others, is nonetheless constitutive for their being in their present time.

Jesus is Really 'Present'

That Jesus is present in a manner in which no other man is or could be is the primary conviction of the New Testament, avers Barth. Jesus' past can never be merely a tradition or recollection of the events which transpired in his existence from Bethlehem to Golgotha.[54] At the same time this presence of his past is not merely a perspective or understanding of this past ventured at some point in the future. Jesus' history transcends the notion of history which employs the assertion that any event is known only when all the possibilities of history have drawn to a close with history itself. Jesus is present in the person and power of his Spirit, the Holy Spirit, whom he has given to his church: 'Note that if there is anything doubtful for Christians here, it is not His presence but their own. And if there is anything axiomatically certain, it is not their presence but His.'[55] So fundamental is this presence of Jesus that Barth sees fit to assert its reality as of an order more basic than even his real presence in the sacraments:

> There is obviously no baptism or Lord's Supper without His real presence as very God and very Man, both body and soul. But this presence cannot be regarded as restricted to what were later called the 'sacraments.' For these are only a symbolical expression of the fact that in its worship the community is gathered directly around Jesus Himself, and lives by and with Him, but that through faith He rules over the hearts and lives of all even apart from worship.[56]

It is the universal presence of Jesus on the basis of his resurrection which for Barth sets the context for understanding the unique status of the presence of Jesus in the sacraments of the church.

But what is it that occurs in this resurrection presence of Jesus to all times and all human beings? According to Barth 'the history of Jesus itself becomes history again', or in other words, 'past time becomes the time of His renewed presence.'[57]

---

53 Ibid., p. 467. It is interesting to note that Barth here includes the resurrection, with Jesus' past life and death, in the whole which is lifted up and given the force of an immediate event in every time. We will see later that the question of whether the resurrection is to be included with Jesus' life from Bethlehem to Golgotha in his reconciling being and action is indeed a significant one.

54 Ibid.

55 Ibid.

56 Ibid., pp. 467f.

57 Ibid., p. 470.

The fact of the resurrection means that the history of Jesus can no longer be merely a thing to be remembered:

> The fact that He is this [the object of recollection] certainly cannot mean that He is to be sought among the dead. ... This shows Him to be the effective appearance of God, which is not only unforgettable but makes itself felt again and again. Thus, while there is recollection and tradition from the standpoint of the action of the community, objectively and in fact He Himself is the acting Subject who lifts the barrier of yesterday and moves into to-day, making Himself present, and entering in as the Lord. This is the inner connexion between Easter and Pentecost.[58]

What this means is that 'the Jesus of that earlier time is still at work.' The way and work and witness of the apostles rests completely in the reality of his presence. 'Their whole recollection and tradition concerning Him is not centred on a figure of the past, on a dead man, but on One who even after His earthly time is still an acting Subject, doing new things, creating in history.'[59] The force of the apostolic witness was nothing other than that in the resurrection of Jesus '[t]he limitation of the past had been burst. The past of Jesus had become a present reality.'[60] The historical Jesus had not remained merely historical, that is, among the dead, but astonishingly he again became an actor in history, removing 'the veil of the merely "historical" from their eyes and [coming] to them as the Lord, the same yesterday and to-day.'[61] That is to say it is the ongoing act of the risen Jesus that he 'not allow the first history to lose its significance or sink into the mere past in the final history to which he himself belongs.'[62]

It is crucial to note that there are at least two important ideas at work here. One pertains to the *action* of the rendering present to all times the unique time of Jesus, the other to the *actor* who effects this action. We have already sufficiently elucidated the former, but the latter requires more attention. Barth names this actor as 'the Jesus of that earlier time', who had indeed died and was buried. That is, as in the death of every other human being, his existence as an acting subject of his own life in the course of human history had come to an end. But astonishingly, he appears nonetheless as 'an acting Subject' in time. It is not merely that his history is rendered present to all times, but that he himself actively renders and mediates this presence. The resurrection involves the utterly surprising and incomparable reality that he who was dead appears once again as a subject of his own history in history. But this entails the notion of a new subjectivity, the movement from the end of an active subject in death to a new subjectivity in a newness of life. Barth's casting the theme of the resurrection in the mold of the relation of the unique time of Jesus to all other times does little to account for the movement of the subject enclosed in his

---

58   Ibid.
59   Ibid., p. 471.
60   Ibid., p. 472.
61   Ibid.
62   Ibid., p. 473.

history to becoming the subject of this relation. How does Barth account for the emergence of this new subjectivity? Here, as elsewhere, Barth is reluctant to speak about the resurrection as the transition from the dissolution of subjectivity in death to a new subjectivity in resurrection life, though without it his depiction of resurrection remains incomplete. We shall have occasion to take up this theme in greater detail as we proceed.

Jesus is Really 'Past'

Furthermore, Barth asserts that to claim Jesus' life-history is present to all other times is not to diminish the reality that he is also past: 'Jesus not only is; He has also been. … Our gaze is directed backward from this present.'[63] Even the 'mystery, power and dignity' of the days of the apostles is derived from the 'yesterday' of the life history of Jesus, for it is there in that yesterday that 'it takes place first and properly that the kingdom of God comes and is proclaimed in parable, but also by signs and wonders.'[64]

By Jesus' past Barth refers not only to his pre-Easter life, but also to the history of the covenant between God and his people. It is in the light of Easter that the mystery of Yahweh's persistent and patient interaction with Israel is revealed:

> The apostolic community of Jews and Gentiles regarded itself as the people of Abraham, Isaac and Jacob now come to its promised goal. The Lord Christ was for it the Messiah to whom the Old Testament had pointed forward, the Son of Man and Servant of God. His teaching was the authoritative exposition of the Law, the Prophets and the Psalms of Israel. … The acts of Jesus, and His resurrection as the crown of all His acts, was the disclosure or revelation of the reality, so long concealed, of the covenant between God and this people; the declaration of the election of this lost people.[65]

In Barth's view Jesus appeared to his disciples as 'the reality of the divine covenant.'[66] It was in his light that they came to the magnificent perception that the One who had been prefigured and expected for so long had actually come as the consummation of that history in the life and time of Jesus of Nazareth.

Jesus is Really 'Future'

Just as surely as the being of Jesus in time is a real present and a real past, Barth insists it is also 'a being in the future, a coming being.'[67] It is not simply that Jesus' life-history is made contemporaneous and in that way present to individual persons in their time in the future, but that he as our contemporary in the present is also at

63 Ibid., p. 474.
64 Ibid.
65 Ibid., p. 475.
66 Ibid., p. 476.
67 Ibid., p. 485.

the same time the presence of our future. Christians not only live in recollection of his past presence but also in expectation of his coming presence. As a result the Church's preaching is not only essentially soteriological and pneumatological but also eschatological. The Church proclaims 'His future and the approaching end of time' just as surely as it preaches 'His past in which time has found its beginning and centre' and 'His present in which we move from that beginning and centre to the end of time.'[68] Barth explains:

> The New Testament always thinks and speaks eschatologically, but never with full logical consistence. Its only logical consistence is to think and speak on all sides and in all dimensions and relationships christologically. And it is for this reason that with equal emphasis and seriousness it can always think and speak eschatologically as well.[69]

In further explication of the eschatological orientation of the New Testament Barth argues that the apostles did not look forward merely to 'a progressive immanent development of the new life opened up by the resurrection.' Such a Utopian vision is surely other than what the New Testament affirms:

> No, the New Testament looks forward, not merely to a better future, but to a future which sets a term to the whole time process, and in its perfection includes and surpasses absolutely all the contents of time. This future will be a wholly new order, quite independent of all creaturely and even Christian development.[70]

Barth is quick to describe this as 'a sure and immediate hope,' not one which can be put off as a remote and rather inconsequential prospect.[71] This new future is Jesus himself once again, that is: 'His own person and work, in a new mode and form.'[72] In Barth's view the New Testament does not concern itself with the hope of a gradual and progressive improvement of present circumstances toward a set of ideal conditions, but rather with 'the coming of the Lord–*Maranatha* (I Cor. 16:22) – in a definitive and general revelation.'[73] The same Jesus who lived from Bethlehem to Golgotha and who lives again in the Easter time, was believed upon and loved 'as the One who comes.'[74]

According to Barth what the first disciples saw in the forty days in Jesus' Easter revelation was nothing less than 'the great *consummatum est.*'[75] They witnessed the being and action of Christ in its entirety and fulfillment, including 'its effectiveness in and to His own, and even in and to the lost for whose sin and salvation he died,

68   Ibid.
69   Ibid.
70   Ibid., p. 486.
71   Ibid.
72   Ibid.
73   Ibid., pp. 486f.
74   Ibid., p. 487.
75   Ibid., p. 488.

and for whose enlightenment concerning His death He was raised again.'[76] The first witnesses saw not only the man Jesus alive again, but in him, the consummation of all things, which included even the efficacy for the corresponding *in nobis* aspect of believing response.

Upon the close of the forty days what was seen and heard and felt directly was now to be embraced only in hope. What had been experienced immediately in the forty days was the 'real beginning of the justification which abolishes sin, of life victorious over death,' but as a genuine temporal event it was 'only an indication and a promise of the general revelation of glory still to come.'[77] Though the consummation was witnessed by the first disciples in those forty days, it was not yet revealed for every eye to see. According to Barth:

> What [the post-ascension followers] now saw and heard and felt was certainly the word of proclamation, the sacraments of baptism and the Lord's Supper, the fellowship and gifts of the Spirit between brothers and sisters, but also the great 'not yet,' the almost overwhelming difficulties and tasks arising from their witness to Jesus in the world, the convulsions of the Roman Empire moving to its climax and its fall, the frailty of Christian flesh requiring constant exhortation and comfort and warning and punishment, much weakness and tribulation in which even the voice of the Spirit could only be a sigh and a stammering, a cry of yearning.[78]

The period following the forty days is a time between the times, a time of remembering, and yet, because it was a time of remembering precisely this *Easter* time, it was also a time of eager expectation:

> To look back to this event is necessarily in this recollection to look forward to the same event, which, having begun at this point, could only be interrupted, but is destined to be consummated when this interim period has run its course and the existence and mission of the community have served their purpose.[79]

Barth takes pains to explicate the unity of the revelation of the resurrection, the forty days and the coming again of the risen Lord. Again this unity is grounded christologically:

> He who comes is the same as He who was and who is. The Resurrection Himself, therefore, is already He who comes, who restricts His coming to the circle of His then followers, and then interrupts it, to resume and complete it at a later point. ... Nothing which will be has not already taken place on Easter Day – included and anticipated in the person of the one man Jesus.[80]

---

76   Ibid.
77   Ibid., p. 489.
78   Ibid., p. 488.
79   Ibid., p. 489.
80   Ibid.

How then does Barth account for the temporal division between the resurrection and the *parousia*? His answer is that the unity of the glory of the Reconciler and the glory of the reconciled has become a future, but not a present, unity:

> The unity of His glory and our glorification already achieved in His resurrection has again become the future, His future, for us. For us, therefore, the resurrection and the parousia are two separate events. But for Him they are a single event. The resurrection is the anticipation of His parousia as His parousia is the completion and the fulfillment of the resurrection.[81]

Last things, for Barth, are only to be seen and embraced christologically. It is not upon last things that the early church set its hope, but upon the One who comes as the consummation of all things:

> The New Testament community does not hope for the attainment merely of abstract blessings. … Strictly speaking, there are not 'last things,' i.e., no abstract and autonomous last things apart from and alongside Him [Jesus Christ], the last One. Consequently there is no diffused hope, but only the one hope concentrated upon Him, and therefore full and perfect.[82]

The Imminent Return of Christ

With the perspective gained by this insight we are able to see more clearly why the unshakeable and persistent hope of the New Testament community was for the imminent arrival of the kingdom of God. If Jesus Christ was the resurrection and the life, if he was the King who is the fullness of the kingdom, how could the kingdom be anything but close at hand? As Eberhard Busch has it: 'In joyful hope, we may expect in the future the One who has come already. Thus, our waiting upon him – impatient and at the same time patient – is "expectation of what is near".'[83] Claims Barth, 'If this is the One whom we expect, we cannot expect Him the day after to-morrow, but to-morrow.'[84] We must not grow weary in hope as did some according to 2 Peter. Having forgotten the promise of the yesterday and today of the Lord, they grew suspect of an imminent expectation for tomorrow.[85] We must rather eagerly await the summing up of all things in his return:

> Like the apostles and prophets, like Christians themselves, the angels wait for the consummation of the process inaugurated by the resurrection – a consummation which according to I Pet. 4:7 will also be 'the end of all things.' The word used to denote the 'looking into' of the angels (παρακύψαι) is the same as that which in Jn. 20:5 is used of Peter when he looks into the empty tomb.[86]

---

81   Ibid., p. 490.
82   Ibid., p. 490.
83   Busch, *The Great Passion*, p. 283.
84   Ibid., p. 491.
85   Ibid., p. 492.
86   Ibid., p. 497.

Hence Barth's eschatology takes shape as a further development of his threefold depiction of the perfect time of Jesus Christ. He is really past, present and future, but now in a way more specific to the perspective of the church – He is past in his Easter time, present in the time of his Spirit and future in the time of his consummate *parousia*.

According to Barth, once we recognize that the event of Easter and that of the *parousia* are different moments of one and the same act, we will see that the supposition that 'there was unforeseen delay in the *parousia*, or that hope in the *parousia* was repeatedly deferred, or that the primitive Church … [was] disillusioned or mistaken on the subject in consequence of an exaggerated enthusiasm' is baseless and 'condemned from the very outset.'[87] The New Testament has no need for recourse to such a 'thoroughgoing eschatology.'

But what then shall we say of our present experience of the kingdom of God? According to Barth:

> The kingdom of God is real but not operative. It has come, but not come. It has still to be prayed for. It is present in reality, but not in revelation. To the extent that the New Testament contains good news, but not yet Easter news, the prophetic history of the Old Testament is continued in the New.[88]

The Gospels, says Barth, look not only to the past revelation of Jesus but also to his future revelation. According to Barth, the goal of Jesus was not the saving event of his death alone, but also 'the subsequent revelation of the meaning of His death, and therefore the putting into effect of the salvation won in Him for men, for the community, for the whole world.'[89] We must not see the death of Jesus as an end in itself, but rather as the securing of his kingdom which is yet to be made visible in glory. Busch aptly explains that for Barth the 'Kingdom of God' might be called the 'revolution of God' for it introduces something entirely new vis-à-vis the given world, 'something that inaugurates its total renewal.'[90] For Barth, the New Testament community of believers exists in the movement from commencement to conclusion. That is, 'it has the completion inaugurated with the resurrection of Jesus as a driving force behind it and the consummation in His *parousia* as a drawing force before it.'[91]

We have examined Barth's most important mid-career depiction of the resurrection in *CD* III/2, and have found convincing evidence of his abiding conviction of the centrality of the resurrection as the movement of Jesus Christ in the completion of his reconciled human being and action to the revelation and embrace of that reconciliation in others. Barth has portrayed this movement as one in and with time, yet also above time. It does not compromise the finished nature of the work of Christ

---

87   Ibid.
88   Ibid., p. 498.
89   Ibid.
90   Busch, *The Great Passion*, p. 280.
91   *CD* III/2, p. 508.

from Bethlehem to Golgotha, but shows that this same Jesus is Lord of this particular history and of all history. What has been completed in his life-history as the God-man has, in his resurrection, been freed from the limits of its yesterday, to-day and to-morrow, such that it takes on its own new eschatological time of past, present and future revelation *in nobis*.

Chapter Four

The Resurrection in *CD* IV as the Movement from Jesus Christ to Others

We now turn our attention to an explication of Barth's resurrection material in the fourth volume of the *Church Dogmatics*, for it is there that we find the latest and most complete development of his much earlier insights. In this chapter we shall note that Barth's resurrection discourse takes the form of a 'transitional' section which depicts the new and gracious act of God in raising Jesus from the dead. This transition neither reflects primarily the historical problem of temporal, nor the philosophical problem of existential distance nor of the separation of objective and subjective poles, nor even the theological problem of the divide between divinity and humanity. Rather, Barth's doctrine of the resurrection of Jesus Christ has to do with the evangelical problem, that is, of the movement of Jesus Christ in his completed reconciling being and action – *extra nos* and *pro nobis* – to us in our as yet opposed and unaffected anthropological sphere. Cognizant of the unsurpassable ontological depth of the death of Jesus Christ and us in him, Barth marvels at the reality and possibility of the resurrection. The force of Barth's thought accentuates both the utter impossibility of this transition except as an act of God and the fact of this transition as the scandal of the gospel of Jesus Christ.

Overview of the Problem

Barth's answer to the fundamental problem of the relation of God and human beings is not a philosophical one[1] but a dogmatic one.[2] He begins with the New Testament

---

1   To attempt to understand this problem as predominantly the philosophical one of the relation of God to the human creature is to mythologize the particular problem Barth identifies in the history of Jesus Christ. A prime example of this sort of misunderstanding can be found in Philip J. Rosato's work, *The Spirit as Lord* (Edinburgh: T. & T. Clark, 1981), where the distinction between the mediation of reconciled being and action in Christ to others in his resurrection revelation is blurred with various abstractly and loosely construed conceptions of the divine-human relationship.

2   For more on the historical development of this problem see the following: Karl Barth, *Protestant Theology in the Nineteenth Century*, pp. 458–72; Wolfhart Pannenberg, *Jesus, God and Man*, pp. 38–49; Rosato, *The Spirit as Lord*, pp. 11–22; Gordon Spykman, *Reformational Theology: A New Paradigm for Doing Dogmatics* (Grand Rapids: William B. Eerdmans Publishing Company, 1992), pp. 17–39; Thomas F. Torrance, *Biblical*, pp. 29–39.

conviction that divine and human natures are perfectly united in the person of Jesus Christ. The true relationship which obtains between God and the human creature is none other than that which occurs in the incarnation of Jesus Christ, that is, in his distinct history from Bethlehem to Golgotha. He is the mediator, the mediation, and that which is mediated, between the divine and the human. It is this assertion which Barth upholds when he insists upon the particularity and concrete nature of this relationship: 'We must realize,' says Barth, 'that the Christian message does not at its heart express a concept or an idea, nor does it recount an anonymous history to be taken as truth and reality only in concepts and ideas.'[3] Rather the gospel recounts the history of God with us and speaks of the 'inclusive power and significance' of this history 'in such a way that it declares a name, binding the history strictly and indissolubly to this name and presenting it as the story of the bearer of this name.'[4] The implication of this for our description of this relationship is that 'all the concepts and ideas used in this report (God, man, world, eternity, time, even salvation, grace, transgression, atonement and any others) can derive their significance only from the bearer of this name and from His history, and not the reverse.'[5] That is to say, 'the Christian message (in all its content) means Jesus Christ.'[6] Barth refuses to describe God and the human creature as abstract and unrelated objects. Such a description derives from an origin other than Jesus Christ, and hence would not be a description of the One under whose name perfectly coheres the relationship of divine and human being and action.

Jesus Christ is Barth's primary and exclusive answer to the question of the relationship of God and the human creature. But it is at this point that Barth is often misunderstood. That is, the problem of the relation of God to human beings is confused with the problem of the relation of Christ to others, the problem of the relation of theology to anthropology is conflated with the problem of the relation of christology to soteriology, the problem of the incarnation is confused with the problem of the resurrection. To maintain awareness of this distinction in Barth's discourse is particularly poignant when we come to his doctrine of the resurrection, for the doctrine of the resurrection deals with the problem of the relation of Christ and others, and only as such with the problem of the relation of God and human beings. That is to say, the problem of the relation of God to the human creature is particularized in such a way that it becomes the problem of the distance between the crucified Christ and others in their contrary and opposed anthropological sphere. It is the problem of the fact that 'the Christian message dares to address man too as an active subject in the event of redemption.'[7] That is, that the message of 'God with us' includes and encloses the message of 'We with God,' the truth and actuality of which

---

3   *CD* IV/1, p. 16.
4   Ibid.
5   Ibid.
6   Ibid., p. 20.
7   Ibid.

can be grasped only in the resurrection of Jesus Christ, 'in the fellowship between Him and us created by His Spirit.'[8]

The problem of the relation between God and human beings in Barth is as complex as it is crucial a notion. It opens up an important set of questions in Barth concerning the relation of the incarnation, the life and history, and the resurrection of Jesus Christ. In each case for Barth there is a form of universality. In the incarnation the Word takes on the sinful flesh shared by all humanity. In this manner he declares his love, demonstrating his willingness to be called our brother, having become like us in all points, yet without sin. It is the particularity of his humanity which effects and guarantees the integrity of his relation to every other human being. He shares in our being, and so rescues it from sin and darkness.

But how is it that his humanity has this *universal* force and significance? Again Barth's answer is subtle and multifaceted. In one respect, it is the fact that he is not merely a man, but also God in the flesh, which effects and guarantees the universality of his being and action. Because his every act is not merely a human act but also a divine act, his action has consequence for every human being. He has, as a man, indeed in all the particularity of a first century Jewish man, acted as none other than the Creator, whose creative power is expressed throughout the created realm. That is, his humanity, unlike that of other men and women, comprehends and transforms the whole of humanity because he has taken and bound to himself sinful human nature and dealt with it in divine power. In another respect, it is the sheer fact that Jesus Christ is the chosen one of God, the one elected to be the representative of humankind, the unsurpassable high priest, who alone mediates between God and human beings. Thus, in his representative capacity he gathers every other human being into himself. In still another respect, his very participation in human being, that is, his taking upon himself all that which distinguishes and characterizes human being, connects him integrally with every other human being. (One must be careful here to understand this not as the embrace of the essence of human being, as if the secret of the being of humanity can be reduced to some inalienable essence. But whatever it is that makes humans beings truly human – this is what he embraces). This reflects Barth's understanding of christology as anhypostatic–enhypostatic union.

Yet even this does not exhaust the manner in which Barth speaks of the work of Christ in reconciling God and humankind. He also speaks of the progressive union brought about in the life and work of Jesus Christ himself, in whose history from Bethlehem to Golgotha the sinful human nature is wrestled to death and the true human nature, as faithful covenant keeper, is enacted and guaranteed. This is the reconciliation brought about in and through the life history of Jesus Christ as he effects the destruction of sinful human being and enacts and establishes faithful human being. It is the actual (being-in-act!) destruction and reconstruction of human being, bringing it into the fullest fellowship with the Father. This too, for Barth, is a transformation which affects the whole of humanity, for the substance of humanity

---

8   Ibid.

itself has been made right with God in Christ. Hence this work of Christ has universal import, yet is localized in the being and action of Jesus Christ.

In addition to this there is in Barth what we might call the evangelical union between God and humanity which comes about in the declaration of the gospel in the power of the Spirit in which men and women are newly created and set free to enact their new humanity which has been graciously given in Christ. This facet of the reconciliation of God and man obtains a universal force of sorts, but in the specific mode of the Spirit of Christ moving outwards, in the proclamation of the gospel, from Christ to human beings of every tribe, tongue and nation. But in this case Barth does not see this as a matter of absolutely necessary universality. Rather, giving due recognition to the freedom of God, Barth announces the good news of indomitable hope for each and every human being, yet stops short of *apokatastasis*, the affirmation of universal salvation. There is then in Barth a universalist tendency, but one which stops short of universalism as an inviolable principle, out of deference to the very freedom of God who cannot be bound by external principles.

This briefly summarizes some of the complexity of Barth's understanding of the universal significance of the being and action of the God-man, Jesus Christ, in the work of the reconciliation of God and humankind. As we shall see, it is important to be aware not only of the narrative context but also the dogmatic context of the various passages of Barth we are reading. Barth's development of the material has brought us to a highly refined and specific set of ideas, which can only be properly understood as such, and which virtually always loose their coherence and logical force when abstracted from this specific context and treated as a discourse of general terms and approximate ideas. In this instance we are dealing with a highly refined conception of the relation of God and humankind, namely, the relation of reconciled human being and action as it is in Christ and that as yet (logically prior to the resurrection) unaffected and contradictory human being of the wider anthropological sphere. This is the problem which comes to the forefront as Barth considers the theological subject matter of the resurrection of Jesus Christ. Once again our thesis is that Barth develops his doctrine of the resurrection in the dogmatic context of the way of the crucified Lord to others, which in itself is a highly particular and distinct set of issues. Let us now turn to a detailed analysis of this problem of transition.

Barth's Resurrection Discourse as a 'Transitional' Paragraph

Barth's development of the resurrection of Jesus Christ, of the theme of transition to others, its impossibility and yet its reality, does more than any other to underscore the significance of this move to which the New Testament narrative does indeed bear witness. Upon it hinges the whole of the reality of human being and understanding – the question of the existence and nature of human being, of human knowledge of God, and of human self-understanding. The whole of Barth's pneumatology, soteriology, ecclesiology, anthropology, and eschatology hangs on this transition. In each of the three prime aspects of the movement of the God-man – Jesus Christ as Priest,

King and Prophet – Barth asks about the movement from the christological sphere proper to the anthropological sphere. In each case he asserts the enclosure of the turn from the narrower christological sphere to same anthropological sphere within the christological sphere. The question of the turn from the narrower christological sphere to the anthropological sphere, the question of the resurrection, is that which shapes the architectonics of each part-volume, and offers an indication of the great significance which it was accorded in Barth's thinking. It is to be noted that this is not a transitional section for the sake of clarity or convenience of presentation. It is rather, to Barth's mind, a substantial transitional moment in the subject matter he seeks to elucidate. The really problematic issue for Barth is that at this point the matter itself involves, rather, *is* this transition [*Übergang*].

The doctrine of the reconciliation, *Church Dogmatics* IV, – and here we are in fundamental agreement with most commentators – forms the structural and material centre of the *Church Dogmatics*.[9] It finds its place after the doctrine of Creation and before the proposed volume on Redemption. It recounts the event of God's fulfilment of the covenant in Jesus Christ as 'God with us.' Reconciliation presupposes the covenant and founds and promises the redemption. Paragraph 58 of the *Church Dogmatics* is given over to an important survey of the entire doctrine of reconciliation. The person and work of Jesus Christ are seen and understood synoptically in a threefold development. Chapters 14, 15 and 16 unfold in parallel fashion. Chapter 14 deals with the self-humiliation of God, the Lord as Servant. In chapter 15 we see the Servant as Lord, the exaltation of the human person by God in Jesus Christ. And in chapter 16 we see Jesus Christ as the mediator and revealer of his own glory as the peerless one in whom God and humanity are unified. Thus chapters 14, 15 and 16 focus upon the priestly, kingly and prophetic offices of Christ respectively.

Each of these chapters is divided similarly into five paragraphs. The first has to do with the personal work or working person developed individually according to each of these offices. The second provides an account of human sin in the forms of pride, sloth and falsehood. Following this is a paragraph on the objective reality secured in the event of reconciliation, namely, the justification, sanctification, and calling of human beings. The fourth paragraph expounds the subjective appropriation of reconciliation as the work of the Holy Spirit in the gathering, upbuilding, and sending the community of Christian believers, that is, the Church. The final paragraph deals with the new being of Christians in Jesus Christ as a being in faith, in love, and in hope. Barth was unable to complete the project of his *magnum opus*, and was compelled to stop just short of the completion of the doctrine of reconciliation. His writing comes to a close with the chapter on special ethics published as a fragment, in which Barth deals with the matter of Baptism (of the Spirit and of water). Though

9   John D. Godsey, ed., *Karl Barth's Table Talk, Scottish Journal of Theology Occasional Papers*, No. 10 (Edinburgh: Oliver and Boyd, 1963), p. 9.

he was unable to complete his projected work on the Lord's Supper, some lecture texts remain on the Lord's Prayer, published posthumously as *The Christian Life*.[10]

The Three Christological Aspects

For Barth, the entire doctrine of reconciliation is committed to an explication of Jesus Christ as very God, very man, and very God-man in his reconciling work. Having no principle which forms the starting point of his exposition, Barth simply takes the second article of the Apostles' Creed, 'I believe in Jesus Christ,' as his confessional basis. Concentrating upon the being of Jesus Christ, he delineates *three christological aspects*, which when understood in connection with the mission and work of Christ, form three perspectives on the event of the atonement.[11] Says Barth, 'Christology is the key to the whole.'[12] Each perspective describes a unique and unsublatable aspect of the being of Jesus Christ in action depicting a threefold movement from above to below, from below to above, and from the centre outwards. The first two movements are simultaneous and achieve their concealed culmination in the cross, representing the being and act of Jesus Christ *extra nos* and *pro nobis*. The third follows upon the completion of the first two as an entirely new movement radiating outwards from the christological centre to its appropriation in the wider anthropological sphere. Here we refer to the self-revelation of the being and act of Jesus Christ *in nobis*.

The first aspect then has to do with Jesus Christ, very God, who humbles himself and thereby reconciles the human being with himself. God has in Jesus Christ become a man, at once establishing and crossing the infinite gulf between God and human beings. He retains and exercises his deity absolutely and exhaustively, but he does so as a man. This is how God determines God shall be God: in all the limitation and fullness and reality of human being. It is at once his condescension and his glory, that he gives himself up to creaturely limitation and human suffering, and dying as a man the death deserved by all others: the very same quality, character and action which marks 'His distinctness from and superiority to all other reality.'[13]

Whereas in the first christological aspect we have to do with Jesus Christ as *vere Deus*, in the second we have to do with Jesus Christ as *vere homo*. He is in all reality a true human being who is exalted by God. He is lifted out of his need and limitation and suffering to stand with God as a free and noble man: 'In Him humanity is exalted humanity, just as Godhead is humiliated Godhead. And humanity is exalted in Him by the humiliation of Godhead.'[14] In Jesus Christ 'true humanity' is realized.[15] Because

---

10   Karl Barth, *The Christian Life, Church Dogmatics*, IV/4, trans. By Geoffrey W. Bromiley (Grand Rapids: William B. Eerdmans Publishing Company, 1981).

11   *CD* IV/1, p. 128.

12   Ibid., p. 138.

13   Ibid., p. 129f.

14   Ibid., p. 131.

15   Ibid., p. 132.

Barth believes that a doctrine of reconciliation must witness to both the deity and the humanity of Jesus Christ and also his humiliation and his exaltation, Barth describes the event of the atonement twice over, beginning with a discourse focusing upon the God who humbles himself in Jesus Christ and then secondly focusing upon human being which in Jesus Christ is exalted.

Barth describes the third christological aspect as both 'the simplest and the highest.'[16] The first two arise out of it and are comprehended by it. This aspect has in view Jesus Christ himself as the unity of the being and action of God's atoning work. In this aspect the view of Jesus Christ moving from above to below and the view of Jesus Christ moving from below to above are held together. Jesus Christ is the one who is both God and man, not a third between the two, but both in absolute unity. This third aspect according to Barth does not add anything materially new with respect to Jesus Christ and the atonement accomplished in him. This has been covered exhaustively in the description of the first two aspects. What remains to be elucidated is that these first two aspects must be seen in their historical unity and completeness, that is, the viewing of Jesus Christ himself in whose personal history the two lines cross – he himself is the selfsame lord who became servant and the selfsame servant who became lord; he is the single subject, the reconciling God and the reconciled human being. As he is in himself this reconciliation, he is the mediator and pledge of the fulfilled covenant.[17] 'This is the new thing in the third christological aspect. Jesus Christ is the actuality of the atonement, and as such the truth of it which speaks for itself.'[18] Barth gives the title 'Jesus Christ, the Guarantor' to this third christological aspect to indicate that Jesus Christ himself is at once the material content of the atonement and the sole and sufficient mediator of that content. In this way Barth develops his unique view of the work of Jesus Christ as Prophet.

It is illuminating to note that for Barth the transition carried out by the third christological aspect is very similar to that carried out under the rubric of the resurrection. For instance, Barth describes his development of the third christological aspect as fulfilling two functions. It both 'concludes' the development of the doctrine of reconciliation, and functions as 'a transition to the doctrine of the redemption or the consummation.'[19] Similarly, the doctrine of the resurrection functions both as the conclusion of the doctrine of the atonement and as the transition to the doctrine of the redemption. Furthermore, just as the third christological aspect establishes, coordinates and upholds the first two, so the resurrection establishes, takes up and carries forward all that has preceded it. And again, under the heading of the first two christological aspects Barth discusses the life history of Jesus Christ from Bethlehem to Golgotha, but under the heading of the third christological aspect Barth deals with the transition from that peculiar history to the history and consummation of

---

16   Ibid., p. 135.
17   Ibid., p. 136.
18   Ibid.
19   Ibid., p. 137.

the world. In like manner Barth's discussion of the resurrection is absorbed with the question of the power of the transition from the particular christological sphere to the anthropological sphere. In other words the relationship of the first two christological aspects to the third has remarkable similarities to the relationship of the history of Jesus Christ from Bethlehem to Golgotha to his Easter reality. The crucial issues at the forefront of Barth's thinking as he writes about the third christological aspect and about the resurrection of Jesus Christ from the dead are identical. The doctrine of the resurrection is bound up with the doctrine of Jesus Christ as Prophet. Barth clearly asserts, 'The testimony of the New Testament witnesses ... is testimony to His resurrection (Acts I:22) as His self-attestation in respect of the universality, inclusiveness and continuity of His particular being and action,' of its outreaching, embracing and comprehensive character.'[20] And furthermore, in the resurrection event there 'has taken place the self-declaration of Jesus Christ ... and therefore the revelation of the reconciliation of the world with God, the immediate and perfect prophecy, by a new and specific divine act.'[21] That is, 'it is the reference to the living Jesus Christ risen from the dead which makes it possible and necessary for us to give this particular answer. The particular event of His resurrection is thus the primal and basic form of His glory, of the outgoing and shining of His light ..., of His prophetic work.'[22] Hence our understanding of the resurrection is greatly enhanced by an understanding of the Jesus Christ in his office as Prophet and *vice versa*. For now it will be sufficient to note that in his discussion of both the Prophetic ministry of Christ and the resurrection Barth is dealing with the transition from his pre-Easter to his Easter existence. Hence we may conclude that the whole structure of the fourth volume of the *Church Dogmatics* is set with a view to the reality of the resurrection of Jesus Christ from the dead as the beginning, interpretive centre and continuing wonder of the whole of Barth's doctrine of reconciliation.

All three of Barth's extended discussions of the resurrection in Volume IV of the *Church Dogmatics* – §59.3, 'The Verdict of the Father' and §64.4, 'The Direction of the Son' and §69.4, 'The Promise of the Spirit' – take place within the context of a transitional subsection as he moves from a consideration of the christological basis of reconciliation to its embrace of the anthropological sphere, from the sphere in which the atonement accomplished in Jesus Christ has already and definitively taken place *for us* to the sphere in which it takes place *in us*. For it is the anthropological sphere which is in need of atonement and it is into this that Jesus Christ has come. Crucial to our understanding of these passages is our notice of the fact that Barth discusses the doctrine of the resurrection in the context of the question of how we can proceed and build on the christological foundation in our own sphere. Repeatedly he reminds the reader that this is the question which has been put by the very being and action

---

20   *CD* IV/3.1, p. 281.
21   Ibid., p. 290.
22   Ibid., p. 281.

of Christ for us.[23] The irrefutable 'answer' to the problem, according to Barth, is 'the resurrection'.[24]

Accordingly, Barth believes that before we can rightly speak of the anthropological sphere, we must give consideration to the relation of the anthropological sphere to its christological basis. Barth's development of the doctrine of the resurrection begins with what is essentially an exegesis of the meaning of the crucified Jesus Christ *in nobis*, who became victor and reconciler in bringing his fallen creatures with him into death, for us. Barth formulates the question in this way: 'What is the power of the existence of the one man Jesus Christ for all other men? To what extent is there a way from the one to the other, from Him to us?'[25] The question comes into sharpest focus as Barth develops the reality and meaning of the resurrection of Jesus Christ, which, more than any other theological *locus*, takes the form of a hinge or a pivot between christology proper and soteriology.

The Primary Structural Divisions are Aspectual

From the preceding overview of the structure of *CD* IV, we are immediately struck with the observation that an important feature of Barth's development of the doctrine is that it is aspectual. That is, the event of the reconciliation resists being viewed from a single vantage point.[26] The nature of the object (reconciliation) requires aspectual elucidation, yet can only be grasped in its completeness when these various aspects are held together. The fact in no way suggests that the object in view is anything other than singular and coherent. The nature of reconciliation as a genuinely divine-human work always bears the distinction of the hyphen which holds the two aspects together without identifying them. This 'twofold fact ... cannot be further reduced conceptually but only brought together historically.'[27] Jesus Christ himself is the 'middle point,' the vantage point, 'the one thing from which neither the God who turns to man nor man converted to God can be abstracted, in which and by which both are what they are, in which and to which they stand in that mutual relationship.'[28] The point of this aspectual approach is that the first two aspects cannot be brought together under some higher conceptual principle. Divine action and human action remain unresolved in their distinct courses and theaters of action except as they are united in the single subject, Jesus Christ.

Moreover, the three christological aspects are not simply three equal and symmetrical vantage points from which to see the whole. The division cannot be accorded to Barth's supposed admiration of triadic exposition. Much more than a nominal division of the material into pedagogically appropriate parts, Barth's

---

23   Cf. *CD* IV/1, pp. 293ff., 312, 314, 347ff.
24   Ibid., p. 349.
25   *CD* IV/2, p. 265.
26   Cf. *CD* IV/2, p. 3 and *CD* IV/3.1, p. 5.
27   *CD* IV/1, p. 136.
28   Ibid., p. 122.

development of this material according to these aspects is an attempt to come to terms with the material itself. The third christological aspect differs markedly from the first two. And it is by force of the demand of the third christological aspect that the first two must be taken into account. According to Barth, the third christological aspect 'is the source of the two first, and it comprehends them both.'[29] In his view, 'The history of Jesus Christ with which the history of reconciliation is identical is the parallel but opposing fulfillment of two great movements, the one from above downwards and the other from below upwards, but both grounded in his person in the union of its true deity and true humanity.'[30] Barth describes this third christological aspect as 'the formal problem' of the doctrine of reconciliation in distinction to the first two christological aspects, which he describes as 'material problems.'[31] The third christological aspect is the 'How' in its distinction from the 'What' of reconciliation. Without the pressure of the third the development of the first two can never be made except in 'opposition.' What is more, the subject matter of each of the first and second aspects remains in complete concealment except in light of the third aspect. That is, apart from a view of Jesus Christ as the subject and mediator of his being and act as the Lord who humbles himself as a servant and the servant who is exalted as the Lord, neither of these come to light at all. Apart from the light of his resurrection the history and crucifixion of Jesus can be seen neither as the self-humiliation of God nor as the exaltation of humanity. Rather it appears only to be the tragic ruin of the man Jesus.

In this respect the only premise for holding together the first and second aspects, the only basis which warrants the Chalcedonian description of the ontological reality of Jesus Christ (that is, that he is both *vere Deus* and *vere homo*) is that Jesus Christ reveals himself as the selfsame subject in and by whom both of these aspects cohere in perfect unity. Indeed, 'the material content of the doctrine of reconciliation is … exhausted by what has to be thought and said from these two christologico-soteriological standpoints.'[32] In this 'strange twofold movement … we are dealing with the whole of the history in which God gives to man salvation but also causes man to give him glory.'[33] The third christological aspect is neither a simple aspect balancing the first two, nor is it a sublation of them into a quite different third. The third christological aspect is rather the source and foundation out of which arise and upon which stand the first two aspects.

The third christological aspect describes an outgoing revelatory event which grounds and holds together the distinct acts of each of the first two christological aspects, and presents their reality in immediate and inescapable proximity and force. The third christological aspect has to do not with a general revealing of these things as from a distinct and disinterested source, but with the absolutely unique rendering

---

29   Ibid., p. 135.
30   *CD* IV/3.1, p. 4.
31   Ibid., p. 8. Cf. also p. 279.
32   Ibid., p. 6.
33   Ibid., p. 7.

radically present of the non-substitutable person of the mediator. Because it is the subject of this history who is raised and who draws near, this revelation must be described in terms of concrete encounter. The revelation of the mediator is living and dynamic; he turns to us; he carries his history with him as he moves from his central place to our place of infinite remoteness. The reconciliation described in the first two christological aspects cannot be revealed and embraced except in the immediate presence of the mediator who is in himself this reconciliation. It is this coming to us, this free rendering of himself immediately present in the fullness of his being – the fact that it is so – which is the object in view in Barth's third christological aspect. The importance of this aspect in Barth reflects the importance of his understanding of the resurrection of Jesus Christ.

The Narrative of Incarnation, Crucifixion and Resurrection

The development of the three basic christological aspects of the doctrine of the reconciliation is to be described neither as an *ad hoc* locus by locus procession of more or less distinct theological themes, nor as an argument in which axioms are affirmed, deductions made and conclusions drawn, but rather the subject matter cumulatively rendered by the narrative is the focus of observation and exposition. The history itself is a unity and can only be properly grasped as such. It is the history of Jesus Christ as a whole which is the controlling object of the investigation and the focal point of the exposition. While Barth is careful to hold the being and work of Jesus Christ together in the unity of his person and history, he recognizes the need and legitimacy of a distinct discussion of the 'nature' of the person Jesus Christ. Thus in each of the three parts Barth begins with the account of the incarnation. Even in the third part Barth begins with the prologue of John's Gospel, the counterpart to the nativity stories of Matthew and Luke. In a separate though integrally related discussion Barth moves on in each part to speak about the atoning work of Jesus Christ, namely, his approach to and embrace of the cross. From there Barth continues to follow the unfolding narrative in his discussion of the resurrection as the outward movement of Jesus Christ *in nobis* in the power of his Spirit.

It is not sufficient to claim, however, that the history of Jesus Christ is a unity. We must also note Barth's corollary assertion that this unity is a history, an event. As such it can only be described in processive or narrative terms. The doctrine of the resurrection plays an important role in the successful exposition of this account of Jesus Christ as history. In each part-volume the doctrine of the resurrection is discussed in the context of a transitional sub-section in which the movement of the objective content of the history of Jesus Christ to the as yet untouched anthropological world is in view. As the third christological aspect preserves and punctuates the event character of the unity of the divine and human action in Christ, so Barth's doctrine of the resurrection gathers up, preserves and punctuates the event character of the entire history of Jesus Christ. This history of Jesus Christ is not a history which dissolves meaninglessly into the unending expanse of time. It is rather a special history in relation to all of history. In the resurrection the history of Jesus Christ itself, because it is the history of the risen one, is raised up and made contemporaneous with all of history. Here the matter of the resurrection comes to the fore. The focal centre of the three christological aspects of the doctrine of reconciliation is the history of Jesus Christ precisely because it is this history which is taken up in the resurrection as the history of all history. The history of Jesus Christ from Bethlehem to Golgotha is understood to be the subject matter of the doctrine of reconciliation because it is lifted up and illuminated as such in the resurrection of Jesus Christ. Hence, the structural composition of *CD* IV bears out the fact that the resurrection of Jesus Christ is to be seen, in Barth, as the crucial event of movement from Christ to others.

The Dogmatic Question

Barth's doctrine of atonement follows, though not uncritically, in the Athanasian tradition and is among the strongest expressions of vicarious or substitutionary atonement to be found in Christian theology. Such a strong statement of the objective nature of the atonement however demands an equally strong account of its subjective aspects. This turn from the objective to the subjective side is the question the answer to which, in Barth's view, is the resurrection of Jesus Christ.

Barth's development of the doctrine of reconciliation comes to a full stop with the crucifixion and death of Jesus Christ. As the life of Jesus Christ reaches its foreordained culmination in his vicarious and inclusive death, all creation (and at its centre, human existence) is gathered up and brought with him into death. The completion of the work of Jesus Christ *pro nobis* on the cross then must be taken to be the consummate finality for which there can be no beyond. To speak at this point of something other is wholly impossible. Yet this is precisely what Barth is forced to do as he turns his consideration to the resurrection of Jesus Christ from the dead. Far from employing a facile leap of historical imagination, or a de- and re-mythologization into the categories of human existence, or a moralistic abstraction, to bridge the chasm between the crucified Jesus and ourselves, Barth takes great pains to depict the chasm itself in all its ominous immensity.

What is the Way and Power of the Crucified In Nobis?

In this transitional discussion Barth concerns himself with the task of understanding the grounds, warrants and impetus for proceeding and building upon the christological basis previously delineated. The question which needs to be posed in Barth's view has to do with the relationship of Jesus Christ in the completion of his saving work and others, or more specifically, the movement of Jesus Christ to those who occupy the anthropological sphere which stands in contradiction to him. How is the Son of God in his being and activity not entirely closed off from our sphere? The question is 'whether and to what extent we can and must proceed from the obedience which

Jesus Christ rendered for us to the thought of its relevance for us.'[34] How can we come to the conclusion of the mutual belonging of Jesus Christ and ourselves? According to Barth:

> The kernel of the question is simply the incompatibility of the existence of Jesus Christ with us and us with Him, the impossibility of the co-existence of His divine-human actuality and action and our sinfully human being and activity, the direct collision between supreme order and supreme disorder which we perceive when we start with the fact that our contemporaneity with Him has been made possible in the most radical form. ... For what will become of us if the real presence of Jesus Christ is going to be a fact in our time and therefore in the sphere of our existence? ... How dare we ever count on the fact that we are His, and therefore move on from Christology to an anthropology which is embraced by Christology, and in which we have to understand ourselves, us men, as His?[35]

The question has to do with the radical way in which Jesus Christ has taken our sinful human existence and borne it to its irreversible end in death. The work of Jesus Christ means nothing less than the absolute end of our existence as being and acting in sin.

In the second part volume Barth again picks up the theme of transition with respect to his discussion of the resurrection, however, in this section he discusses it with greater emphasis upon 'the *power* of the existence of the one man Jesus for all other men.'[36] Again, this question in no way casts doubts upon the real operation or effectiveness of this power; rather, as before, the question proceeds from the firm reality of its solution. The reality of his being with us and acting for us is our indisputable point of departure. 'It has its basis in the resurrection of Jesus from the dead.'[37] What is yet to be explained, according to Barth, is 'the fact that we are the ones to whom He is already on the way as the Resurrected.'[38]

Once again, in his discussion of 'The Promise of the Spirit',[39] Barth returns to the same question. And again the decisive answer to the question as to what constrains the transition from the christological sphere in the narrower sense to the anthropological sphere is given in the person and work of Jesus Christ. That is, the glorious mediator is in the process of glorifying himself in and among and through the human person such that the human person is ordered and set free for an active and receptive participation in his glory. As Barth says, 'Jesus Christ is never without His own, but always is and acts inclusively, and particularly in the transition from himself to the world, to us.'[40] According to Barth it is in the resurrection that the prophecy of Jesus Christ 'is initiated in its primal and basic form.'[41] It is in the

---

34   *CD* IV/1, p. 312.
35   Ibid., p. 348.
36   *CD* IV/2, p. 265. Emphasis mine.
37   Ibid.
38   Ibid., p. 266.
39   *CD* IV/3, pp. 274–367.
40   Ibid., p. 284.
41   Ibid., p. 281.

exercise of his prophetic office that Jesus Christ moves out from the christological
sphere in the narrower sense to the whole range of the anthropological sphere:

> In His revelation, shining as light, He discloses and manifests and announces and imparts
> Himself, moving out from Himself to where He and His being and work are not yet
> known and perceived, to where there is not yet any awareness of the alteration in Him of
> the situation between God and man, to where the consequences of this alteration have not
> yet been deduced, to where the sin of man, his pride and sloth, already overcome in the
> justification and sanctification of man accomplished in Him, still maintain a foothold, in
> a twofold sense *per nefas*.[42]

It is of crucial importance first to understand that Barth sees the issue to be that of the
movement from the christological sphere proper to the anthropological sphere. All
other concerns are to be illuminated and expounded in relation to this centre.

In addition we must note, second, that the resurrection marks a unique moment
of transition. It cannot be understood simply as a link in an historical chain of
interrelated events. The transition carried out by the resurrection involves also the
movement from the narrower sphere of the redemptive activity within Jesus Christ
himself to the larger sphere of the world of men and women in which we live. It is
a real transition which can only adequately be described in *dogmatic* terms. It arises
not from idealistic speculation or phenomenological observation. Rather, it arises
from and concerns itself with the specific, new and free action of God. Thus, for
Barth, the defining issue is neither a subjective–objective duality, nor a problem of
faith and history, nor a problem of time and eternity, but *the* problem of Jesus Christ
and we others. Hence Barth upholds dogmatic discourse as a credible language
of scientific description. John Webster is quite correct when he claims that Barth
replaces twentieth-century christology's 'formal preoccupations' of 'history and
hermeneutics' with doctrinal affirmations: 'about the resurrection as the luminosity
of the Christ-event, and about the Holy Spirit as the *doctor veritatis*.'[43]

The Pseudo-Problem of Faith and History

In a further attempt to come to terms with the problem of the transition from Jesus
Christ *in nobis* Barth considers the extent to which this problem may be conceived of
as merely a theological implication of the problem of time.[44] Thought of in this way
the issue becomes: 'How can that which has happened once, even if it did happen
for us, be recognised to-day as having happened for us, seeing it does not happen
to-day?[45] Again we note that for Barth the problem is clearly not about the matter of
the happening being for us, but about how that happening for us can be *recognised*

---

42   Ibid., p. 280.

43   John Webster, *Barth's Ethics of Reconciliation* (Cambridge: Cambridge University
Press, 1995), p. 87.

44   Cf. *CD* IV/1, pp. 287ff.

45   Ibid., p. 287.

and *experienced* as such if it does not happen within the space-time realm of our experience? The problem defined in this way, according to Barth, is none other than the problem of faith and history, and is identical with Lessing's puzzle regarding the relationship between contingent truths of history and necessary truths of reason.

It is important to note here that Barth's answer to the problem is not what many have mistakenly claimed it to be: the radical suspicion and rejection of uncertain facts of history as sufficient grounds for faith. That the problem has this temporal and spatial aspect Barth does not deny. But to identify this with *the fundamental* problem would be erroneous. Barth agrees that the historical distance between Jesus of Nazareth and ourselves is great and that this can generate problems of our historical understanding, though he acknowledges that there are many things, historical and otherwise, which we can accept with full confidence on the testimony of others. Having noted these formulations of the problem, however, Barth warns of the danger of a preoccupation with the spatial and temporal and even existential distance which separates Christ from us. He raises the question whether this formulation of the problem might have more the character of a 'technical difficulty in thinking', of a 'formal antithesis of the then and now' than of an underlying 'spiritual' or 'genuine theological' problem,[46] and he challenges the notion that we can accept 'the being and activity of Jesus Christ for us and in our place' upon the basis of recollection.[47] He rejects the thought that such a message can come to us 'in any but a direct way, removing the distance altogether, establishing between the one remembered and our recollection a contemporaneity which ... is real, enabling that distant event to become and to be true to us directly and therefore incontrovertibly.'[48] Barth advises against attempting to remove the difficulty exclusively in the light of its historical aspect, for: 'In it it is only formally and not in substance, only incidentally and secondarily and not primarily and centrally, that the question concerns God and ourselves, Jesus Christ and His cross and our reconciliation. It is a methodological question.'[49] Methodological problems and their solutions, for Barth, rightly come to the fore only in the context of the proper object of investigation. Methodological issues, taken in abstraction from the prime object in view lead inevitably to reductionist conclusions. Hinting to the fact that 'the real scandal is grounded ... in the event of the atonement itself,' Barth asserts that the solving of this pseudo-problem only marks the beginning of our real problem: 'the strangeness and remoteness of this event.'[50] Preoccupation with the technical difficulty of the temporal and spatial distance between Christ and us merely eclipses the real problem, that is, 'what has taken place and been done to us with the incarnation of the Son of God, in His appearance in our place, in His effective action for us now as well as then and here as well as there.'[51] The

---

46   Ibid., pp. 288f.
47   Ibid., p. 288.
48   Ibid.
49   Ibid., pp. 288f.
50   Ibid., p. 189.
51   Ibid., p. 291.

question of faith and history is one which assumes that the death of Jesus Christ is a contingent truth of history and by definition not a universal truth of reason. Barth objects to this conceptuality and rejects it on the grounds that it is inappropriate to the reality of the death of Jesus Christ as an act of God. The death of Jesus Christ cannot be understood for the reality it is except that it is understood as the reality of the whole of humanity in him, immediately and directly embracing all of history. To pose the question of faith and history is to deny that what has come to us definitively and finally in the crucifixion of Jesus Christ is our judgment, end and death which we have no capacity to transcend. Barth is indefatigable in his opposition to the separation of the question of the absolute comprehensiveness of the being and act of Jesus Christ from the question of the relation of faith to its historical referent.

Many of Barth's critics come up short at this point, because of an inadequate understanding of the grounds of Barth's refusal to grant interpretive priority to presuppositions and contingent issues which arise from various critical standpoints external to the gospel. Barth comes to terms with the problem as one that is inherent in the gospel and arises out of the gospel, and hence, for Barth, is as such a real and substantive issue.

For Barth, Lessing's question is understandable in as much as it represents a supreme interest to disguise our relationship to Jesus Christ as one which is 'purely historical and therefore mediated and indirect' to be apprehended as a mere recollection.[52] In Barth's view the question of faith and history is a question which arises from a pervasive human need, that is,

> the need to hide ourselves (like Adam and Eve in the garden of Eden) from Jesus Christ as He makes Himself present and mediates Himself to us; the need to keep our eyes closed to that about which we ask with such solemn concern, taking ourselves and our 'honesty' with such frightful seriousness; the need to safeguard ourselves as far as this movement of flight allows against the directness in which He does in fact confront us, against His presence, and the consequences which it threatens.[53]

It is only in this attempt to elude the real problem that the question of historical distance takes on such importance. The question merely reflects our desperate attempt to flee from the reality which confronts us in the risen Jesus. The only way to explain our fear of this reality, the reality of our death in him, is that this reality is really present in his resurrection, and as such is the occasion of our fear of and flight from it. Hence, for Barth, even our rejection of him has its ground and occasion in Christ's resurrection presence with us.

---

52   Ibid., p. 292.
53   Ibid.

The Problem as the Scandal of the Gospel

Barth does not stop at the discussion of the temporal and spatial distance between the crucifixion of Jesus in his time and space and our own historico-spatial particularity, but rather tries to understand the problem of distance with an appropriate seriousness. The 'real scandal' in Barth's view 'is grounded ... in the event of the atonement itself.'[54] The real problem is that God appears in the human sphere, that he acts and speaks for us in this sphere, that he confronts us.[55] That is to say, because the atonement accomplished in Jesus Christ is so thoroughly objective, because he stands so completely in our place, the problem of the distance between himself and us others is profound. The difficulty of the problem does not betray a weakness of the doctrine of vicarious atonement, but rather draws its force from that very reality. It is the problem of the direct encounter of the anthropological sphere by and in the christological sphere:

> There are two orders (or, rather, order and disorder), two opposite world-structures, two worlds opposing and apparently excluding one another. ... On the side of man the only possible word seems to be a deep-seated No, the No of the one who when God comes and acts for Him and tells him that He is doing so is forced to see that his day is over and that he can only perish.[56]

The scandal of the gospel is the impossibility of our present existence, our being-in-sin, because this very existence has been negated once for all in Christ.

The Inclusiveness of the Being and Action of Jesus Christ

Surely one of the most decisive issues apparent within Barth's theological understanding is the absolute supremacy and precedence of christology over anthropology. For Barth, anthropology must be christological anthropology – it can only be thought out correctly as an ancillary sphere to the christological sphere proper, one that finds its source, origin, meaning and warrant within christology itself. Hence to bring previously established anthropological ideas, concepts and categories to bear on christology, that is, to invert this fundamental order, is in effect to reduce christology to anthropology and thus to eclipse the very source of light under the illumination of which the investigation is attempted.

The anthropological sphere has existence and meaning for Barth only as it remains within and is responsible to the larger christological sphere. That is not to underestimate the appreciable distinction which Barth makes between what he calls the 'narrower christological sphere' or 'Christology proper' and the wider sphere of christology which includes the anthropological sphere, but it is to assert that the anthropological has no independence from the christological sphere. Barth

---

54   Ibid., p. 289.
55   Ibid., p. 290.
56   Ibid.

has made it very clear that his sole basis for consideration of the question of the anthropological sphere and of movement from the narrower christological sphere to the anthropological sphere rests upon the warrants provided within the narrower christological sphere itself, that is, in as much as the Word has taken upon himself human flesh, thereby creating, establishing and drawing the anthropological into inextricable relationship with himself:

> In the glory of the Mediator as such there is included the fact that He is in process of glorifying Himself among and in and through us, and that we are ordained and liberated to take a receptive and active part in His glory. ... Jesus Christ is not without His own. ... Virtually, prospectively and *de iure* all men are His own. Actually, effectively and *de facto* His own are those who believe in Him, who know Him, who serve Him and who are thus the interconnected members of His body, i.e., Christians.[57]

Yet there is a gap between this reality as it is completed in Christ and the recognition and embrace of it in the world-time existence of other men and women. This in no way signals a limitation to the radical inclusion of the anthropological sphere within the christological. On the contrary, it points to the fullness of its inclusion for it indicates that even the richness of the historical unfolding of this reality is grounded and occasioned in Christ. That is to say, even the very movement – historical, spatial, and existential transition – from Jesus Christ to us is established and determined from its basis in the narrower christological sphere. No human response is required or even possible except that which is generated, grounded and guaranteed in advance in the being and action of Jesus Christ. According to Barth, Jesus Christ at the same time is and enacts and empowers this transition:

> He Himself is not merely there in His own place, but as he is there in His own place He is also here in ours. He is the One who is on the way from there to here. ... He is and acts on His way from His own particular sphere to our surrounding, anthropological sphere. ... The reconciliation which has taken place in Him, in His person and work, is as such an occurrence which reaches beyond its own particular sphere, which embraces our sphere, the sphere of human life generally.[58]

Thus, for Barth, the anthropological sphere is completely and without remainder anticipated and comprehended and determined in the christological sphere. Likewise, the question of the transition from the christological sphere proper to the anthropological sphere must be accountable to the actuality of the primacy and power of Jesus Christ *extra nos* and *pro nobis*.

The way and power of the crucified Lord *in nobis* is, according to Barth, already inherent in the being and action of Jesus Christ. The way, power and knowledge of Jesus Christ *extra nos* and *pro nobis* on the cross is communicated to us in the resurrection of Jesus Christ, in which he comes to us revealing himself as our crucified yet risen Lord and ourselves as his reconciled and obedient people. The resurrection

---

57   *CD* IV/3, p. 278.
58   Ibid., p. 279.

is the decisive moment in which the actuality and power of our reconciliation in Christ on the cross becomes present and known. Barth's justification for the move from the christological basis to the anthropological sphere lies in the not immediately apparent fact that the christological basis includes within itself the move from Jesus Christ to us as already executed and actual in him, and hence already *per definitionem* we are included in his being and activity as those for whom he is and has acted. Barth wants to avoid all distinction between an objective atonement and a quite different subjective atonement. Rather, the fact of the inclusion of the movement from the christological basis to the anthropological sphere already in the being and activity of Jesus Christ Barth describes as the turn outward already achieved in the narrower christology.[59]

Here Barth makes an important theological decision. He does not see the power of the turn from Christ to us as a subsequent thing, an added essence or extension, or the completion of something left undone in Christ. His discussion of this basic transition is self-confessedly nothing more than an attempt to disclose and confirm that 'it is He Himself in whom this turn has already been executed and is a fact.'[60] All of our knowledge of the relevance of his being and act for us is to be referred back to this irrevocable fact. But, since ours is 'the sphere of the unreconciled world, of man contradicting and opposing God' it is not as such 'qualified for this novelty.'[61] Says Barth:

> There is a great gulf between 'Jesus Christ for us' and ourselves as those who in this supremely perfect word are summoned to regard ourselves as those for whom He is and acts. ... [B]y what right or power dare I make the corresponding minor, or draw the simple conclusion, that I myself am one of those for whom Jesus Christ is and acts?[62]

What are we to take from this whole discussion? That Barth looks firstly and steadfastly to the unassailable being and activity of Jesus Christ, and he asserts that this being and this activity is in the most basic sense *for us*. The question then is whether we in our contradiction and opposition to God are able to see ourselves as those for whom Jesus Christ is and acts. The great gulf is not between Jesus Christ in his work and us, but between 'Jesus Christ for us' and 'we ourselves against God.' How are we to describe this gulf? It is decidedly not a gulf of relevance. It is not a question of the relevance of his being and act for us as we are in our contradiction and opposition to God. It is the gulf wrought by our inability to embrace this relevance. It is the question of the inability of our darkness to comprehend his light. It is the problem the christological sphere – in which human being in contradiction and opposition to God has been put to death and yet has been made whole and elevated to covenant faithfulness to God – presents to our anthropological sphere of contradiction and opposition to God. It is the clash of radically antithetical anthropological spheres.

---

59   *CD* IV/2, p. 280.
60   *CD* IV/1, p. 284.
61   Ibid., p. 286.
62   Ibid.

Here we note that it is in the one particular man, Jesus, that the reality and essence of all other human persons is shaped and determined. Human being is thoroughly recreated in Jesus Christ, though it is 'in Him' and not as yet 'in us.' The doctrine of the resurrection of Jesus Christ concerns the transition from 'in Him' to 'in us.' Thus Barth does not refrain from using language about 'essence' though he is quite careful about the manner in which he defines it. Barth says,

> It is in perfect likeness with us, as our genuine Brother, that He was and is so unique, so unlike us as the true and royal man. ... To human nature in all its nature and corruption there now belongs the fact that in the one Jesus Christ, who as the true Son of God was and is also the true son of Man, it has now become and is participant in this elevation and exaltation.[63]

Hence,

> There can ... be no question of our not being in Him as the elected, called, instituted and revealed Lord and Head of all men, of our not being in His representative existence, as if our own obedience were not anticipated and virtually accomplished in His.[64]

The danger is that we overlook the seriousness and radicality with which Jesus took up our cause and, with us and for us, lived in perfect covenant keeping fellowship with the Father:

> For what took place ... is that the covenant between God and man was maintained and restored on both sides: on both sides perfectly, because in this history the Son of God became also the Son of Man; and for the same reason representatively ... all men being included in this One in the covenant as it is perfectly maintained and restored on both sides.[65]

Barth insists that the statements of the New Testament concerning the being of the man Jesus, and therefore of the being of all other men and women, must be taken as 'statements of an ontological character.' That is not to deny that they are statements of faith, but as statements of faith they are statements of the knowledge and power of this *being*.[66]

Death as the Télos of Christ's Life

The inclusiveness of the being and action of Jesus Christ arrives at the height of its scandalous nature in his crucifixion and death. It is in his end that our own end is effected. For Barth the entire movement of the Gospel narratives is toward the death of Jesus Christ. If we are to take the synoptic Gospels seriously as they present

---

63   *CD* IV/2, pp. 269f.
64   Ibid.
65   Ibid., p. 271.
66   Ibid., p. 281.

themselves, *that is*, as essentially passion narratives with lengthy introductions, then we must see the crucifixion as the sweeping theme and *terminus* of the story. The whole of the representative humiliation of the Son of God as well as the whole of the representative exaltation of the Son of Man achieves its definitive and unsurpassable conclusion in the death of Jesus Christ. There on the cross it is finished.

Barth describes three theological aspects of the meaning of this orientation of the Son of Man to death and the attainment of his goal in his death. The *first* of these is that the crucifixion of Jesus is the presupposition of the incarnation.[67] The *second* aspect of the decisive answer to our question is that the cross was and is the close and crown of the life of Jesus. For in his crucifixion decisively and irrevocably he took to himself the situation of the human being under the judgment of God. As such Jesus has become our brother and liberator without reserve.[68] The *third* aspect of the answer to our question is, Barth claims, that the 'final and controlling function' of the cross is:

> grounded in the fact that the life of Jesus has and reveals in this determination the character of an act of God. It is this determination which gives to His life the power to be a life which intercedes for us and all men, which is lived in their place, which includes and controls their life and being.[69]

It is the proper will and act of God that the life of Jesus should have its orientation and *télos* in his crucifixion. God's act of self-humiliation and of the exaltation of human being comes to its fitting and ultimate conclusion in the concealment of the cross.

Unlike everything else in the cosmos, though the life of Jesus moves towards death and takes its mature form in death, death is not the end, but the goal or *télos* of this life. According to Barth 'it has power and significance as it moves towards this death and really derives from it.'[70]

> [His life] had and has power from death, from the frontier of all life. But this means that it is not just a limited power. It is the unlimited power of the merciful God, who alone can act in this world from that absolute beyond of all creaturely being and life, of whom it is characteristic to act from that beyond, who in so doing demonstrates and reveals that He is the merciful and omnipotent God.[71]

The answer to the question of why we should speak of Christ's death as the *télos* of his life, for the moment, is given only as the assertion that the question is indeed that of Jesus Christ *pro nobis*, and in particular, of the reality of the death of the human being in Jesus Christ. The fearsome reality of the death effected and mediated in Jesus Christ is the real and pressing issue. It is the reality and finality of this death

---

67   Ibid., pp. 292f.
68   Ibid., pp. 293f.
69   Ibid., p. 294.
70   Ibid., p. 295.
71   Ibid.

which so forcefully imposes itself upon us such that we cower under this word and make a last gasp effort to perceive the word as something less final, less definitive than death.[72] It is with this understanding that Barth makes the following claim:

> That Jesus Christ died for us does not mean, therefore, that we do not have to die, but that we have died in and with Him, that as the people we were we have been done away and destroyed, that we are no longer there and have no more future.[73]

Barth argues that we would be wrong to dismiss too quickly this possibility as absurd. It is in keeping with the freedom of God to exercise his good and holy will in this way, a radical undoing of creation. The positive answer to the problem, the resurrection, demands that we confront the negative possibility which was within the realm of possibility for God.[74]

Because the life of Jesus is so fundamentally oriented to his death the scandal arises. True self-knowledge is the knowledge of ourselves as those who are in Christ, as those for whom Christ is. But if the fundamental orientation of the life of Jesus is his death, and if his death is a black hole of concealment from which no light can escape, how can we have any true knowledge of Christ and ourselves in him? Jesus Christ is hidden from us, and hence who we are in Christ is also hidden from us. The question is 'how can the unknown become for us the known reality, reality in truth? ... What does it really mean to see the Crucified?'[75] 'One thing is sure', says Barth, 'If His cross is the mystery with which we have to do ... no penetration to the truth is in fact possible from our side. For this mystery is a matter of His will and power and act. ... He Himself has concealed Himself in it.'[76]

It is Barth's belief that this concealment is a necessary one, willed by Christ and exercised in his lordship:

> Far from competing with His love and its revelation, or opposing our knowledge of His love and its revelation, this concealment of Christ and the existence of this concealing factor are themselves a necessary, and perhaps even a decisive, element in the work of His grace.[77]

That we do not know who we are in Jesus Christ, that such knowledge is hidden and humanly unattainable, is neither a result of the limitations of human knowing generally derived nor evidence that our human being and knowing is genuinely to be found elsewhere. It is rather a result of the wise, gracious and atoning action of God in Jesus Christ. This concealment is the reconciling concealment of all that we human persons once were apart from Jesus Christ. This concealment is the

---

72   *CD* IV/1, p. 294.
73   Ibid., p. 295.
74   Ibid., p. 294.
75   Ibid., p. 297.
76   Ibid.
77   *CD* IV/2, p. 289.

epistemological correlate to the ontological reality of what was accomplished in Jesus' atoning death.

It is important to note here that Barth is careful not to define this transition in terms of the christological or anthropological poles generally conceived, that is, independent of the concrete saving being and action of Jesus Christ. Rather, the anthropological sphere in question is given its specific determination in the person and work of Jesus Christ. As a sovereign reconciling act God has permitted this remaining anthropological sphere to be as yet not affected by his saving being and action. That is to say, this is a deliberate act of God in which he has determined to bring about reconciliation in what may be provisionally described as first ontic, then noetic, moments.

The real question is then, how can we who are no longer there and who have no more future come to terms with this our reconciled being in Jesus Christ? But the very fact that we are presented with this genuine problem suggests that we are really asking another question:

> Is there a sure place and basis from which the judgment which has fallen upon us, the end in which we are posited, and the death which has overtaken us in that Jesus Christ died for us, can be seen in all their frightful seriousness and yet not accepted as final and absolute, but only in a certain relationship and connexion and subordination?[78]

In attending to this fundamental question Barth concludes that the problem of the distance between the crucified Reconciler and ourselves is not one of our own making, neither is it one we have discovered apart from the reconciling work of Christ as another thing which must still be considered, such as the application of reconciliation through yet another agency (our own). It is rather a problem inherent in the reconciling work of Christ itself. That is to say, it is a basic aspect of his reconciling work on the cross that it be a matter concealed from within with such authority and seriousness that no penetrating of its secrets from without can be achieved.

It is further to be noted that this concealment cannot be explained as the consequence of human sin. Provision has been made in Jesus Christ to destroy the consequences of sin and to establish in their place the rewards of righteousness. But even with the defeat of sin and the conversion of human being in Christ this concealment remains. When we inquire into the purpose and power of this concealment Barth reminds us that 'everything took place in this crucifixion – the whole reconciliation, the whole restoration of peace, between man and God.'[79] Sin no longer has mastery over those who are in Christ, for in his death he has destroyed the dominion of sin: 'In His death He has not only reached His own goal, but made this new beginning for us, in our place, and with us, with men.'[80]

---

78   *CD* IV/1, p. 297.
79   *CD* IV/2, p. 290.
80   Ibid., p. 291.

In addition, we can be certain, claims Barth, that the answer to our question does not lie in introspection. We cannot know ourselves as we really are, as those justified and sanctified in Christ, by looking at ourselves as we stand apart from Christ. Because we are who we are only in Christ, 'we cannot be too strict or consistent in looking away from ourselves' to Christ.[81] This looking beyond ourselves is not a looking to a beyond spun out of ourselves or an empty beyond. In either case we would not be looking beyond at all; we would still be looking most intently at ourselves. If we are to look truly beyond we must look at that someone who 'irresistibly draws' our gaze.[82] We must look to Jesus Christ.

But looking to Jesus Christ means looking to that which is thoroughly concealed, for his is a hidden being.[83] The great mystery is that the truth is concealed, not in some partially concealing yet partially revealing cloak, but in its opposite, in what contradicts it. The 'Yes' is given the form of a 'No'.[84] There can be no even indirect or analogical perception of the reality by virtue of that which conceals it:

> It does not prove, but denies, the being of Jesus Christ and our being in Him. What it proves and demonstrates is that Jesus Christ is not the Lord, that there is no such thing as His kingdom, that we are not therefore His, and that we are not elevated and exalted to be the saints of God in Him.[85]

Therefore, 'if we are to see what is hidden ... it will not be by looking through that which hides.'[86]

The question which underlies all that Barth says here is that of the transition of the reconciling being and action of Jesus Christ to the anthropological sphere. Taking the New Testament at face value, Barth underscores the ontological force of the biblical claims concerning Christ and therefore concerning other men and women. The question though is, if we are to take this seriously – that Jesus Christ stands in our place and that we stand in him – how can we know and embrace our real human being in Christ, seeing as our real human being stands in such radical contrast and opposition to our false existence apart from Christ? The genuine secret of the question lies in the real and inescapable question with which, in Barth's view, the Christ event presents us:

> Granted the possibility of an actual contemporaneity of Jesus Christ with us, and therefore of the directness of our encounter and presence with Him, and of the overcoming of the temporal barrier between Him and us, we are forced to put the question with a final and

---

81   Ibid., p. 283.
82   Ibid., p. 284.
83   Ibid., p. 285.
84   Ibid., p. 287.
85   Ibid.
86   Ibid. This constitutes the primary basis of Barth's renowned rejection of natural theology.

true seriousness: how will it stand with us when we are alongside Jesus Christ and follow Him, when we are in His environment and time and space?[87]

One might ask the question why Barth concentrates upon our radical destruction in the immediacy of the presence of Jesus Christ in his being and completed act. The answer lies, in part, in the fact that in the first part of this volume Barth is dealing with the Lord as Servant, that is, the doctrine of Justification, in which Barth argues that human beings as sinners are put to death in and with Jesus Christ. Hence the radical presence of Jesus Christ means precisely our end as men and women of sin. The great threat is that it is not at all self-evident that there is any beyond of this end. One would expect in the second part-volume a development of the radical presence not of our end as sinners but of our new beginning as faithful covenant partners with the Father, for in the life history of Jesus Christ both are accomplished: the wrestling down to death of the man of sin and the lifting up into life of the man of righteousness. But we do well to recall that this second aspect of the reconciling work of Christ, that of the exaltation of human being to the nobility of covenant faithfulness is equally threatening for the existential anthropological sphere because just as it means the end of what we are – sinners in contradiction to God in Christ – it also means the beginning of what we are not – free, righteous servants of God. Both negate our existence in sin and death. Hence our feeble objections are attempts to evade the radical presence of the conversion of our human being in Jesus Christ.

The question is taken up again in the third part-volume in which Barth describes the transition as the turn from 'Christology in the narrower sense' to 'the remaining sphere of our own life and the life of man generally.'[88] Just as it could not be taken for granted that the justification and sanctification wrought in Christ for us would have effect in us so 'it cannot be taken for granted that the shining of the light of life as the being and action of Jesus Christ will demonstrate its range and power in occurrences in the very different sphere in which we exist.'[89]

> Between Jesus Christ as the Word of God and what becomes of this Word when we think we can receive and accept and assimilate and attest and pass it on, there yawns a deep cleft. Who are we other men, the rest of humanity, that the question can even arise ... of a true and genuine continuity of this Word, and therefore of a real presence of the prophecy of Jesus Christ ... in our receiving and attesting of His being and action?[90]

The question is indeed a serious one. Failure to grant due consideration to this fundamental puzzle is to gloss over a defining element of the Christian gospel.[91]

Barth claims we know real human being when we look to our death. But our death is not a nothingness on the other side of our known or unknown limits. It is rather our

---

87   *CD* IV/1, p. 293.
88   *CD* IV/3, p. 276.
89   Ibid.
90   Ibid., p. 277.
91   Ibid.

death in Jesus Christ. This question to which Barth attends so rigorously can only be raised and answered in light of the reality that the being and action of Jesus Christ does indeed have power and relevance for us. It is only because the crucified yet risen Jesus Christ, in the fullness of his being and action, actually comes to us that we can recognize that our existence is already caught up in the reality that he is for us. In other words the fundamental question of the way and power of the crucified *in nobis* is already raised and answered in the light of the resurrection.

The Answer is the Resurrection

To the question 'Is there something beyond this death, this conclusion, this end, in the light of which Christology is not exclusive but inclusive ... ?'[92] Barth responds:

> The answer is the resurrection of Jesus Christ from the dead, His life as the Resurrected from the dead, the verdict of God the Father on the obedience of His Son as it was pronounced in this event and as it is in force in His being from this event.[93]

That Jesus Christ has risen from the dead means that 'He discloses Himself to us with the same will and power and in the same act as He closes Himself off from us.'[94] That is to say, it is in the resurrection revelation, in the fact that he who has closed the door has now opened it again, that we are able to penetrate the concealment of his death and gaze upon his true being and ours in him.[95] This is the event and power of the resurrection; this is the way and force of the transition from Jesus Christ to others.

At this point Barth turns his focus from the discovery of a problem to the recognition that the discovery of the problem comes in the wake of the reality of its solution. It is only in the brilliant light of the resurrection that the reality and depth of the matter is fully disclosed. The subject matter of reconciliation itself involves the question of the great gulf between Jesus Christ and we others in the most radical manner. Yet the profound crisis of the crucifixion could not possibility be understood of itself apart from this light. That is, it is not so much the distance, of whatever form, which is the problem, but the immediacy of the Christ-event, of Jesus Christ himself to us others. Barth works backwards as it were from the reality of the resurrection to the illumination of the meaning of the crucifixion in its light. From the perspective of the crucifixion we are faced with the utter dissolution of our existence – of our existence as beings-in-sin-and-death – with the annihilation of all that we are and have and do. Yet this can be known only from the perspective of the resurrection in which Jesus is declared with power to be the Son of God. This in turn illuminates the event of the cross as an act of God in which the whole of humanity, in its Representative, is borne to its death. It is only from the standpoint

---

92   *CD* IV/1, p. 349.
93   Ibid.
94   *CD* IV/2, p. 298.
95   Ibid., p. 299.

of the resurrection that we are confronted with the immediacy and inescapability of this condition.

The Revelation of the Inclusion of Humanity in Christ

Together with the ontological question Barth clarifies the epistemological question of humanity in Jesus Christ. In this form the question becomes: 'how can we know ourselves to be those who are so included in Christ?' Barth's answer to this question shares the same orientation and character as the ontological question. That is to say, human knowing finds its complete and undifferentiated basis in the self-knowing of Jesus Christ just as human being finds its complete and undifferentiated basis in his being:

> It is a matter of knowing ourselves but of knowing ourselves in Christ, and therefore not here in ourselves but there outside ourselves in this Other who is not identical with me, and with whom I am not, and do not become, identical, but in whose humanity God himself becomes and is and always will be another, a concrete antithesis.[96]

The question concerns the way in which we see and know our being in Jesus Christ. How is it that we are able to perceive ourselves as no longer turned away from and rejected by God but rather as those who are established in Christ as regenerate and converted, as saints of God, as genuine Christians?[97] The answer to the question is the resurrection in which the transition is made from the concealment of the being and activity of Jesus Christ to its revelation to and in us.

The cross is absolute darkness. No human enterprise can discover its inner secrets, for it entails the end of all human enterprise. From the side of the human the cross is shrouded in darkness and gloom. Thus, the question becomes 'how can we understand ourselves as those who are included in Christ?' Barth's answer is that we do know because the risen Lord sovereignly chooses to reveal this mystery in us and to us. He has, in his resurrection, opened the door to this understanding and hence our anthropological sphere is flooded with his light. Barth comes to understand that the radicality of the reconciling work of Christ on the cross cannot be known from the cross. Only in the light of the risen one can we perceive and know the great darkness of the crucified one. Jesus Christ himself mediates the reconciliation he has wrought in his own being and act:

> This is the outreaching, embracing and comprehending of reconciliation in its prophetic determination. ... Its peculiar feature in this determination is that it shares with the world the fact that it is the world already reconciled with God. By this impartation it awakens and allows and commands it to know and experience and take itself seriously as such, to act as such, and therefore to exist as the reconciled ... world.[98]

---

96   Ibid., p. 283.
97   Ibid., p. 296.
98   *CD* IV/3, p. 280.

In his own turning to God and recognition of himself as turning to God, Jesus Christ has made actual and determinate the turning of all other human persons to God and the recognition of themselves as turning to God. His resurrection is his self-revelation and in his self-revelation we too are revealed:

> The particular event of His resurrection is thus the primal and basic form of His glory, of the outgoing and shining of His light, of His expression, of His Word as His self-expression, and therefore of His outgoing and penetration and entry into the world around and ourselves, of His prophetic work.[99]

The Necessity of the Resurrection

Barth consistently argues that the finished reconciling work of Jesus Christ was complete, requiring nothing further. But this begs the question: 'What is the reason for the resurrection?' While Barth asserts that the resurrection does not augment the crucifixion, he insists that without the resurrection the completed being and action of Christ 'would have remained shut up in Him.' It would have remained completely unknown and 'without practical significance.'[100] The resurrection was necessary not as a completion of the reconciling work of Christ on the cross but as the revelation and effective outreaching of that work to include the world. Indeed Barth claims without the resurrection, 'The world reconciled to God in Him would then be practically and factually unreconciled as though nothing had happened.'[101] In this case the world would have no true knowledge of the Reconciler and therefore no true knowledge of itself as the world reconciled:

> Whatever else we might know or not know concerning Him, we could know nothing of His inclusive being and action embracing the world, the Church and ourselves, nor of Him as the declaration of this inclusive being and action. ... A precise and conscientious affirmative can be given to the question of this movement and connexion only in the power of His self-witness as the living One, and therefore as the Resurrected from the dead. It can have its origin only in this event.[102]

Thus Barth claims that though complete and conclusive and effective the inclusive work of Christ on the cross without the event of the resurrection would have been in fact practically incomplete, inconclusive and ineffective. But how can this be seen as anything but non-sensical and paradoxical? Barth's answer to this apparent contradiction is given, at least in part, in his explication of the nature of the inclusiveness of the being and action of Jesus Christ:

---

99   Ibid., p. 281.
100   Ibid., p. 282.
101   Ibid.
102   Ibid., p. 285.

Jesus Christ and His being and action in His life and death have penetrated to us in the particular event of His resurrection, thus becoming truth in their reality, and as truth reality for the world, for the community, *pro nobis* and *pro me*.[103]

Because the transition of true human being and action in Jesus Christ to us is real and effective in the resurrection, and hence cannot be adequately 'captured' in our descriptive formulations, the resurrection remains an astonishing and incomprehensible miracle. According to Barth, 'If we really see and understand [the resurrection, the transition from Jesus Christ to us], it is never under our mastery, and therefore we can never cease to be astonished.'[104] Seeing as this transition is God's own act and therefore both real and inconvertible to something other (that is, cannot be accomplished in the human reproduction) it 'has the stamp of the axiomatic, the first and the last, and therefore the self-evident.'[105] It is therefore that upon which we can depend without reserve. This transition, as effected in the resurrection of Jesus Christ, is not merely a possibility nor even an enthusiastic hope; it is rather 'the reality of the way on which Jesus Christ strides into the world and to us as the One He is for the world and therefore *pro nobis* and *pro me*, not remaining alone but already present among us and with us.'[106]

Conclusion

Our analysis thus far has concentrated upon the general context and meaning of Barth's development of the doctrine of the resurrection of Jesus Christ in *CD* IV. We have demonstrated that this doctrine occupies a pivotal place not only as a transitional section in the overall structure of his doctrine of reconciliation, but also as a material transition rooted in the fundamental dogmatic structure of Barth's theological understanding. For Barth the ominous nature of Jesus' crucifixion opens up the problem of the transition of reconciled human being and action to others. The comprehensive nature of Jesus' reconciling work looms so large that it appears to threaten the existence of all other reality. The reason for this is twofold, by virtue of the utter ontological depth of his representative work and by the consummation of that work in his death.

However, Barth speaks at this point of transition because this supreme end of all human possibilities does indeed have a beyond in the miraculous, creative possibility of God. This beyond is that to which the New Testament testifies as it bears witness to Jesus' resurrection. In this way Barth distinctively develops the doctrine of the resurrection of Jesus Christ as the movement of the crucified Lord to us in our opposed and contradictory anthropological condition.

---

103   Ibid., p. 284.
104   Ibid., p. 286.
105   Ibid., p. 288.
106   Ibid.

Chapter Five

The Resurrection as the Beyond of the Crucifixion

Our thesis states that for Karl Barth the resurrection of Jesus Christ is the reality, revelation and power of the crucified Lord *in nobis*. To the question, 'can the reconciliation of the world with God accomplished in [Jesus Christ] consist in anything but the dissolution of the world?'[1] Barth answers a confident 'Yes.' What is yet to be understood is the manner in which that transition comes about. How is it that there is this beyond to the finality of the crucifixion and death of Jesus Christ? What is the nature of this transition? These are the questions Barth addresses in *CD* IV/1, §59.3, 'The Verdict of the Father.' And this is the matter which occupies our attention in this chapter.

As we have already noted, Barth takes seriously the finality and decisiveness of the work of Jesus Christ on the cross, in his sacrificial death: 'What has come to us in the crucifixion of Jesus Christ would not be our judgment, end and death if we could (even theoretically) transcend it, if we could even hypothetically place ourselves on an upper level of this event, and view and penetrate and understand and interpret it from this level.'[2] However, quite apart from all anticipation, the resurrection occurs as a new act of God beyond that act which brought Jesus Christ to his death. In the resurrection Barth finds the verdict of the Father pronounced on the Son, God's 'Yes' inclusive of, yet subsequent to and superseding his 'No'. An exposition of the resurrection is, in a most important manner of speaking, an exposition of that aspect of our christological basis which is the already executed and factual happening of the turn from Jesus Christ to us. That is to say, having taken the first step in hearing of the being and activity of Jesus Christ *pro nobis*, we can also take the second step in which we can, furthermore, believe and accept as true, of ourselves and for ourselves, the being and activity of Jesus Christ *in nobis*.[3]

For Barth the resurrection is the central point of illumination from which to look back upon the life, crucifixion and death of Jesus Christ as he moves toward this ultimate end. The event of 'the awakening or resurrection from the dead of the crucified and dead Jesus Christ':

---

1   *CD* IV/1, p. 293.
2   Ibid., p. 297.
3   Ibid., p. 285.

is undoubtedly the sure ground and basis from which the New Testament witnesses could look back to the crucifixion and death of Jesus Christ, but also to the way which led and had to lead to this goal, to what this way and goal implied for themselves and all men, to the happening which broke catastrophically upon us all in and with Jesus Christ. We can say confidently ... that the whole New Testament thinks and speaks in the light of this event, and to understand it we must be prepared to think with it in the light of this event.[4]

There can be no doubt that for Barth the resurrection constitutes the certain beyond of the crucifixion of Jesus Christ. Those who view his doctrine of the resurrection as little more than the making visible of the life history of Jesus fail to account for the substantial material describing this character of the resurrection.

The Resurrection of Jesus Christ as a Real Event

Barth begins with the resurrection of Jesus Christ *de facto*. It is an enacted and present reality. It does not require establishment or validation. It is in itself already the reality in which we stand in Jesus Christ. It is not a matter which can be subjected to serious question and doubt, for it is an objective reality which precedes all human questioning and doubting.

Though Barth's development of the material moves from an exposition of the problem to its solution, the solution has determinative priority over the problem. He consistently takes an *a posteriori* approach, reasoning from the reality to its possibility and exposition.[5] For Barth the reality of the resurrection of Jesus Christ must control our understanding of the conditions of its possibility. Our reasoning must be retrospective rather than prospective. Hence he defines the problem, the knowledge and acceptance of our reconciled being in Jesus Christ, in terms of its established solution: the crucified Reconciler lives and turns to us.

Hence, while at first glance it may seem that Barth attempts to understand the resurrection under the rubric of external criteria drawn from a class of supposedly similar events, a closer look reveals that he permits his descriptive language to be shaped by this particular event itself. His talk of the 'five conditions' which must be fulfilled if an event is to be a genuine beyond of the crucifixion and death of Jesus Christ must then be taken as idiosyncratic language necessitated by this real, peculiar and non-substitutable resurrection. Barth makes it clear that these conditions are wholly determined by the object itself:

---

4   Ibid., p. 299.

5   For more on this important aspect of Barth's theological understanding see Thomas F. Torrance, *Reality and Evangelical Theology: The Realism of Christian Revelation* (Downers Grove: Intervarsity Press, 1982, 1999), pp. 14f., 77. Cf. also Ingolf U. Dalferth, 'Karl Barth's Eschatological Realism' in *Karl Barth: Centenary Essays*, pp. 14–18, especially p. 17 where he claims for Barth 'God's saving action in Jesus Christ is true independently of our believing or not believing it.'

We have not spun these five conditions out of the void. ... The New Testament witness to Christ knows and names an event which corresponds to and satisfies all the five conditions of the actuality of such a beyond. We have, in fact, taken the conditions from the event.[6]

It is to be noted then that Barth's is a description of *features* of the resurrection of Jesus Christ. In this sense, too, it is a realist description, for it seeks not to replace its object with conceptual terms – all such attempts are understood to be clearly inadequate – but to point to various aspects of the reality, which remains distinct from and transcends every attempt to describe it. Barth asserts that it is necessary to speak of this event if we are to understand the positive aspect of the reconciliation of the world with God which took place in the being and act of Jesus Christ.[7]

Five Features of the Resurrection

Barth identifies *five features* characteristic of the resurrection of Jesus Christ from the dead as depicted in the New Testament. The resurrection is then: i) an *act of God*, ii) a *non-necessary novum*, iii) meaningfully and substantively *following upon and corresponding to the crucifixion*, iv) as an *historical event*, v) in the *historical existence of the selfsame Jesus Christ*. The fact that these features of the resurrection of Jesus Christ are real demonstrates in what way this is a genuine beyond to his crucifixion and death, and hence, how the transition from the crucified Lord *in nobis* is indeed real and effective.

An Act of God

As regards its material content, the resurrection of Jesus Christ, according to Barth, is to be understood first as an undeniable act *of God*. Divine action alone is possible, for all creaturely possibilities have been brought to their end in the representative death of Jesus Christ. 'To be dead means not to be. Those who are not, cannot will and do, nor can they possibly be objects of the willing and doing of others. ἀνάστασις ἐκ νεκρῶν is not one possibility of this kind with others.'[8] If there is to be any beyond to the act of God in bringing to death all human-being-in-sin, it must be solely by a new act of the same God.

In distinction to the event of the crucifixion of Jesus Christ, his resurrection, in Barth's view, is exclusively and inimitably an act of the Father. That is to say, the resurrection of Jesus Christ 'is unequivocally marked off' from his crucifixion 'by the fact that it does not have in the very least this component of human willing and activity.'[9] The cross, according to Barth, as the occasion of the outpouring of God's judgment is 'exclusively the work of God' too, and hence is an act of God. It must

---

6   *CD* IV/1, p. 299.
7   Ibid.
8   Ibid., p. 301.
9   Ibid., p. 300.

also be asserted, however, that, in as much as it also involves the obedience of the man Jesus of Nazareth and the decisions and actions of sinful human persons, 'it has a component of human action.'[10] And to the degree that human decision and action is discernible here, Barth argues for an understanding of the event of the crucifixion of Jesus as 'historical.' As such, it is available to be understood, comprehended and interpreted in the concrete context of human decisions and actions, though it will inevitably be misunderstood and misinterpreted if not perceived also as the genuine work of the hand of God. Barth, however, in distinction to the crucifixion, compares the work of the resurrection to the act of God in creation: 'To raise (ἐγείρειν) the dead, to give life (ζωοποιειν) to the dead, is, like the creative summoning into being of non-being, a matter wholly and exclusively for God alone.'[11] This exclusivity applies not only to the purpose and ordination of the event but also to its actual fulfilment: 'It takes place quite outside the pragmatic context of human decisions and actions.'[12] And hence it takes place without our being able to ascribe to it the 'historical' character of human decision and action. It takes place nevertheless, but as a sovereign act of God alone.

The significance of the claim that the awakening of Jesus Christ from the dead is a pure divine act is that it guarantees that we are indeed dealing with the one true God and no other. This act is exclusively a divine act and therefore we can emphatically conclude that God himself performs it, and in performing it reveals himself. Its exclusivity ensures that we are not confusing the divine Subject with another for all other subjectivity is eliminated. It is nothing less than God's very being which is revealed in his action. The resurrection of Jesus Christ from the dead is, for Barth, nothing less than divine revelation. Thus, Barth is careful not to reduce the resurrection merely to its character as an event devoid of human decision and action. As such the resurrection could be seen merely as 'a miracle accrediting Jesus Christ,' but not necessarily as 'the revelation of God in Him.'[13] This negative depiction requires the complementary positive depiction for its clarification and completion. In other words, though it is true, it is not enough, to say that the resurrection of Jesus Christ from the dead is an event devoid of all human decision and action and as such an event which falls outside the normal characterization of what is historical. It must also be said that this is indeed the act of God, in which God's own being and activity is made known. Far from being something merely formal and noetic the resurrection was also the 'true, original, typical form of the revelation of God in Him and therefore of revelation generally, the revelation which lights up for the first time all God's revealing and being revealed (in Him and generally).'[14] The creative act of resurrection, in which life is given to the dead, is the genuine form of the revelation

---

10   Ibid.
11   Ibid., p. 301.
12   Ibid., p. 300.
13   Ibid.
14   Ibid., p. 301.

of God. That is to say, this event admits of no other possibility than to be understood as the sovereign self-revealing act of God.

As the true form of the revelation of the Father the resurrection event is the mediation of an understanding which otherwise was closed and inaccessible to the community of Jesus, namely, the apprehension that God was in Christ. The members of the community were witnesses to the fact that 'in the man Jesus, God Himself was at work, speaking and acting and suffering and going to His death.'[15] This was the basis of the indisputable certainty of their knowledge:

> He came amongst [the disciples] again in such a way that His presence as the man He had been (had been!) was and could be exclusively and therefore unequivocally the act of God without any component of human will and action. ... This was the formal side of the resurrection of Christ which made it the true and original and typical form of the revelation of God made in Him. This was what gave it as an act of God its special and distinctive character for the first community, deciding and underlying their whole knowledge of Jesus Christ.[16]

Thus, in saying that 'Jesus is risen!' we summarize the controlling *content* of Christian confession, for it is in this act that the secret of the identity of Jesus Christ is revealed. That is not to imply that the resurrection of Jesus Christ from the dead is the only matter with which theological reflection concerns itself, but that this is the specific content which brings the wider field of theological reflection into proper place and focus. It is from this centre and on this basis that Barth reasons to the periphery in his theological reflection. Hence, in Barth's view, it is only in the light of the resurrection of Jesus Christ from the dead that we have a true understanding of the event of the crucifixion, of the incarnation, and even of the history of Israel and of the world.

In addition, the act of raising Jesus from the dead must also be described, in Barth's view, as a *gracious* one. Not only must we acknowledge the divine character of this act, but also and as such we are compelled to understand it as an act of divine freedom, grounded solely in the good pleasure of God. Barth, believing himself to be following the New Testament, does not describe the event of the resurrection of Jesus Christ from the dead as the work of the Son of God in as much as this weakens and obfuscates the character of the resurrection as an exclusive and gracious act of the divine Father. Drawing upon John 11:25, 10:18, Rev. 5:12, John 5:26, Rom. 1:4 and Phil. 2:7ff. Barth argues for a distinction between the resurrection as the act of the Father and Spirit upon the God-man and the resurrection as the self-revelation of the one raised again: 'It is one thing that He 'rises again' and shows Himself (ἐφανερώθη) to his disciples as the One raised again from the dead (John 21:14). Quite another thing is the act of this resurrection.'[17]

---

15   Ibid.
16   Ibid., p. 302.
17   Ibid., p. 303.

[T]he facts themselves tell us decisively that the event of Easter has to be understood primarily as the raising which happens to Jesus Christ, and only secondarily and (actively) on that basis as His resurrection. For in the New Testament it is everywhere described as an act of divine grace which follows the crucifixion but which is quite free.[18]

Barth continues: 'His [Jesus Christ's] resurrection did not follow from His death, but sovereignly on His death.'[19] Thus, the resurrection of Jesus Christ is not to be seen as merely the impersonal and mechanistic unfolding of what was already achieved in his representative life and death, but rather the free and gracious act of the Father upon the Son:

Certainly in the resurrection [*Auferweckung*] of Jesus Christ we have to do with a movement and action which took place not merely in human history but first and foremost in God Himself, a movement and action in which Jesus Christ as the Son of God had no less part than in His humiliation to the death of the cross, yet only as a pure object and recipient of the grace of God. We must not be afraid of the apparently difficult thought that as in God Himself ... in the relationship of the Son to the Father ... there is a free and pure grace which as such can only be received, and the historical fulfilment of which is the resurrection [*Auferstehung*] of Jesus Christ.[20]

Thus, the first instance of the transition from Jesus Christ to others does not occur as an extension or further act of the crucified in himself in his own power. This movement, rather, is wholly dependent upon the gracious act of the Father upon Jesus Christ.

In so far as the emphasis is placed upon the primary agency of the Father, Bertold Klappert is right to note that Barth distinguishes the resurrection in the sense of the awakening [*Auferweckung*] of Jesus Christ by the Father, from the resurrection appearances [*Auferstehung*] of Jesus Christ.[21] While Barth most frequently uses *Auferstehung* to refer to the self-revelation of Jesus Christ, he does on occasion use the term to describe both the passive (*Auferweckung*) and the active aspect of resurrection. *Auferweckung* however, he reserves for the specifically passive awakening of Jesus Christ, that is, by a subject other than himself, and by an authority and power not his own. In the awakening of Jesus Christ from the dead the Father alone, but unmistakably, is active, while Jesus Christ is wholly passive.

At this point we come upon an ambiguous element of Barth's depiction of the resurrection which lies at the basis of a good deal of confusion. Barth appears to

---

18   Ibid.

19   Ibid., p. 304.

20   Ibid. *KD*, IV/1, p. 335. We will have occasion later to criticize Barth for not developing this very important observation. Why does he not take up this notion of Jesus Christ as 'pure object' in the resurrection as a foundation for a development of the Holy Spirit as *Creator Spiritus* and not only the Spirit of the Lord? Surely this has vastly significant implications in Barth's understanding of the Trinity, not to mention of the notion of what has become object being made subject again in the resurrection.

21   Klappert, *Kreuz und Auferstehung*, pp. 391f.

be making two contradictory claims. On the one hand he asserts that the basis and power of the transition from Jesus Christ to others rests more properly in the action of the Father upon Jesus as an act of sheer grace. But on the other hand, he stresses (much more frequently and strenuously, and in greater detail) that reconciling being and action of Jesus Christ comes to its culmination and completion (the perfection of which admits of no addition) in his crucifixion and death.[22] How are we to make sense of this apparent contradiction? Are Barth's critics right? Does his understanding of the completion of reconciling being and action in the death of Jesus Christ reduce the resurrection to merely the declaration of this accomplished act, thereby rendering all further human action superfluous and meaningless?

While our answer to this question can be given in full only in the light of the completion of this study, we may declare at this point our contention that while Barth appears to rest content with terms which hover between the options, the force of his thought tends more consistently to the inclusion of the passive reception of the resurrection grace of the Father by Jesus Christ as a materially new act and dimension of the being and act of reconciliation. In other words, Barth's assertion that the resurrection adds nothing new to the accomplishment of reconciliation in the death of Jesus Christ must be understood in the context both of Barth's distinction between the awakening of Jesus Christ and his self-revelation, and of his assertion of the completion of the justifying and sanctifying work of Jesus Christ in his crucifixion and death. Our answer then is that Barth more consistently holds to the view that Jesus Christ's passive reception of the Father's gracious verdict is a constitutive element of the objective accomplishment of reconciliation.

From our analysis to this point Barth clearly views the resurrection – the awakening of Jesus Christ from the dead – as the Father's divine act of sheer grace upon the Son, in which Jesus Christ can only be the passive recipient of this grace. But in Barth's conceptuality this passive receptivity is another aspect of Jesus Christ *pro nobis*. In no way can this be understood as an extra-christological event for the object of this act is particularly the non-substitutable Jesus Christ, the man for all others. Hence while Barth is able to place the awakening of Jesus Christ under the head of the completed work of Jesus Christ (as an element of his passive work), he is also able to assert the resurrection (self-revelation) of Jesus Christ as the effective revelation of that which is already complete in him and therefore requiring no further reconciling act.

In and with the Father's free and gracious act in raising Jesus Christ from the dead are clear implications for the sphere of other men and women. According to Barth, the transition of reconciled human being and action in Jesus Christ *in nobis* is made sure and certain in this act of resurrection. For in as much as the Father acts upon the Son, unmistakably and irrevocably, he acts upon those whom the Son represents. That is to say, in the one self-revealing act of the resurrection of Jesus

---

22   In response to the question 'Was Jesus' resurrection necessary?' Barth asserts, 'Certainly not in the sense that at Golgotha everything had not taken place which had to take place for the reconciliation of the world with God.' *CD* IV/1, p. 306.

Christ, the Father has revealed: i) that God was in Christ reconciling the world to himself; ii) that Jesus of Nazareth was indeed the Son of God; iii) that Jesus Christ stood in the place of every human being as their representative and head; iv) that he has received grace from the Father on our behalf as our representative; v) and that because he lives we too shall live (*that is*, the existential meaning of his resurrection for us)! Hence, this act of the Father's grace – the raising of Jesus Christ from the dead – plays a decisive role in the transition of reconciled being and action from Jesus Christ to us.

A Non-necessary Novum

The *second* feature of the resurrection of Jesus Christ, noted by Barth, is that it is a *new*, *distinct* and *free* act of God. That is the act of the Father in raising Jesus from the dead is free of any necessity of its occurrence linked to the event of the crucifixion. The resurrection is neither the undoing of the crucifixion, nor the noetic converse of it, nor simply the illumination and declaration of the positive meaning and relevance of it. It is, rather, according to Barth, an event of its own inherent significance.[23] Neither enclosed within nor entailed by the crucifixion the resurrection follows it as a differentiated event. That is to say, the resurrection of Jesus Christ is a non-necessary *novum*. Yet the resurrection cannot be understood in isolation from the crucifixion for it follows in a sequence of free acts which includes both. 'The *theologia resurrectionis* does not absorb the *theologia crucis*, nor *vice versa*.'[24] Here Barth deals with the event character of the resurrection. Its meaning is not exhausted in the fact that it is an act of ontological import, but it takes place within a meaningful history of related such acts of God. It therefore requires description in terms of these other acts of God. It is necessary then to discuss the *historical* relatedness of this divine act (ontological event) in the field of all other divine acts and especially its relation to the crucifixion.

The events of both Good Friday and Easter remain in indissoluble connexion with each other, while at the same time each retains it own content and form. Easter is bound up with, but not necessitated by, the crucifixion. In the dying of Jesus Christ on the cross for us and as our representative there took place everything which had to take place for the reconciliation of the world with God. Barth strongly emphasizes that any reduction of the τετέλεσται of the work of Christ is 'quite alien to the New Testament.'[25] But Barth clarifies, saying it is:

> to death that He bows His head and commits Himself. In and with the fulfilment there of the will of God it is nothingness which can triumph over Him. ... The reconciliation of the world with God ... had therefore the meaning that a radical end was made of Him and therefore of the world.[26]

---

23   *CD* IV/1, p. 304.
24   Ibid.
25   Ibid., p. 306.
26   Ibid.

Barth could not be more determined to maintain the New Testament emphasis upon the 'finished-ness' of the reconciling work of Christ.

The resurrection of Jesus Christ did not nullify, but rather, confirmed his death. In this new, gracious act, the Father confronted the being-in-death of Jesus Christ, that is, '[Jesus Christ's] non-being as the One who was crucified, dead, buried, and destroyed, as the One who had been and had ceased to be.'[27] The resurrection was God's answer to and acknowledgement of the life and death of Jesus Christ. The resurrection was the Father's second judicial sentence – following and superseding his condemnation, now his vindication of the Son, the pronouncement of the Father's pleasure with the Son's action and passion as the obedient servant in our place. The raising of Jesus Christ from the dead and us in him is the Father's free and merciful act, consequent upon nothing but his gracious and loving will. Barth employs the terms 'answer, confession and sentence' to draw out the uniqueness of the resurrection of Jesus Christ as depicted in the New Testament. 'To sum up, the resurrection of Jesus Christ is the great verdict of God, the fulfilment and proclamation of God's decision concerning the event of the cross.'[28]

When Barth comes to address the question 'What gives this justification its true and decisive power?', he answers that this was an act of God himself alone. In the resurrection of Jesus Christ from the dead God justifies *himself*. It might have been, says Barth, that in the death of Jesus Christ the Father willed to turn away from us absolutely and eternally. 'It might have been,' says Barth, 'that by the same eternal Word by which as Creator He gave being to man and the world He now willed to take away that being from them, to let them perish with all their corruption and sin.'[29] He would still have been in the right, asserts Barth, even had he determined to give death and nothingness the final word over the creature.

But had he done so, 'He would have been in the right only in complete concealment.'[30] Furthermore, 'He would not have justified Himself,'[31] in as much as by recognising the power of death and nothingness over the creature he would have left unconfirmed his primal election 'between heaven and earth on the one hand and chaos on the other, His decision for light and His rejection of darkness.'[32] He would not have justified himself, but rather 'would have been in the right only in and for Himself.'[33] '[L]ike His right as Creator and Lord of the world,' his would have been and remained 'a completely hidden love: without witnesses, without participants, because without proclamation, without outward confirmation and form, concealed in the mystery of the inner life and being of the Godhead.'[34] But God did choose to assert his right to the world over death and nothingness, not because of any external

---

27   Ibid., p. 305.
28   Ibid., p. 309.
29   Ibid., p. 306.
30   Ibid.
31   Ibid.
32   Ibid.
33   Ibid.
34   Ibid., p. 308.

compulsion, but because He, sovereignly and graciously, so chose: 'He willed to give to the inner and secret radiance of His glory an outward radiance in the sphere of creation and its history. He willed to give to His eternal life space and time.'[35] In this manner, in calling Jesus Christ to life from the dead, God justified himself, his Son, and in his Son, all sinful human beings.[36] God elected to create the human being anew,

> to cause him to be born again from the dead, freed from his sin and guilt, freed from the claim and power which death and nothingness and chaos necessarily had over him in his former corrupted state, freed for life for Him and with Him, and therefore for life everlasting.[37]

For Barth, then, the resurrection of Jesus Christ from the dead is the Father's 'Yes' to life, order and being, the corollary of the Father's 'No' to death, chaos and non-being. It is the re-affirmation of his creative will.

Barth then radically redefines justification as the declaration and affirmation of our new being in Jesus Christ. Justification is not merely the declaration of a judicial discernment of guilt or innocence, which may or may not affect the being of the defendant. Nor is it strictly an execution of justice in which due penalty is meted out for infraction of a moral code. It is rather an ontological event, affirming and making so in space and time the new human being in Jesus Christ. It is a moving out of this eternal ontic reality to its full expression and illumination in the created order. It is the transition of reconciled human being and action in Jesus Christ *pro nobis* to us.

Let us pause at this point to consider the adequacy of Barth's depiction of Jesus' resurrection as the transition from Christ to others. Is his account of the completion of reconciliation in the crucifixion and death of Jesus true to the New Testament, or does he underplay the role of the resurrection in reconciliation? With respect to Barth's speculative entertainment of the possibility of a reconciliation without the resurrection, it must be asserted that the New Testament knows nothing of the possibility of a crucified Saviour who remains forever concealed, nor of a Father whose being is disclosed in the light of this (rejected) possibility. Barth's effort is to guard the transition of reconciled being and action in Christ from the narrower christological sphere to our anthropological sphere from any external human subjectivity. However, there is substance to the criticism that his concern here has led him to underplay the passive role of the Son in being raised from the dead and the active role of the Father and Spirit in raising him from the dead. In this respect it may be accurate to say that Barth falls to the accusation made by some that his development of the Trinity is incomplete, at least as regards this aspect of his view of the resurrection. Had Barth worked out in greater detail the distinct action of the Father and the Holy Spirit in the reconciling being and action of God, he might have more thoroughly developed the *Auferweckung* (the act of the Father upon the Son

---

35   Ibid.
36   Ibid., p. 309.
37   Ibid., p. 307.

in the power of the Holy Spirit) in distinction to the *Auferstehung* (the primordial self-disclosure of the Triune God in the raising of Jesus Christ from the dead). That is, he may have developed his discourse on the *Auferweckung* of Jesus Christ more clearly as a fundamental aspect of the reconciling work God, leaving the notion of *Auferstehung*, the free self-revelation of Jesus Christ, to address the problem of the active movement of Jesus Christ to others. Barth claims that the resurrection adds nothing materially new to the crucifixion of Jesus Christ. However, we must disagree, insisting something indeed is added in the resurrection in as much as it asserts the passive reception of grace by Jesus Christ on our behalf, a fundamental aspect of reconciliation. Barth's point might better have been secured by saying that the *Auferstehung* adds nothing materially new to the saving being and action of Jesus Christ, for it refers to the resurrection appearances, the self-revelation, of Jesus Christ and the impartation of his reconciled being and action to us. In other words, there is an aspect of the transition of the reconciled being and action of Jesus Christ to us which is not an active deed of Jesus Christ. Rather it was as he was acted upon by the Father in raising him from the dead (and us in him) that the transition from death to life, from darkness to light, from concealment to revelation was initiated. That is to say, there is an aspect of the self-revelation of God in the resurrection event which does not come out so clearly in Barth, a self-revelation which is not purely christological, though purely christologically mediated. The resurrection of Jesus Christ from the dead involves a trinitarian self-revelation, which is mediated in turn by the self-revelation of Jesus Christ. Here Barth's understanding of the resurrection of Jesus Christ is too strongly influenced by the rubric under which it is discussed, namely, that of the transition of reconciled being and action in Jesus Christ *in nobis*. The issue of the transition from the ontic aspect of reconciliation to its noetic aspect casts its shadow over the event of the resurrection making it difficult to see the broader implications of this act. In other words, in Barth's development of the resurrection of Jesus Christ, he too quickly passes over the passive role of Jesus Christ and consequently develops the import of the resurrection event in a manner almost indistinguishable from that of the mediatorial role of Jesus Christ, as developed fully in *CD* IV/3.

An Act of the Same Divine Subject and History

In his description of the *third* feature of the resurrection of Jesus Christ, Barth underscores the fact that the crucifixion and the resurrection of Jesus Christ reveal as their true subject the same God who is unified in his will and way in this history. The resurrection of Jesus Christ from the dead must be understood as an act of the same God who judged and made an end of sinful human being in the crucifixion and death of Jesus Christ. As such it is a supremely sovereign, effective and irrevocable act of the same gravity and comprehensiveness as the judgment of God in the crucifixion with its definite implication for all human persons.[38] The judgment and crucifixion

---

38   Ibid., pp. 300ff.

of Jesus Christ forms the necessary 'presupposition' for the act of God in raising Jesus Christ from the dead. Just as 'the judgment of the grace' of the Father executed on Calvary was a work of God which could be fulfilled by God alone, so in the resurrection of Jesus Christ from the dead 'the grace of this judgment' occurs as an exclusive act of God.[39] Because of the unity of the divine Subject, the crucifixion and resurrection are also to be understood as a unity. In these two events is effected and expressed the 'Yes' of God in the fulfilment of his single reconciling will. In the crucifixion the 'Yes' of God is concealed under its opposite, the 'No' of God. In the resurrection the 'No' of God is revealed as the specific negative act which cannot be separated from its positive intention. As an implicate of this, Barth avers the historicality of the resurrection. That is to say, the resurrection is necessarily an event in human history, for it follows meaningfully upon the historical crucifixion of Jesus.

We note first that Barth nowhere treats of the resurrection in isolation but rather always with a view to the entire doctrine of reconciliation. This is not merely a pedagogical decision; it is rather a crucial theological decision essential to Barth's understanding of the resurrection of Jesus Christ. Not only is Barth interested in the relationship of the resurrection to the other aspects of reconciliation but he is convinced that the resurrection can only be understood in the context of the unfolding event of reconciliation. It is the whole event character of reconciliation which is attested in Barth's unwillingness to treat the resurrection in any fashion distinct from its historical narrative connections to other aspects of reconciliation. Reconciliation has indeed 'occurred'; the resurrection of Jesus Christ from the dead can only be understood, therefore, in the context of the interconnected events which make up this unified occurrence.

In this third and decisive feature of the resurrection Barth expounds what he calls the 'positive connection' between the resurrection of Jesus Christ and his sacrificial death.[40] These two events reveal as their subject the same God unified in his will and way in the one history of God with a rebellious world. In these two events is effected and expressed the 'Yes' of God in the fulfilment of his reconciling will, the conversion of the human person to God. The 'Yes' of God is proclaimed upon the obedience of his Son in our place and is similarly proclaimed and made effective in his Son, again in our place, as the first recipient of the grace of God the Father.[41] The relationship of these two events is neither one of repetition, nor the unity of two factors in which one might just as easily be superfluous to or enclosed in the other. We must speak rather of 'a genuine sequence and correspondence in a differentiated relationship in which both factors have their proper form and function.'[42] A *terminus a quo* must be distinguished from a *terminus ad quem*. The first is a negative event with a positive intention; the second, a positive event with a negative presupposition. In the light of

---

39   Ibid., p. 300.
40   Ibid., p. 310.
41   Ibid.
42   Ibid.

the resurrection we recognize the crucifixion of Jesus Christ as the negative act of God with a hidden positive intention. The positive event of the resurrection has as its negative presupposition the 'total removing of man in his earlier form.'[43]

Barth's understanding of the indissoluble interrelatedness of the crucifixion and resurrection is clear. The two are inalienably held together in the unified and singular will and act of the Father. The relationship, too, which binds the two events together in this unity, is grounded in the will of the Father. Hence the momentous transition from the crucifixion to the resurrection of Jesus Christ (and us in him) is grounded primarily in the will and verdict of the Father. So integrally tied are these two events that each demands the other for its fullness and meaning. As a negative event with a positive intention the crucifixion could in no sense be complete without the resurrection; as a positive event with a negative presupposition the resurrection could never stand on its own.

In further support of the claim that Barth's statement regarding the resurrection adding nothing to the completion of reconciliation in the death of Jesus Christ is to be understood as applying only to justification and sanctification, let us consider the fact that Barth's own development of this third feature of the resurrection contradicts the view he appears to leave open on this matter. The crucifixion is only known in the light of the resurrection and the resurrection can only be properly understood as the resurrection of this crucified one. The resurrection is the (historical) verdict of the Father in answer to the event of the cross. The event of the cross cannot be complete without its one and only answer: the resurrection of Jesus Christ from the dead. Furthermore, Barth's fifth feature of the resurrection – that it is part of the unified history of God's saving act in Christ in fulfilment of his one and indivisible will – implies a certain necessity of the resurrection as the fulfillment of the positive intent of the one reconciling will and action of God in the crucifixion and resurrection.

According to Barth, the crucifixion and resurrection of Jesus Christ, in which took place the alteration of the human situation, the reconciliation of the world with God, are held together in 'differentiated relationship.'[44] This term indicates not a specific instance of a general concept of the relation of historical events, but the unique relationship of this particular crucifixion and this particular resurrection event. It cannot be doubted that the New Testament witness to these events views them not in isolation but as an indissoluble unity. Only within this 'differentiated relationship' can these two events be properly understood. That is to say, the crucifixion of Jesus Christ is this particular crucifixion only as it is followed upon by his resurrection. And likewise the resurrection of Jesus Christ is this particular resurrection only as it follows his crucifixion. In other words the relationship of these two distinct events is integral to their unique essence. Apart from this specific relationship these events simply cannot be what they in fact are. Thus, Barth affirms: 'The justification which

---

43   Ibid.
44   Ibid.

took place in the resurrection of Jesus Christ confirmed and revealed in what sense God was in the right in His death.'[45]

A further important feature of this 'differentiated relationship' is that these events follow in sequential order. According to Barth, the fact that the crucifixion and the resurrection of Jesus Christ stand as distinct events in sequential relationship is the decisive point in the solution to the main problem which occupies us, namely 'whether and to what extent we can and must proceed from the obedience which Jesus Christ rendered for us to the thought of its relevance for us.'[46] The fact that these two events stand in sequential relationship *in time* entails, in Barth's view, that we must proceed from the one to the other. Because the resurrection of Jesus Christ follows his crucifixion and death as its beyond, because these events stand in this particular sequential relationship advancing from the one to the other, we must conclude that the decisive step from Jesus Christ to us has indeed taken place, that the reconciled human being and action in Jesus Christ reaches to us. As Barth claims:

> It is because according to the Scriptures this took place on the 'third day' that we can and must positively and thankfully confess what took place on the 'first' day, the day of His cross: He died for our sins 'according to the scriptures' (I Cor. 15;3f). He, the risen One, opened up the Scriptures to them and opened their eyes to the Scriptures (Lk. 24;25f.).[47]

Two aspects or forms of this temporal relation require explication. The *first* is simply that the resurrection has a 'temporal togetherness' with the crucifixion. The resurrection of Jesus Christ follows upon and moves beyond his crucifixion, and hence declares the dominion of Jesus Christ over death. He lives to die no more. No reversal of this order is possible. His being in his history from Bethlehem to Golgotha is eternal and ever present in our own time. And as such his being has been made effective for us all. According to Barth:

> That which took place on the third day after His death lifted up the whole of what took place before in all its particularity (not in spite of but because of its particularity) into something that took place once and for all. It is in the power of the event of the third day that the event of the first day – as something that happened there and then – is not something which belongs to the past, which can be present only by recollection, tradition and proclamation, but is as such a present event, the event which fills and determines the whole present.[48]

Jesus Christ, in his resurrection, has ceased to be enclosed within the limits of his life from Bethlehem to Golgotha; he became, is and will be Lord of all time, and therefore present, actual and supremely relevant in all time. He was once, is now and always will be our representative, reconciler and redeemer. He is this, not merely

---

45   Ibid., pp. 310f.
46   Ibid., p. 312.
47   Ibid., p. 299.
48   Ibid., p. 313.

for the people of his own age, and for certain other men and women of other ages as would be the case if all that could be relied upon was the recollection of him or of the tradition concerning him. If this were the case he would 'be alive only in virtue of the life breathed into Him as a historical and therefore a dead figure by the men of other ages.'[49] But his has become a living history, an 'eternal history,' a history contemporaneous with all times, and as the One whose history this is he ever lives as the mediator between himself and human persons: 'The eternal action of Jesus Christ grounded in His resurrection is itself the true and direct bridge from once to always, from Himself in His time to us in our time.'[50]

It is in this event, claims Barth, that we have the solution to our problem 'of the transition from the understanding of the person and work of Christ to soteriology proper, to the question of the *applicatio salutis.*'[51] Barth argues that had this recognition been taken seriously Lessing's problem of the unbridgeable divide between contingent facts of history and necessary truths of reason, which plagued 18th Century theology, would surely have been discredited and denounced. For, Barth claims, 'The moment of this particular `contingent fact of history' was the moment of all moments.'[52] Because the day of the resurrection of Jesus Christ is the day of all days, the day of the movement of Jesus Christ from his historical particularity enclosed within universal history to the universalization of his historical particularity, today, our day, is the day of the transition of reconciled being and action in Jesus Christ to us.

The *second* aspect of the fact that these events, the resurrection of Jesus Christ following upon his crucifixion, are events with and in time, has to do with the fact that the resurrection itself has an unfolding history; it follows upon, and, in this way, moves beyond and supersedes the crucifixion: like the existence of Jesus Christ from Bethlehem to Golgotha, the period of the forty days has a beginning, an ending and a beyond. 'The resurrection of Jesus Christ, His living presence, His *parousia* in the direct form of the events of Easter was ... a happening in time with a definite beginning and end like other happenings.'[53] Accordingly, Barth develops his understanding of the *parousia* as the singular event of the self-revelation of Jesus Christ in three distinct forms.

We will defer our treatment of Barth's important development of the *parousia* to the chapter in which we discuss Barth's doctrine of the resurrection in *CD* IV/3, for there Barth takes up this theme afresh in a more extensive manner. For the moment it will be sufficient to claim that here too Barth understands the resurrection appearances of Jesus Christ as the first form of the *parousia*, that is, of the movement of Jesus Christ from his place of infinite distance to us. It is in the light of the differentiation of the *parousia* in its three forms that it becomes necessary to understand the crucifixion

---

49   Ibid., p. 314.
50   Ibid., p. 315.
51   Ibid., p. 314.
52   Ibid., p. 315.
53   Ibid., p. 318.

and death of Jesus Christ 'not as a conclusion, but as a beginning,' a possibility which is 'necessitated' and 'disclosed' by the resurrection of Jesus Christ.[54] Hence in answer to our fundamental question, Barth says, the possibility of understanding the death of Jesus Christ, not only as an all-encompassing conclusion, but also as an all-encompassing beginning is disclosed 'by the being of the crucified Jesus Christ raised from the dead in His twofold form as the One who has come and is present and the One who is present and has still to come, by the verdict of the Father.'[55] Hence, 'On the resurrection of Jesus Christ there depends the permission and command to proceed from Him, from his person and from the work which He completed in His death.'[56] But this turn requires still further amplification in two important ways.

An Event in History

As a *fourth* feature Barth advances the notion that the resurrection of Jesus Christ from the dead must be a particular *event* in history if it is to be an event which meaningfully follows upon the crucifixion of Jesus Christ. That is, the resurrection is a particular history within history generally, a 'concrete factuality' within the nexus of space and time. According to Barth the first *parousia* of Jesus Christ in his appearances to his disciples was an historical happening of the same order as his crucifixion. In the same manner Barth claims that the final return of Jesus Christ will be historical, will belong to time and space, though as the final moment of time and history.

According to Barth, it was the resurrection appearances of Christ that was the originative force and abiding focus of the apostolic faith: 'That He appeared to them, with all that this implies, that this history took place, is the content of the apostolic *kerygma*, the theme of the faith of the community which it awakened (I Cor. 15[14]).'[57] That this took place is at one and the same time the sign and real beginning of the immediate and unsurpassable manifestation of our justification and altered situation, awaiting their final form to be revealed in the Lord's final coming.

If we are to perceive these events correctly, says Barth, we must lay hold not only of the fact that the crucifixion and the resurrection are alike in the sense that they are both particular historical events within general history, but also of the fact that they are different. That difference Barth explains in this way:

> They differ in substance as God's right and God's justification, as end and new beginning, as work and revelation. They also differ as the act of the obedient Son and the act of the gracious Father. They also differ formally in the way in which they take place in the human sphere and human time, and therefore in the way in which they have to be understood as history.[58]

---

54   Ibid., p. 333.
55   Ibid.
56   Ibid.
57   Ibid., p. 334.
58   Ibid.

In further clarification of this idea, Barth offers the following:

> We cannot read the Gospels without getting the strong impression that as we pass from the story of the passion to the story of Easter we are led into a historical sphere of a different kind. ... Here we can think only of the act of God which cannot be described and therefore cannot be narrated, and then of the actual fact that Jesus Himself stood in the midst (Luke 24[36]). Whether we take the accounts of the resurrection appearances in detail or put them together, they do not give us a concrete and coherent picture, a history of the forty days. Rather we are confronted by obscurities and irreconcilable contradictions, so that we are surprised that in the formation of the canon no one seems to have taken offence at them or tried to assimilate the various accounts of this happening which is so basically important for the New Testament message.[59]

The resurrection as attested in the New Testament is according to Barth an *indescribable, unnarratable* event. Whereas the crucifixion of Jesus Christ, in so far as it was an event in the normal flow of human history, could be described most accurately in terms of the historical narrative of the Gospels, the resurrection of Jesus Christ defies historical narrative description for it is history of a different kind. The transition then from Jesus Christ to us effected in his resurrection is not simply a matter of historical continuance of his person after his death. In this transition he comes again as the eternally living one.

The resurrection of Jesus Christ is a unique reality. It knows neither comparison nor likeness, except perhaps, with the divine act of creation. This means that we cannot arrive at the meaning of the resurrection of Jesus Christ on the basis of theodical hope, that is, that in some unknown and inscrutable future prolongation of this existence, justice will be served; that is, with eternity conceived of as the future realm in which present injustices are rectified, where the unjust are punished, the just are rewarded, and amends are made to victims of injustice. Barth rejects this kind of extrapolation from the realm where death reigns into the realm of resurrection life. Barth argues rather that the New Testament speaks of a life which is radically new, and, therefore, completely unexpected: 'What has come to us in the crucifixion of Jesus Christ would not be our judgment, end and death if we could (even theoretically) transcend it.'[60] The resurrection is an external reality; it comes to us from outside our world and experience and expectation and hope.

Because this is indeed the case Barth asserts that the New Testament does not intend to fit or wish to be adjusted so as to fit into the category of historical artefact as understood by modern historical scholarship:

> If in modern scholarship 'historical ground' means the outline of an event as it can be seen in its 'How' independently of the standpoint of the onlooker, as it can be presented in this way, as it can be proved in itself and in its general and more specific context and in relation to the analogies of other events, as it can be established as having certainly taken

---

59   Ibid., pp. 334f.
60   Ibid., p. 297.

place, then the New Testament itself does not enable us to state that we are on 'historical ground' in relation to the event here recorded.[61]

The New Testament authors wished to witness to the reality of God, a reality beyond the constraints of time and space, yet also within time and space, a reality in which all things including time and space are brought to a close and all things are begun anew. How might they be expected to achieve this if restricted to the canons of historical critical science? Barth denies the need for proof of the historical nature of this history and argues against the possibility of such proof. The history of the *parousia* of Jesus Christ does not have historical ground in the sense described by modern scholarship. In Barth's own words:

> After all that we have seen of the nature and character and function of the resurrection of Jesus Christ as the basis, and in the context, of the New Testament message, it is inevitable that this should not be the place for the 'historicist' concept of history.[62]

For Barth, 'The death of Jesus Christ can certainly be thought of as history in the modern sense, but not the resurrection.'[63] Hence Barth suggests we should be prepared to accept the account of the resurrection as the story of the creation and many others, as 'saga' or 'legend.' The movement of Jesus Christ to us, then, cannot be depicted without remainder under the canons of historical-critical science.

That is by no means to suggest, however, that the message of the New Testament can be understood properly at all, if one were to attempt to interpret it as though it did not actually and objectively happen, or did not happen in time and space in the same way as did the crucifixion of Jesus Christ, or happened only in the emergence and formation of apostolic faith.[64] Quite to the contrary, 'If Jesus Christ is not risen – bodily, visibly, audibly, perceptibly, in the same concrete sense in which He died, as the texts themselves have it – if He is not also risen, then our preaching and our faith are vain and futile; we are still in our sins.'[65] Barth explicitly denounces the use of the term 'myth' in relation to this history while encouraging the use of the term 'pre-historical,' signifying an event 'which has actually happened although it cannot be grasped historically.'[66]

From this engagement with historical criticism, Barth turns to a deeper investigation of the biblical text. And again he returns to the theme of the transition from the reconciliation accomplished in Christ on Golgotha to the concrete history of faith in him. As Barth reads the New Testament, it was primarily at Pentecost and not so much during the period of the forty days that there took place the inception of the community and the sending out of the apostles as bearers of the *kerygma* to

---

61   Ibid., p. 335.
62   Ibid.
63   Ibid., p. 336.
64   Ibid.
65   Ibid., pp. 351f.
66   Ibid., p. 336

the people of Jerusalem and to all nations. For Barth the forty days constitutes the presupposition for the events of Pentecost and afterwards. What took place in the forty days was the laying of the foundation, the act of God awakening and developing the faith of the disciples.[67] That is to say, the faith of the disciples becomes a historical factor 'only in and with the outpouring of the Holy Spirit,' for '[i]t is only there that the community develops from its original form as the company of disciples believing in the living Jesus Christ into the Church which grows and expands in the world.'[68] The great concern of the biblical narratives is not the manner of the rise of the faith of the disciples, but 'who and what brought and impelled and drove the disciples to this [Easter] faith.'[69] Barth argues strenuously that the New Testament texts speak of the objective foundation of the faith of the disciples, a faith which comes to them from outside of themselves, a faith which lives by and is defined in terms of the priority of its object. According to Barth:

> The texts do not speak primarily of the formation of the Easter faith as such but of its foundation by Jesus Christ Himself, who met and talked with His disciples after His death as One who is alive. ... According to the texts, this event of the forty days, and the act of God in this event, was the concrete factor – the concrete factor in its externality, its objectivity, not taking place in their faith but in conflict with their lack of faith, overcoming and removing their lack of faith and creating their faith.[70]

Interestingly, Barth understands the necessity of the sign of the empty tomb, not as a proof but as a 'safeguard' against a misunderstanding of the apostolic witness 'in terms of a being of the Resurrected which is purely beyond or inward.'[71] The empty tomb, for Barth, is 'the negative presupposition of the concrete objectivity of His being.'[72] And Barth warns those who reject the empty tomb that they take care lest they fall into Docetism.

For Barth the Easter event can be understood faithfully in no other way than as the New Testament presents it, namely, as a real historical encounter with God, God himself confronting the disciples and speaking with them in the person of the Risen Jesus Christ:

> In this sense the rest of the New Testament looked back to that which is attested in the Easter texts as the beginning of the parousia of the Lord in glory, the history which underlies and impels and legitimates and authorises the kerygma, the history which follows the history

---

67 Ibid.

68 Ibid.

69 Ibid., p. 339.

70 Ibid., p. 341. At this point Barth corrects his earlier comment on the force of the empty tomb, made in *The Resurrection of the Dead*, by claiming that it is an 'indispensable' component of the apostolic witness.

71 Ibid.

72 Ibid.

of the life and death of Jesus Christ and precedes that of the community in the world, itself a real history within the history of the world.[73]

This and nothing other was the presupposition of the faith and action of the disciples.

Once again we note the significance of Barth's depiction of the resurrection as the transition or movement of Jesus Christ *in nobis*. Barth describes the resurrection as a concrete, objective event in conflict with the unbelief of the disciples. Quite contrary to the notion that the resurrection narratives of the New Testament refer to a reality which originated in the existence of the disciples, Barth argues that the New Testament witnesses to an encounter, initiated by the same Jesus who was crucified, as an external, objective happening in the lives of the disciples. Furthermore, Barth asserts this encounter was a personal one between Jesus Christ and his disciples. Furthermore, this transition transcended a mere remembrance of the person and work of the historical Jesus; it surpassed even ever new understandings of the existential meaning of his person and work. This transition was nothing less than the re-entrance of that person and work into the nexus of space and time in which the same Jesus mediated the encounter between himself and his disciples. The product of that encounter was the faith and community of the disciples.

An Event United in the One History of Jesus Christ

The *fifth* and final feature of the resurrection of Jesus from the dead according to Barth is that this new historical act of God must form a unity with the crucifixion of Jesus Christ as a sequence of historical events in the existence of the selfsame historical subject. That is both the crucifixion and the resurrection follow in sequence as moments in the history of Jesus Christ, and, in him, in the history of all other human persons.[74] These two distinct events, both acts of God, must also be seen in their unity, that is, as the one act of God involving the crucifixion (with its presupposition, the history of Israel and the incarnation) and the resurrection (understood as the entirety of his *parousia* as it began with the events of Easter and achieves its completion as the end of all time):

> It is an inseparable unity. We can and must explain each of these two moments by the other. We do not speak rightly of the death of Jesus Christ unless we have clearly and plainly before us His resurrection, His being as the Resurrected. We also do not speak rightly of His resurrection and His being as the Resurrected if we conceal and efface the fact that this living One was crucified and died for us.[75]

---

73 Ibid., p. 342.

74 Hence the understanding of Douglas Farrow – that, for Barth, Jesus-history ends with his crucifixion and death – is quite inadequate as an exposition of Barth's position. (Cf. Farrow, *Ascension and Ecclesia*, p. 246.) Barth clearly sees the pre- and post-Easter history of Jesus as the single unified history of the self-same subject.

75 *CD* IV/1, p. 343.

It is the one God who has accomplished both on the basis of his eternal election of Jesus Christ and in him the world in the singular objective of the reconciliation of the world with himself. In other words these two events fulfil and proclaim the one supreme will and act of God in the conversion of human persons to himself.

But more than this, this unity of event has an irreversible sequence. The crucifixion of Jesus Christ took place once, never to take place again. Following his crucifixion was his resurrection, and as the one crucified but now resurrected his is eternal life, a life which is continuous in and with time. According to Barth, 'There is no Crucified *in abstracto*.' Thus, there can be no preaching of the cross in abstraction from the resurrection. As Barth sees it, 'There is no going back behind Easter morning. To the extent that they may contain or express such a going back, all theologies or pieties or exercises or aesthetics which centre on the cross – however grimly in earnest they may be – must be repudiated at once.'[76] Barth insists that the 'community is not called up to repeat this act of God, let alone to expect and demand that the world should be ready to do so.'[77] According to Barth:

> The way of God the Father, Son and Holy Spirit, the way of the true God, is not a cycle, a way of eternal recurrence, in which the end is a constant beginning. ... Rather we are invited, indeed required, to accept this [that is, God's way and action] as something that has happened for us and to us, in order that we may go forward with this decision already behind us. God in His own action has Himself gone further along this road, and He summons us to go further.[78]

God's action over us, against us, for us, and among us in Jesus Christ constitutes the final word and action which can never admit of reversal or adjustment. Human history is linear, not because of some general law, but because God's history is linear, and precisely with this linearity. The final word possesses absolute force: 'death is swallowed up in victory.' The transition from Jesus Christ to us is not one of many such transitions which occur over and over again in endless repetition; it is not a transition which requires imitation or representation or repristination. It is the once for all movement of Jesus Christ to us. The way of God among us calls us into the forward advance of God's own history, a history of the existence of the human person in Christ in hope, a history of death defeated and life eternal.

Against Barth one must ask, does this repudiation apply equally to his development of the transition from crucifixion to resurrection with its accompanying speculation that God would have been in the right even if he had not raised Jesus from the dead? One might argue that this contradicts Barth's assertion of the revelatory primacy of the resurrection, expressed so unmistakably here:

> If the crucified Jesus Christ is alive, if his community is the company of those among whom this is seen and taken seriously, as the axiom of all axioms, then the community

---

76   Ibid., p. 344.
77   Ibid.
78   Ibid., p. 345.

cannot take account of any other word that God might have spoken before or after or side by side with or outside this word, and that He willed to have proclaimed by it.[79]

In further objection to this same aspect of Barth's view of the resurrection we ask whether the unity of Christ's being is jeopardized if we conceive of the resurrection (glorification) aspect of reconciled being as incidental to Christ's being in a manner similar to that which Barth rejected in relation to the other two (justification and sanctification) aspects of Christ's being?

Conclusion

Having completed his description of the five features of the resurrection of Jesus Christ, Barth returns to the overall question which has guided him all along: 'How dare we ever count on the fact that we are His, and therefore move on from christology to an anthropology which is embraced by christology, and in which we have to understand ourselves, us men, as His?'[80] He asks:

> Is there something beyond this death, this conclusion, this end, in the light of which Christology is not exclusive but inclusive, in the light of which it is false if it is exclusive, in the light of which it can and must comprehend within itself as yet another element in the doctrine of reconciliation a perception of our sin first, but then of our justification, of the community as the people of justified sinners, of what makes men members of this community, our faith?[81]

Barth answers decisively – the resurrection is this beyond. In the resurrection of Jesus Christ from the dead we have the effective transition of reconciled human being and action in Jesus Christ *pro nobis* from him to us. For 'if it is true that this Jesus Christ who was crucified and delivered up to death for us is risen and alive, then it is also true that we who are crucified and dead with Him have a future and hope.'[82] The 'question' concerning the significance of his being and activity as it embraces us, as it embraces the anthropological sphere: is 'answered' in the resurrection of Jesus Christ from the dead. This 'creative and revelatory divine verdict ... is ... both the ontic and also the noetic ... basis of our being.'[83]

From the above it is clear that Barth develops the doctrine of the resurrection of Jesus Christ from the dead as the effective, revelatory transition of the reconciling being and action of Jesus Christ, culminating in his crucifixion and death, from his place of infinite remoteness and concealment to our counterpoised anthropological sphere. Barth argues that if this transition from him to us is real and true, it must be on the basis of a genuine beyond to that event in which he brought human being-

---

79   Ibid., p. 346.
80   Ibid., p. 348.
81   Ibid., pp. 348f.
82   Ibid., p. 350.
83   Ibid., pp. 354f.

in-sin to its final end in his own death. Barth further argues that the resurrection of Jesus Christ from the dead is that genuine beyond of his crucifixion and death, and hence, it is also *our* genuine beyond. Clearly Barth's account of this transition is a trinitarian one, involving the agency of Father, Son and Spirit. Our difference with Barth concerns the adequacy of his description of this transition as almost exclusively expounded in its active christological aspect, that is, where Jesus Christ is active subject in this transition, for while this is undoubtedly the dominant consideration of the transition effected in the resurrection, it is not the exclusive one. That is not to deny the fact that Barth's description has a strongly trinitarian character, but merely to point out that it does not go far enough. The independent action of the Father and Holy Spirit upon the wholly passive Jesus Christ in the carrying out of this transition does not receive sufficient exposition. However, this objection does not undermine Barth's contention that this transition as such is christologically focused and grounded and not anthropologically so.

Chapter Six

The Spirit of the Lord as the Power of the Transition

If the event of the crucifixion of Jesus Christ precludes penetration to its inner truth, as the reality of the utter concealment of death entails, how are we to know and take ourselves as included in it? That is, as Barth sees it, the unavoidable question raised by the fact of the radical being and action of Jesus Christ *pro nobis*; it necessarily rules out any apprehension and appropriation of this *in nobis* from our side. The answer, he asserts, is to be found only in the resurrection of Jesus Christ from the dead, in his being among us once again as the risen One. Once again the rubric of transition, of the movement of Christ to other human beings, of the way and power of the Crucified (and of reconciled human being and action in him) from his place of infinite remoteness to his place of proximity and encounter with human beings, governs Barth's development of the doctrine of the resurrection of Jesus Christ. In the light of the resurrection it is revealed that the Crucified is no longer infinitely distant, untouchable and unknowable. Rather he has drawn near to us, encountering us, declaring himself to us, setting us free to receive and embrace him.

In this chapter we turn our attention to §64.4, 'The Direction of the Son.'[1] Four key questions comprise our investigation. First, 'What is the nature of this transition effected in the resurrection?' In this, we examine Barth's development of the reality concealed in Christ as truth pressing for subjectivization. Here we see that reconciled being and action in Christ does not require the assistance of an external subject to objectify and in that way to know it, but rather that this reality possesses within itself the power to reveal itself fully and effectively to human subjects external to itself, thus rendering them true and proper human subjects. Second, 'Who performs this transition?' We thus turn to Barth's understanding of the Spirit of the Lord as the power of the revelation of this reality. It is in this context that we begin to understand Barth's conception of the essential relation of Jesus Christ and the Holy Spirit. Third, we inquire concerning the 'Whence?' of this transition, and accordingly attend to Barth's grounding of the problem of the transition from Jesus Christ to us in the life of the divine Trinity. At this point we come to understand our problem of transition as a reflection of the problem of transition between God the Father and God the Son in the power of God the Holy Spirit. Our fourth question concerns the 'How?' of this transition, and hence we consider Barth's depiction of the manner in which the Holy Spirit effects this transition in us. But before we address any of these questions,

---

1   *CD* IV/2, pp. 264–377.

it will be profitable to note Barth's important distinction between resurrection and exaltation, so as not to confuse the two, and not to confound the specific importance of the resurrection event.

The Relationship of Resurrection and Exaltation

As is well known, Barth's understanding of the humiliation and exaltation of Jesus Christ differs from that of earlier theology. Barth's doctrine of the exaltation of Jesus Christ concerns the transformation of human being to faithful covenant partnership with the Father as accomplished in the life of Jesus Christ culminating in his obedience in his death on the cross, as a pre-resurrection reality. In distinction to this Barth sees the ascension of Jesus Christ (the elevation of human being to the right hand of the Father) as the *sign* of the exaltation of human being and not as its accomplishment, and as the beginning of the faithful covenant partnership of other human beings with God.

Barth's propensity to follow the Reformers in the design of his theological discourse, especially that of Calvin, is acknowledged by Barth himself.[2] Since he was not easily moved from the pattern of systematic development established by the Reformers, it is especially noteworthy that here Barth makes some very basic and substantial changes in his outline of the field. Certainly among the most telling of these are the inclusion of the exaltation of the Son of Man with the humiliation of the Son of God in the life of Jesus culminating simultaneously in his death, and the development of the prophetic office of Christ in which the resurrection is seen as the first form of the radiance of the glory of the mediator.

One of the most significant modifications of Classical and Reformed christology as it relates to the resurrection is Barth's radical re-interpretation and re-presentation of the doctrine of the humiliation and exaltation of Jesus Christ. As Barth has it, the matter is not to be viewed as two sequential historical states but as a double movement of a single divine and human action which begins at Bethlehem and reaches its culmination at Golgotha. The humiliation and exaltation of Jesus Christ have in view different aspects of the same unified event which occurs cumulatively as the life history of the single subject Jesus Christ. The humiliation and exaltation of Jesus Christ must not be developed as a movement from the former to the latter, as in traditional Reformed christology, but rather as a twofold movement occurring simultaneously in the life history of Jesus Christ, the *vere Deus vere homo*, in a singular historical progression from its beginning in exaltation and humiliation to its ending in humiliation and exaltation.

Berkouwer faults Barth's view precisely on this point. He correctly understands the self-humiliation of God to be coincident with the exaltation of man in Barth's view, for he notes Barth's view 'replaces the idea of *succession* in the humiliation-exaltation relationship by the idea of *contemporaneity*. ... The resurrection is the

---

2   *CD* IV/1, pp. 108f., 132ff., 137f., 366, and others.

absolute revelation of this.'³ However, he mistakenly asserts 'The substitution of Christ lies for Barth not in the 'not *we* but *He*' as the confessions of the Reformation teach, but in the resurrection of the *new* man, while the *old* man is struck by the catastrophe and thereby *disappears, no longer has a future*.'⁴ Berkouwer's difficulty rests in the identification of the temporal transition from crucifixion to resurrection with that of humiliation to exaltation, and thus he is forced to separate temporally the justifying work of Christ from his sanctifying work. This leaves Berkouwer open to the very charge he praises Barth for adeptly avoiding, namely, that a further future realization of reconciliation is required *in us*. However, the difficulty is overcome if we recognize with Barth that the temporal transition of crucifixion to resurrection is identified in Scripture with the transition from concealment to revelation, from Christ *pro nobis in se* to Christ *pro nobis* on his way to others. As the fullness of what was accomplished in the work of Christ culminating on the cross is revealed in his resurrection, both the depth of his humiliation and the height of his exaltation in their unassailable unity are revealed. This is the revelation of his glory. A closer examination of Barth's reasons for a more thoroughly integrated development of these doctrines will help to clarify this distinction.

The first reason Barth gives for understanding the doctrine of the two states in the light of the doctrine of the two natures and *vice versa* is that in no place does the New Testament speak of the single work of Jesus Christ as 'divided into different stages or periods of His existence.'⁵ The New Testament rather describes the being of Jesus Christ in the twofold form, involving at all times both his humiliation and his exaltation. The second reason is that in no place does the New Testament develop these doctrines independently. The real humiliation and exaltation of Jesus Christ, asserts Barth, 'is not something incidental to His being.' This humiliation and exaltation is rather 'the actuality of the being of Jesus Christ as very God and very man.'⁶ Says Barth, 'We cannot, therefore, ascribe to Jesus Christ two natures and then quite independently two states.'⁷ As a third and most compelling argument for developing the doctrine as he does, Barth asserts that the referenced humiliation is the humiliation of God, and conversely, the referenced exaltation is the exaltation of human being: 'the humiliation of God to supreme glory, as the activation and demonstration of His divine being; and the exaltation of man as the work of God's grace which consists in the restoration of his true humanity.'⁸ Barth claims it is mere tautology to assert that Jesus Christ is lowly as a man, just as it is to assert that Jesus Christ is exalted as God. Thus Barth develops the doctrine of reconciliation in its first two forms, beginning with the discussion of the God who humbles himself in Jesus Christ, and continuing with the discussion of the human person who in Jesus

---

3   Berkouwer, *Triumph of Grace*, p. 134.
4   Ibid., p. 317.
5   *CD* IV/1, p. 133.
6   Ibid.
7   Ibid., pp. 133f.
8   Ibid., p. 134.

Christ is exalted. The traditional correlation of the crucifixion with the humiliation of Christ and the resurrection with the exaltation of Christ in a sequential movement from one state to another is, in his view, inadequate to the reality depicted in the New Testament.

We further note that in Barth's view the doctrine of the self-humiliation of the Son of God and the exaltation of the man Jesus does not follow from the doctrine of the incarnation, still less from the human nature of Christ. Even Klappert's account of the temporal coincidence on the cross of the double movement of the reconciling God and the reconciled man as the establishment of the covenant,[9] while much closer, falls short of doing full justice to Barth's thought for it fails to explain how this coincidence is upheld and known. While Klappert's case is strengthened by his appeal to the 'differentiated relationship' of the cross and resurrection, the cross as a negative event with a positive intention and the resurrection as a positive event with a negative presupposition, the full force of Barth's understanding of the resurrection is not yet clear.

In order to understand Barth here we must recall that the humiliation of the Son of God and the exaltation of the Son of Man on the cross is a completely concealed reality. The two aspects are not merely supplementary aspects to be brought together by an objective observer. They are rather unintelligible assertions as they are veiled in the darkness of the cross. If in the first part-volume we have in view the action of God in Jesus Christ humbling himself, and in no way the work of the human humbling himself (in as much as he is already in a low state), then we have in the first aspect the divine action fulfilling the covenant promises of God. And if we have in the second part-volume the action of the man Jesus perfectly fulfilling the requirements of the covenant from the human side and in so doing enacting the identity of the exalted man, then we have a distinctly human action (in as much as the already exalted God requires no action to fulfill or sustain his exalted status). However only in the resurrection is it revealed that these two different forms of action, divine and human, each performing their distinct and inalienable task, hold together as unified action in a single subject. Only from the perspective of Easter can it be seen that these two histories are in fact one and the same, namely, the history of the God-man Jesus Christ. The unifying perspective of the resurrection alone permits each to be seen and understood for what it is:

> there can be no disputing the fact that, ... prior to any knowledge of His being or temporally conditioned confession of it, He actually was and is and will be what He is represented in the reflection of this witness, the Son of the Heavenly Father, the King of His kingdom, and therefore 'by nature God.' ... The fact that He is this can be known only as He Himself reveals it, only by His Holy Spirit. When the New Testament attests Him to be such, it speaks of His resurrection from the dead.[10]

With respect to the New Testament view of Jesus as the royal man, Barth asserts:

---

9   Klappert, *Die Auferweckung des Gekreuzigten*, pp. 5, 90ff., 387.
10   *CD* IV/1, p. 163.

we have consciously accepted what is surely obvious to any unprejudiced reader ... that the standpoint from which they saw Jesus and told us about Him lies ... in the context of events which took place after His death and which they described as His resurrection and ascension and the impartation of His Holy Spirit to the community. ... Our position in relation to the New Testament, and therefore to Jesus Himself, is not one which is adopted in abstraction from His resurrection. We make no attempt to see and understand His life prior to His death as if it were not illuminated and interpreted ... by what happened after His death, as if we were free to see and represent it later either in this light, in one like it, or in a very different light. Neutrality of this kind is quite illegitimate ...[11]

Hence, in Barth's view, the doctrine of the humiliation of the Son of God and the exaltation of the Son of Man are not inferred from the doctrine of the incarnation, nor from any preconceived schema of the relation of divine and human action, nor even from the temporal coincidence of divine and human action on the cross, but rather from the revelation of the One in whom both these actions cohere in perfect unity: the risen Jesus Christ.

The resurrection, therefore, is not to be understood as the temporal exaltation of Jesus Christ, subsequent to his humiliation culminating on the cross. Crucifixion and resurrection are not to be ordered as signs of distinct states in temporal sequence, but are rather to be understood as divine historical events in a definite temporal sequence, in which the transition from the concealment of reconciled human being and action (justified and sanctified) in Christ to its revelation in him occurs.

Truth Pressing for Subjectivization

If as we have claimed the transition to which we attend is not that of the temporal alteration from the state of humiliation to the state to exaltation, what then is the nature of this transition? How are we to know it? It is in address of these questions that Barth speaks of the reconciling being and action of Jesus Christ not as isolated in and of itself, but as reaching out beyond itself, embracing and informing our anthropological sphere. That is, the reality of reconciled being and action in Jesus Christ is genuinely inclusive of our anthropological sphere and hence moves out from its remoteness and concealment to effect real encounter with human persons. What we speak of is true and essential and unchangeable being. But it is not being which is content to stand alone as such. It is also the objective reality, the truth of which presses for subjectivization in the anthropological sphere. What does this mean? In part it means that the reconciled being and action of Jesus Christ is not only an objective reality, but is also a subjectivizing reality. That is, it has the power to draw human subjects into appropriate correspondence with its reality and truth. It does not require another force or power outside of itself. Rather, it grounds, establishes and sustains the true subjectivity which suitably corresponds to its objective content. In this discussion Barth begins to redefine our distinctions between objective and

---

11   *CD* IV/2, pp. 247f.

subjective realities, insisting upon the subjectivizing power of the objective reality of reconciling being and action in Jesus Christ. He goes to great lengths to understand what he calls the *antithesis* [*Gegensatzes*][12] of the humiliation of the Son of God and the exaltation of the Son of Man in order that he might formulate the question of the transition from Christ to others aright.

The Active Power of Truth

If the being and act of God in Jesus Christ is thoroughly concealed in his crucifixion, to what may we appeal in order to come to terms with this all-comprehensive reality? Barth's answer is that there is nowhere to turn. The secret of the revelation of this truth and of our knowledge of it lies wholly within the truth itself. That is, we know this truth truly, in and of itself, because it is essential to this truth that it be revealed and known. According to Barth, the reality of Jesus Christ must be seen as 'truth which ontologically and essentially presses for subjectivisation.'[13] And yet it is more than merely this. It is an active and manifest power having the full force of truth, of a deed already done. It is not an automatic revealing of its light in a rather mechanistic way. It is rather an act taken in free sovereign decision; it is a power enacted by will. This power is the power of God's self-disclosure in the resurrection.

Once again we do well to note that Barth takes great care to speak about the power of this truth in its concealment and its disclosure because he wishes to avoid at all costs the perception that the concealment of being and truth in Jesus Christ in his crucifixion is an invitation for human beings to attempt to penetrate to its depths from our side. To understand it as such is to completely misconstrue the reality, for the completeness of the concealment undermines all human knowing and willing and acting to disclose its contents. Yet this truth in itself is not content in its remote objectivity. This unique truth not only presses for subjectivization but is also the power of its own subjectivization. Thus Barth attempts to understand the problem of the transition from the being and act of Jesus Christ in himself to genuine human response to it as a christological problem. This ontological truth is not merely the object of knowledge but also its subject, and only as subject of its knowledge can this ontological truth be truly known. Jesus Christ, in all the fullness of his life, death and resurrection, is this ontological truth. Primordially he knows himself and derivatively he includes other subjects in his self-knowledge. It is this derivative knowledge, this inclusion of other knowing subjects within his self-knowing, that Barth speaks of as the subjectivization of this ontological truth.

With this depiction of the relationship of the reality of reconciliation (objective accomplishment) and its revelation (subjective appropriation) in terms of the ontic and noetic aspects of a single reality, we note immediately the emphasis upon the sufficiency of the reality to break free of the constraints of its concealment in the revelation of its truth. Quite apart from any external force or agency whatsoever

---

12   Ibid., p. 348ff.
13   Ibid., p. 298.

the ontic reality possesses the power of the revelation of its own truth. Barth's choice of this conceptual construct appears to suggest that the reality of reconciled being and action in Jesus Christ in his death possesses the power of self-revelation quite apart from the act of the Father in awakening Jesus Christ. Yet the view that Jesus Christ raised himself from the dead on the basis of his own power, Barth has already rejected. Barth's language here has formal similarities with a notion of truth generally derived. The danger of this ontic–noetic descriptive framework lies in the overly naturalistic depiction it yields, tending to reduce the significance of the awakening of Jesus Christ as a distinct act of God. But as we shall see, Barth is vigilant, refusing to surrender the content to the terms of its description. He quickly moves on to describe the transition from this ontic to this noetic in actualist terms conforming to the particular reality of the resurrection and the Holy Spirit. Barth's use of the ontic–noetic description here then is to be interpreted rather loosely as a general framework within which to grasp the distinction of the unique reality (the completed act of reconciliation) and its truth (subjective appropriation) as well as the unique relation of the two (resurrection). The being of completed reconciliation in the crucified Jesus Christ is not to be seen as possessing the power of its own illumination quite apart from the gracious act of the Father upon him. Rather the power of the revelation of reconciled human being in Jesus Christ is conferred upon him in his awakening, the resulting eternal life having the power of its own self-illumination. Hence, Barth's ontic–noetic depiction of crucifixion and resurrection is to be subordinated to, that is, interpreted in the light of, his particular and concrete description of the resurrection of Jesus Christ as firstly the awakening and then the self-revealing of Jesus Christ in the power of his Spirit as he is on his way to others.

Whereas in his crucifixion Christ was concealed, in his resurrection he is revealed. Barth speaks of the concealment and revelation of Jesus Christ in their 'irreversible sequence' of the cross and resurrection: 'He is the Crucified who as such closes Himself off from us, and He is the Resurrected who as such discloses Himself to us.'[14] This concealment and disclosure are both sovereign acts of Jesus Christ: 'He does not close Himself off from us to keep us away. He also discloses Himself to us. ... He not only hides Himself, but also reveals Himself to us.[15] It is clear then that Barth sees the power of this being and truth in its concealment and revelation as the power of Jesus Christ: 'He is risen, and reveals Himself. He Himself, Jesus Christ, declares His majesty. He declares Himself to be the royal man. ... He declares Himself as the Herald and Bearer, the actualisation, of the kingdom of God on earth.'[16] Again the issue here is the penetration into the depths of the concealment by virtue of the revelation of that reality therein concealed, and this by the powerful act of Jesus Christ himself. Therefore to posit any other person or force or mechanism in the mediation of Jesus Christ and reconciliation accomplished in him and ourselves

---

14   Ibid., p. 299.
15   Ibid.
16   Ibid.

in the anthropological world into which reconciliation must come is to misconstrue both the depth of the concealment of human being in the crucifixion of Jesus Christ and the power of the revelation of that being in his resurrection.

Barth believes it is not only meaningful but necessary to speak about the reality of reconciled human being in Jesus Christ as that which is real, concrete and unchangeable, having all the force of ontological reality, yet which is not manifest. Barth conceives of the reality of the humbled and exalted saviour and of us in him prior to his resurrection as an as yet concealed certainty which is not a product of history or historical causes or cosmic forces, but rather the origin and cause, the source and goal, the power and meaning of these others. It is the active power of this truth that is the secret of the transition from the christological sphere of Christ's self-knowing to the anthropological sphere of the human person's knowledge of Christ and of self as self in Christ.

The Resurrection as Revelatory Event

But what, one may ask, is the source and power of this ontological and essential pressing for the subjectivization of reconciliation truth? Our answer, says Barth, is the resurrection of Jesus Christ from the dead. Barth differs from earlier theology in the fact that he sees the resurrection of Jesus Christ from the dead as far more than the *datum* of Christ's exaltation. Rather, Barth believes the New Testament to assert that the *datum* of both the humiliation and the exaltation of Jesus Christ is nothing other than the entirety of his human existence inclusive of his death. But the resurrection, on the other hand, is 'the event, and not merely the *datum*, of the revelation of the One who is exalted in His lowliness.'[17] The resurrection then is not merely another fact in the existence of Jesus Christ. It is rather the revelation that the historical factuality of the life of Jesus Christ concluding in his death is an exalted and majestic existence. As such the resurrection is not to be understood – and here Barth implicitly criticizes Bultmann – as an explanation of human faith and self-understanding. The resurrection is the powerful revelation of Jesus Christ, the God-man, in his fullness.

Furthermore, the resurrection is not only one important element among many in matters of human knowing, for Barth. The resurrection is rather the source, substance and sum of all human knowing. There is no true knowledge, direct or indirect, of divine and human reality, apart from the revelation which is the resurrection of Jesus Christ from the dead in its extension into the anthropological sphere – 'All Christian knowledge and confession, all Christian knowledge of God and man and the world, derives from this self-declaration of Jesus Christ, from His resurrection.'[18] For what was concealed in Christ in his death was not only himself in his humiliation and exaltation but also ourselves, our having been put to death as sinners and our having been raised simultaneously to faithful covenant partnership with God. Because Jesus

---

17   Ibid.
18   Ibid., p. 300.

Christ is the head and representative of all human persons, the revelation of Jesus Christ himself entails the revelation of the genuine being of all human persons.[19]

The Word and the Power of Transition

For Barth, the ontic reality of human being in Christ is not a purely objective reality, as though it could be and remain something quite distinct from the subjective response of those whom it claims. The objective–subjective distinction is a useful descriptive tool as one attempts to account for the reality of Jesus Christ aspectually, but the distinction is not essential. In this matter the objective cannot be isolated from the subjective as a separate matter in itself. Rather, the objective reality, being what it is, must pass over into its subjective side:

> We have kept to the fact that both statements – the first in transition to the second and the second in transition from the first – are attested in the New Testament; that the objective reality of the being of Jesus Christ, and our being in Him, has also the character of objective truth; and that this truth is not satisfied with a purely objective form but demands also a subjective, pressing in upon us and our seeing and understanding and knowing with the aim of the orientation and determination of our existence in the light of it, of awakening and summoning us to love in return the One who has first loved us.[20]

According to Barth, it is as the New Testament message is proclaimed that the unified being and truth of Jesus Christ moves from its objective aspect to its subjective aspect. As the New Testament witness is heard the truth of the objective reality of Jesus Christ moves out illuminating the rest of reality for what it has become in him. The light shines in the declaration of the New Testament witness, dispelling the darkness and evoking the appropriate subjective response in the lives of particular human beings:

> What we have said about the objective content or truth of the reality of Jesus Christ, which includes our own reality, presses in upon us, from its objectivity to our subjectivity, in order that there should be in us a correspondence. We have already seen this from what we find in its human attestation as it concerns us in the New Testament. ... It becomes a historical event in the encounter between this witness and us. In the name and commission of the reality and truth of Jesus Christ we are concretely seized, whether we like it or not, in the course of this address and summons and application and claim.[21]

Thus, Barth claims that this movement of the objective reality of reconciled and reconciling being and action in Jesus Christ occurs in coincidence with the proclamation of the New Testament witness. It is important to note that Barth does

---

19   Ibid.

20   Ibid. We note here Barth's free and flexible use of philosophical language. While he is prepared to use philosophical language as a tool to describe a theological reality, he does not permit himself to be enthralled with any particular philosophical scheme.

21   Ibid., p. 303.

not identify this movement with this proclamation, but avers the indissoluble unity of the two. This has profound consequences for Barth's understanding of Scripture. We must observe that Barth not only sees the New Testament perspective as a thorough-going resurrection perspective, but he also sees its proclamation as coincident with the effective transition to the appropriate subjective correspondence vis-à-vis its objective content.

But to be complete we must go further in our account of this witness. In the preaching of the gospel not only is information imparted, God's claim asserted, and appropriate response demanded, but also the *power of transition* is released:

> when we are confronted by its witnesses, we are already in the circle of the validity of what they say to us, and are no longer the same in the sense that we are now marked, like trees for cutting, for the fulfilment of our own actual acknowledgement of its validity. ... We stand already under the Word.[22]

The derivative human word, though most evident, is neither the only nor ultimate word of the address. The divine witness includes the human witness. This divine word, the creative power of transition, which by God's faithful promise accompanies the human announcement of the good news, brings about the mysterious and miraculous extension of the objective reality into its full subjective domain.

Barth asserts that the New Testament not only brings us under this Word but also depends upon a unique and definite power of transition:

> The power on which [the New Testament] counts is the power to set us ... in a very definite freedom: the freedom to appropriate as our own conversion the conversion of man to God as it has taken place in Jesus Christ, the translation of man from a state of disobedience to one of obedience.[23]

This power is not one which is merely offered to us, but is genuinely made to be our own. It is a power which at one and the same time is external to ourselves yet freeing ourselves to be motivated and impelled of ourselves from within ourselves:

> It is the power to call us effectively to positive decision in relation to ... the freedom of that accompanying and following of conversion. It is the power to keep us in this as a correspondence to our conversion as it is already accomplished in Jesus Christ, so that we live daily in a free fulfilment of this correspondence.[24]

This is the power upon which the New Testament depends, the power of transition which sets us in the specific freedom of true correspondence to the objective reality of Jesus Christ.

Barth notes that this power is greater than the power of the New Testament witness itself, in as much as the evangelists and apostles have power to set us under

---

22   Ibid., p. 304.
23   Ibid.
24   Ibid., p. 305.

the Word but they cannot put us in obedience to it.[25] They cannot set us in freedom for this correspondence and response. It must be said of course that this power makes use of the New Testament witness and has its activity in and with the declaration of it. And the New Testament witnesses live and speak and act on the basis of and in dependence upon this power. Existence upon this basis and functioning in dependence upon and anticipation of this power is the mode of the operation of the New Testament witness. 'It is the power alone which on both sides unlocks the heart so that there is living speech on the one part and living hearing on the other, the Word flying like a well-directed arrow to its target and striking and sticking in the right place, being received with a meaning and content with which it is given.'[26]

Barth summarizes this power, the power of the resurrection which accompanies the preaching of the Gospel, in this manner: 'it is the power of the inconceivably transcendent transition from what is true and actual in Jesus Christ to what is true for us, or even more simply from Christ to us as Christians.'[27]

Barth asks 'What transpires if a human person is to be a Christian in reality?'[28] It is clear from the start that its basis cannot be found in us. There can simply be no question of any human ability in this matter. Rather, this Christian subjectivity:

> denotes a human act without the corresponding human potency, a pure act which takes place because that other and greater power on which the New Testament counts shows itself in might to and in a man, not merely declaring but fulfilling for him a Nevertheless and Therefore which transcend and leave behind both himself and the contradiction which derives from himself, putting him continually in the new beginning and on the way to those new conclusions in spite of his contradiction, setting him in the freedom of conversion.[29]

The Miraculous Character of the Power of Transition

The power of the resurrection is, therefore, in Barth's view, the power of the transition from Jesus Christ in himself *pro nobis* to human persons. Not only is this power of the resurrection active as a revelatory event, it is also clearly a *miraculous* power. It is not to be understood as a factor or phenomenon, albeit extraordinary and striking, in the closed nexus of world occurrence. Nevertheless, it is a definite power with a definite character, the power and character of resurrection. It is the power of God:

> The power of the transition on which the New Testament counts when it looks from the basis and origin of its witness in Jesus Christ to its goal in the existence of Christians is absolutely unique as the power of the resurrection of Jesus Christ.[30]

---

25   Ibid., p. 306.

26   Ibid.

27   Ibid., hearkening back to Barth's much earlier comment: 'Jesus Christ in the power of His resurrection is present whenever men really speak of God' (*CD* I/2, p. 752).

28   Ibid., p. 308.

29   Ibid., p. 309.

30   Ibid., p. 310.

Barth describes the particular character of this power of transition as light, liberation, knowledge, peace and life.[31] Summarizing, he asserts: 'It aims at an enlightened, liberated and understanding life which is at peace in all dimensions. ... The power of the resurrection of Jesus Christ may be known by the fact that it snatches man upwards.'[32] That is to say, this power is 'the power which proceeds from His resurrection, and He Himself as the Resurrected.' As such, this power sows 'a seed which is not only psychical but physical, and gives nourishment which is not only spiritual but material – a whole preservation of the whole man.'[33]

As this miraculous power of transition, the resurrection of Jesus Christ enables human persons to live in the hope of their own resurrection and eternal life. The proof of the power of the resurrection, according to Barth, lay in the fact that it reveals the life of the man Jesus as 'exalted to participation in the eternal life of God' and in so doing it effectively brings the human person 'the promise of eternal life which is given in it, making it his own, and moving him for his part to make it his own, to grasp it, to allow it to be the comfort and confidence and hope of his life as he still lives it in the shadow of death.'[34] No other force can bring about this miraculous result, that is, the enabling of men and women, who receive and possess the promise, 'to live a life which already defies death, and arrests that discontinuity, and persists even in that flight through the times.'[35]

It is on account of this miraculous power of God, says Barth, that it is both possible and actual that a human person becomes and is a Christian. The answer to our plaguing question can only be that:

> deriving from Jesus Christ, i.e., His resurrection, there is a sovereignly operative power of revelation, and therefore of the transition from Him to us, of His communication with us; a power by whose working there is revealed and made known to us our own election as it has taken place in Him ... and therefore the deliverance and establishment of our own being, so that our existence receives a new determination. It is by the operation of this power that we become and are Christians.[36]

Once again, it is in his description of the particularity and definiteness of the miraculous power that Barth adds force to his argument that the resurrection of Jesus Christ from the dead is indeed the transition of reconciled human being and action in him to the remaining anthropological sphere.

---

31   Barth offers a fuller description of the character of the power of this transition on pp. 311–16.

32   Ibid., p. 316

33   Ibid., p. 317

34   Ibid.

35   Ibid., p. 318.

36   Ibid.

The Holy Spirit of Christ as the Power of Transition

Augmenting his argument, Barth makes the very important assertion that this power which the New Testament presupposes is 'the outgoing and receiving and presence and action of the Holy Spirit.'[37] It is the Holy Spirit who awakens others causing them to see Jesus Christ and themselves in him, and therefore to live and speak in a new and corresponding way. He generates the fellowship in which both the witnesses and those who receive the witness become his community. He directs the *kerygma*. He commissions and orders the community's actions. He empowers and controls them. According to Barth, 'the Holy Spirit alone [is] the Alpha and Omega, the beginning and continuance, the principle and power of the Christian life.'[38]

In answer to the question of how it is that the Holy Spirit can be this power of transition from Christ to others without entailing the same problem one step removed, Barth says:

> He is the Holy Spirit in this supreme sense ... because He is no other than the presence and action of Jesus Christ Himself: His stretched out arm; He Himself in the power of His resurrection, i.e., in the power of His revelation as it begins in and with the power of His resurrection and continues its work from this point.[39]

According to Barth it is by the power of the Holy Spirit that the children of God are enabled to live in the presence of Jesus Christ: 'Thus the Spirit who makes Christians Christians is the power of this revelation of Jesus Christ Himself – His Spirit. And for this reason, and in this fact, He is the Holy Spirit. ... He legitimates and proves Himself as the Spirit of Jesus Christ.'[40]

In making this claim Barth seems to all but equate the Holy Spirit with the resurrection. This coupled with his earlier interchangeable use of the 'power of His resurrection in the Holy Spirit' and the 'power of the Holy Spirit in the resurrection',[41] seems to signal a severe reduction of the distinction between the two. He appears to come close to falling to the accusation made of him in his earlier writings by Walter Künneth in which Kingdom of God, Resurrection, Spirit, Redemption, Righteousness, Messiah, Last things, End, God, all merge into one and the same identity. Is there substance to Künneth's charge, even here, against Barth? Is Barth in danger of conflating the resurrection and the Holy Spirit? For the moment we can only assert he does not. Rather, Barth employs a more subtle form of description which does not force the identification of the two, but stresses their interrelationship in such a way that their individual realities are illumined in these relationships. Barth's development of the doctrine of the Holy Spirit in this manner does not negate an understanding of the Holy Spirit in his own right (as we shall see later when we

---

37   Ibid., p. 319.
38   Ibid., p. 320.
39   Ibid., pp. 322f.
40   Ibid., p. 323.
41   *CD* IV/1, p. 159, cf. also p. 163.

consider the implications of this for the ontological Trinity), but demonstrates all the more clearly the unique character and role of the Holy Spirit in transition from Jesus Christ to others. Barth does insist however that we must understand the Holy Spirit in this regard uniquely and truly as the Spirit of Jesus Christ. How could it be any other way if it is to be a genuine transition between Christ and others?

Identity of the Holy Spirit as the Spirit of Christ

In light of his growing awareness of the importance of the doctrine of the Holy Spirit for the question of the transition from Christ to the remaining anthropological sphere, Barth enters into a close examination of the New Testament texts concerning the identity of the Holy Spirit and his relationship to Jesus Christ. The enquiry seeks to answer the question concerning the *holiness* of the Holy Spirit. That the *Holy* Spirit is the Spirit of the Lord is crucial to our being able to proceed from a christological basis to the remainder of the anthropological world.

If we are to appreciate the profundity of Barth's position, it is imperative we understand that he emphasizes not only the consubstantiality, but also the identity of the Spirit and Jesus Christ. It is not enough to affirm the deity of the Spirit, nor even his full and genuine membership in the Trinity. Nor is it sufficient to assert that Jesus Christ has the Spirit in the fullest sense surpassing all others, in every way moved and empowered by the Spirit. This is indeed true, but more must be said. Above all this, the identity of the Spirit as the Spirit of Jesus Christ must be confessed. Only on this basis, that is, of the movement of *his* Spirit to other men and women, can there be a true and actual transition from Christ to others, for only on this basis is Jesus Christ himself present with his own. Jesus Christ could be present to his followers in bodily form during the forty days in a manner analogous to the presence of any human being (in the flesh) with another. But in the power of his Spirit, poured out upon all men and women, Jesus Christ himself is present to *all* without temporal or spatial limit.

We must further note that there are strong parallels between Barth's development of the necessity of the identity of the Spirit as the Spirit of the Lord and the Athanasian development of the soteriological necessity of the hypostatic union. For Athanasius, if Jesus Christ is not fully God, he could not *save* us, for divine presence and power is indispensable to salvation. Likewise, if Jesus Christ is not fully human, he could not save *us*, for full and effective comprehension of human being is also necessary to salvation. In similar fashion, in Barth's construal of this transition, if it is not genuinely the Spirit of Jesus Christ who comes to us, how can we be encountered by our new reconciled human being as it is in Jesus Christ? Moreover, if the selfsame Jesus Christ does not come to *us*, how can *we* be saved? The transition from Jesus Christ to others must be the radical encounter of Jesus Christ himself (not a *tertium quid*) and us others. Only in the Holy Spirit, the Spirit of the Lord, is this possible.

Looking to the New Testament, Barth concludes that the solution given there to the problem of the distance between Jesus Christ in his crucifixion and us, and of the transition from him to us, is '[t]he outpouring of the Spirit as the effect of His resurrection, of His life in His death and in the conquest of His death, and therefore the occurrence of His self-impartation.'[42] On Barth's reading of the New Testament, the holiness of the Holy Spirit is to be understood as:

> the fact that He is the self-expression of the man Jesus, and that as such He is Himself His effective turning to us and our effective conversion to Him; His disclosure for us and our disclosure for Him; and, as this comes to us in this twofold sense, the new thing in earthly history.[43]

Whatever else might be said concerning the Holy Spirit, we cannot moderate the claim of the identity of the Spirit as the Spirit of the Lord, without sacrificing the genuine transition of reconciled human being and action from Jesus Christ to others.

Barth's Pneumatology

Let us at this point briefly interrupt our exposition to inquire concerning the adequacy of Barth's development of pneumatology in the context of the transition from Jesus Christ to others. At least two important criticisms have been mounted against Barth's understanding of the Holy Spirit. The first is that the doctrine of the Holy Spirit is not developed sufficiently, that is, it is developed so strongly in christological terms that the genuine trinitarian character of the Holy Spirit is obscured.[44] The second is that the role of the Holy Spirit in the subjective appropriation of reconciliation looms so large as to obliterate all genuine human response. We will deal with the first criticism here, but will reserve our explication of the second to the final section of this chapter.

Though Karl Barth has often been acclaimed as the preeminent christocentric theologian of the 20th Century, Philip J. Rosato[45] believes he would be more adequately described as a theologian of the Holy Spirit. Barth's impressive development of the

---

42   *CD* IV/2, p. 333.

43   Ibid., p. 331.

44   Important representative examples of this view are to be found in Rowan Williams, 'Barth on the Triune God,' in *Karl Barth – Studies of His Theological Method*, ed. S. W. Sykes (Oxford: Clarendon Press, 1979), pp. 147–93; Philip J. Rosato, *The Spirit as Lord* (Edinburgh: T. & T. Clark, 1981), Gary D. Badcock, *Light of Truth & Fire of Love: A Theology of the Holy Spirit* (Grand Rapids: William B. Eerdmans Publishing Company, 1997), pp. 170–84, and Alan Torrance 'The Trinity' in the *Cambridge Companion to Karl Barth*, ed. By John Webster (Cambridge: Cambridge University Press, 2000), pp. 72–91. Each to a greater or lesser degree seeks to identify the fundamental problem in Barth's pneumatology as a failure to reconcile his emphasis upon the Spirit of Christ as the basis and power of the revelation of God in Christ to Christians and a more complete pneumatology in which the categories of mutual relationality, independence and fellowship feature more prominently. For the sake of brevity our comments will focus on Rosato's larger and more comprehensive work, though they have a bearing on each.

45   Philip J. Rosato, *The Spirit as Lord*, cf. chapter 8.

doctrine of the Holy Spirit, its integral relationship to his christology, and some scattered comments to the effect that Barth could conceive of his work as a veiled theology of the Holy Spirit, lead Rosato to theorize that this is indeed the best way to understand the development and direction of Barth's theology.[46] Hence though reputed to be a *christologian* Barth would be better understood as a *pneumatologian*.

Rosato's thesis unravels, however, in the details of its description. Rosato mistakenly describes Barth's theology as a 'search for a balance,' that is, 'for a conjunction but not a confusion between a theology of Christ and a theology of man.' This, according to Rosato, undoubtedly constitutes 'the germ of Barth's own pneumatology.'[47] Rosato somewhat correctly observes that 'Barth's own pneumatology is at its core a search for a theologically legitimate principle of mediation at the centre of Christian dogmatics – at the point where the transition is made between Christ and the Christian. Only the Holy Spirit, the divine mediator, can validly serve this function.'[48] In this Rosato agrees with us regarding the centre of Barth's dogmatics and the transition between Christ and the Christian, but Rosato wrongly construes it as Barth's search for a philosophically oriented mediation of an idealist sort between the two foci. Whereas Barth clearly has this aspect of mediation, it is not a philosophical device, but an historical actuality. According to Rosato, Barth 'clearly supplants [the] philosophical mediating principles' of 'the theological methodologies of his chief adversaries' with 'a decidedly pneumatic one.'[49] In this, says Rosato, Barth opts 'to keep their dialectical structure intact.'[50] However, we must insist that Barth's anthropology is subsumed within his theology of Christ and that his pneumatology is the outward movement of Christ in the resurrection, not the balancing factor as Rosato would have it. The union of divine and human being, for Barth, is achieved in the incarnation of Jesus Christ, culminating in his crucifixion and death. However, the antithesis Barth deals with here is that of sinful human being outside of Christ in opposition to reconciled human being in Christ. That is the antithesis has to do with the opposition of who we are in Christ with who we are apart from him. And this is the context of Barth's development of the Holy Spirit as the Spirit of the Lord. The dialectical structure is radically different when there is this vector of movement from Christ to Christians without the leaving behind of Christ.

Rosato astutely sees in *Church Dogmatics* IV that 'With [the] identification of the Holy Spirit with the power of the risen Christ, Barth clarifies ecclesial existence as man's direct share in the eschatological event of Jesus' resurrection.'[51] However,

---

46   Ibid., p. v.
47   Ibid., p. 16.
48   Ibid., p. 21.
49   Ibid.
50   Ibid.
51   Ibid., p. 118.

in Rosato's view, the role of the Holy Spirit is underplayed in Barth's theology of Christ and the church:[52]

> the germ of this paradox is the historical irrelevance which marks Barth's theology of the Spirit and of the Christian community because of his pronounced conviction that everything significant has been achieved by Jesus Christ. Barth is hindered from allowing the Holy Spirit's activity in human history to have its own salutary and innovative character, precisely because these general attributes of all God's self-revealing actions are confined by Barth to christology.[53]

Rosato illuminates the point with this question: 'Is the role of Jesus Christ so exaggerated in Barth's account of salvation history that the work of the Spirit, as a distinct salvific self-communication of the Father, is relegated to a decidedly second place in the whole sweep of the *Church Dogmatics*?'[54] He argues that in the *Church Dogmatics* the activity of the Holy Spirit 'is almost totally confined to the part of the spectrum which begins with the resurrection of Jesus and goes on from there. The Spirit is restricted to the domain of the Church since He is the outreaching power of Jesus Christ's resurrection and the penultimate form of His parousia.'[55] While Rosato admits that this is an important aspect of the New Testament understanding of the Holy Spirit, that is, as the Spirit of Christ, nevertheless, he argues, Barth underplays the importance of the New Testament's understanding of 'the Pneuma as the life-giving power of the Father which begins to permeate the cosmos at creation and continues to energize history until the very goal of time itself.'[56] According to Rosato 'Though Barth certainly is well aware of this latter strain of biblical pneumatology, he clearly chooses to emphasize the former throughout most of the *Church Dogmatics*.'[57] The problem with this is:

> Granting ontic validity only to Jesus Christ and according the Spirit and man only noetic significance seem to debilitate against keeping a balanced tension between human and divine freedom. It also curbs the power of God to act in the world before and after the Christ-event in a way which embraces both the first and the last comings of Jesus Christ. The Spirit and man do not have the privilege of developing or furthering the work of Christ in any ontic sense.[58]

While we agree with Rosato concerning the almost exclusively christological explication of the Holy Spirit in Barth's doctrine of reconciliation and with the need for greater development of the Spirit as *Creator Spiritus*, we disagree with the implication that such descriptions are mutually exclusive in Barth's understanding.

---

52   Ibid., p. 157.
53   Ibid.
54   Ibid.
55   Ibid., p. 160.
56   Ibid.
57   Ibid.
58   Ibid., p. 161.

We also point out Rosato's insufficient appreciation of Barth's account of the role of the Spirit in the pre-Easter (and as such concealed) life of the God-man, in which the humiliation of the Son of God and the exaltation of the Son of Man are held together in differentiated unity.

According to Rosato: 'It is necessary, therefore, to disagree with Barth's clear but prejudiced ontic–noetic distinction. Instead, the Spirit and the Son must each be given both ontic and noetic functions.'[59] Continuing his critique, Rosato claims:

> Barth cannot envision the Spirit creating a revelatory event which is ontologically new; all ontic relevance has been rooted in the Word from eternity. The consequence of Barth's position is that his Spirit theology simply reiterates the content of the Christ-event. In a real sense, sanctification has been absorbed by justification, Pentecost by the Cross.[60]

Again we must take issue with these conclusions on the basis of the observation – to which we have already alluded, and which will be developed more fully in the following chapter – that Barth does explicate the outward movement of the Holy Spirit as a divine noetic, but that with all the force of a divine *ontic*. That is, the Spirit does have an efficacious role in the ontic transformation of the remaining anthropological sphere in full correspondence with the finished reconciling work of Jesus Christ.

A few points of further clarification are required. Against Rosato it is here argued that Barth is much more profoundly affected by his attention to the biblico-historical character of the revelation of the Word of God in the power of the Spirit of God and its appropriation than by the search for a mediating principle between two previously established realities, standing in dialectical tension in a static Idealist scheme. If the Holy Spirit is the particular Spirit of Jesus Christ, how is this Idealistic? Is Barth not attending to the reality of the Spirit of Christ and hence to a *real* mediation? Furthermore, Barth's development of the Holy Spirit has to do with the mediation of the God-man to others, not an abstract gulf between God and human beings. That is, it is union with (the presence of) Jesus Christ as the Son of God which is important. As we shall see, it is impossible to reconcile Rosato's idealistic interpretation with Barth's emphasis upon the basis of the turn from christology proper to its anthropological expression as originating within the narrower christological sphere. For Barth there are not two poles which need to be mediated, but the one pole, the objective person and work of Jesus Christ, which contains within itself the power to establish and uphold the anthropological reality outside of Christ. That is to say the person and work of Jesus Christ, in Barth's understanding, is not limited to an objectivity which prohibits its effectiveness in the subjective reality of the human person. On Rosato's view the person and work of Jesus Christ requires something external to itself to mediate between it and the human person. According to Barth's view the human person is established and upheld on the basis of the inherent life and power of the person and work of Jesus Christ to mediate himself. The very existence

---

59 Ibid., p. 162.
60 Ibid., p. 164.

and reality of the human person in faith is evidence of the self-mediating power of Jesus Christ and his reconciling work. The Holy Spirit then in Barth's understanding is not a mediating principle, a third entity between Jesus Christ and others. The Holy Spirit is rather the creative outward movement of Jesus Christ establishing and upholding all other reality and primarily the human person. Most importantly here, in distinction to Rosato's description, Barth denies the requirement of a mediating principle. Barth adeptly avoids and rejects such a scheme, in part, because of his understanding of the doctrine of the resurrection. That is the self-revelation of Jesus Christ in the resurrection is a lordly and gracious act, and in no way a necessary filler between Christ and others. Barth elects to develop the doctrine of the Holy Spirit in the light of the sovereign and gracious act of God, and not as the sublation of a dialectical tension in an Idealistic scheme. He rather asserts the mediatorial character of the reality of Jesus Christ and his reconciling work. This mediatorial activity, this undeniable consequence and effectiveness, is then an act of the Holy Spirit.

It is interesting that in none of this development by Rosato is the historical character of the revelation of the Word of God taken into account, that is, in particular, the sequential relationship of the crucifixion to the resurrection of Jesus Christ and the fact that the ministry of the Holy Spirit in bringing the Word of God to others comes only after the fullness of the objective atonement culminating in the crucifixion. It is the resurrection that secures this movement as from its christological centre to its pneumatological extension and not vice versa. And it is the reality of the resurrection which insists upon both in their place and sequence. Rosato does not account for Barth's understanding of resurrection as an entirely free, new and gracious act of God.

Must we not admit, however, with Rosato and others, that there is a great deal more to be said, and particularly in light of the resurrection event, concerning the person and ministry of the Holy Spirit, in this case not exclusively as the Spirit of the Lord but also as the Holy Spirit of the Trinity in his own right? The Holy Spirit acts upon the crucified and dead Jesus Christ raising him to newness of life. In this regard we have a clear distinction between the subjectivity of the Holy Spirit and that of Jesus Christ, for Barth has already made clear that the Son is in the position of requiring and receiving the grace of the Father. Included in this is also the basis for a development of the life-giving action of the Holy Spirit. This would do much to fill out Barth's near exclusive christological development of the Holy Spirit in the doctrine of reconciliation. George Hunsinger helps us in this regard with the reminder that Barth reserved the term 'redemption' to refer to the future of reconciliation, which he saw as the primary category for the depiction of the saving work of the Holy Spirit in his own right:[61] 'Whereas from the standpoint of reconciliation, the work of the Spirit served the work of Christ; from the standpoint

---

61 George Hunsinger, 'The mediator of communion: Karl Barth's doctrine of the holy spirit' in *Cambridge Companion to Karl Barth*, ed. By John Webster (Cambridge: Cambridge University Press, 2000), pp. 177–94.

of the redemption, the work of Christ served the work of the Spirit.'[62] Yet we must also say that as regards the doctrine of reconciliation, Barth has, in emphasizing the procession of the Holy Spirit from the Son, left largely undeveloped the notion of the Holy Spirit as proceeding from the Father and acting upon the Son. Further development of the Holy Spirit as life-giving Spirit, as *Creator Spiritus*, would do much to elucidate the power and action of the Holy Spirit as that which overcomes death. In such an account the resurrection itself, and not just the crucifixion, would be more clearly seen as part of the ontological overcoming of the deathly forces which assail and enslave human beings. That is, the resurrection, far from simply the revelation of this victory, is essential to the achieving and enacting of this victory. In this respect we would agree with those who call for further explication in Barth's pneumatology as it is developed in these transitional passages.

The Grounding of the Problem of the Transition in the Trinity

Barth at this point broadens the focus of the discussion to include the more fundamental transition which occurs within the immanent Trinity. The antithesis between Jesus Christ and other human beings illuminates the prior and altogether greater antithesis of the Father and the Son in the Godhead. The antithesis there is present yet overcome through the power of the Holy Spirit in the binding together in loving relationship and unity of the Father and the Son. This is not a move from the specific to the general or from the instance to its rule. Rather this is a move from the revelation in Jesus Christ to the God revealed in him. The being of God is revealed by the Holy Spirit, therefore this is not a search for new information or an exercise in generalization but a responsible reasoning out of what is therein revealed. In this manner Barth grounds the activity of Jesus Christ and his Spirit in the inner life of the Triune God.

Barth begins by noting that the New Testament does not describe the Holy Spirit as the Spirit of Jesus Christ with strict consistency. Rather there are many New Testament passages that refer to him as the Spirit of God, or the Spirit of the Lord, or the Spirit of the Father, or simply as the Spirit. And while he is linked exclusively to these names, he is not linked exclusively to the name of Jesus Christ.[63] Barth argues that while the Pauline and the Johannine writings use the name of the Father and of Jesus Christ when speaking of the origin and nature of the Spirit, greater emphasis and frequency mark 'The more narrowly christological description and derivation.'[64] However, in keeping with the freedom of the New Testament to embrace both a narrower and wider description Barth seeks to understand the wider context of the problem of transition, noting that 'the history which takes place between the existence of the man Jesus and that of other men when there is between Him and them a transition, a communication and a union' has a 'background' in the life of

---

62   Ibid., p. 178.
63   *CD* IV/2, p. 332.
64   Ibid., p. 333.

the Trinity.[65] Since this is the case it is important that we not lose sight of the fact that when we are concerned with the unity between the man Jesus and other human persons we are concerned with the totality of the work of God, and therefore with the totality of the being and operation of the Holy Spirit. According to Barth, in the history of the church God himself is at work 'in His own most proper cause,'[66] not as he is operative in all creaturely occurrence in all space-time history, but in the special manner in which he is at work bringing to fulfilment the original purpose and meaning of creation. It is only in this way that we can rightly think of history and rightly think of God's action in history:

> It is the Christian thought of God which, when it is rightly thought, is kindled from the very outset in the history whose origin is the man Jesus, whose goal is Christendom, and whose centre is the Holy [Spirit] in the living transition from the one to the other. ... What we can and must do is to learn to know God from this history.[67]

It is at this point and in this conjunction of questions concerning the transition from Jesus Christ to others that Barth begins to disclose the contours of his understanding of the divine Trinity: 'That God, who is present and active in this history, is the triune God, Father, Son, and Holy Spirit, has emerged only in outline.'[68] Barth acknowledges that in this history we have a *vestigium trinitatis*, a reflection of the divine Trinity in this history. It is in this light and from this central transition from Christ to others in the power of the Holy Spirit that we are able to see the light of the triune God shining in and over this history:

> The fact that in the third and mediating factor of that history, as in the third and mediating mode of being of God, we have to do with the Holy Spirit, in the one case within the undivided *opus trinitatis ad extra* and in the other in His specific *opus ad intra*, is a provisional confirmation that even the formal comparison of the first and second factors of that history with the first and second modes of being of God (however formal it may be) is no mere speculative venture.[69]

And what does the Holy Spirit do? He takes what is for us hidden and unattainable and places it within our reach. Despite its 'invisibility' and 'inconceivability' we have true knowledge of this transition as we pray that it may take place, our prayer testifying already that 'the Holy Spirit is not for us merely the great unknown.'[70] We can proclaim confidently *Credo in Spiritum sanctum* for it is not the case that we are without him. Rather, 'we know His power and efficiency.'[71]

---

65 Ibid., pp. 333f.
66 Ibid.
67 Ibid., p. 336.
68 Ibid., p. 338.
69 Ibid., p. 339.
70 Ibid., p. 340.
71 Ibid.

However, genuine knowledge of the Holy Spirit in the transition from Christ to us does not diminish or remove his hiddenness and inconceivability. Barth asks concerning the reason for this. What lies behind it? The answer is that 'in this mystery of his being and work in our earthly history there is repeated and represented and expressed what God is in Himself.'[72] That is, we have the revelation of the fellowship of the Father and the Son. In this reality, according to Barth, we have to do with the mystery of the very being of God:

> It is with the unity of God, and therefore with God Himself, that we have to do when we have to do with the Holy Spirit in the event of the transition, the communication, the mediation between Jesus and us. This is what makes the mystery so singular and great. This is why the transition is so invisible and inconceivable. ... It takes place first in God Himself. It is an event in His essence and being and life. It falls straight down from above into the sphere of our essence and being and life, repeating and representing and expressing itself in the occurrence of that history, in the unknown and yet known event of that transition.[73]

In this place of transition God does not cloak himself in something other than his true nature, but is what he most authentically is in himself. His appearance and reality are one and the same: 'Nor does He live an alien life. He lives his own most proper life. The Father lives with the Son, and the Son with the Father, in the Holy Spirit who is Himself God, the Spirit of the Father and the Son. It is as this God that God is the living God.'[74] And again, 'The Holy Spirit is not a magical third between Jesus and us. God Himself acts in His own most proper cause when in the Holy Spirit He mediates between the man Jesus and other men.'[75]

The Divine Problem

In an insightful and important move Barth asserts that this problem of transition is primarily a *divine* problem.[76] That is, it is the 'problem of God's own being, and the answer and solution in and with which, by His own personal intervention in the Holy Spirit, He also answers and solves our problem.'[77] We must be careful, warns Barth, not to conceive of this similarity as an apparent similarity with profound substantial differences, nor as a chance likeness which would identify these two problems as of

---

72   Ibid., p. 341.
73   Ibid.
74   Ibid.
75   Ibid., p. 343.
76   Klappert overlooks this important aspect of Barth's conception of the reality of the resurrection transition in his explication of Barth's doctrine of the resurrection under the rubric of the differentiated relationship of the crucifixion and the resurrection. We must go beyond Klappert to see not only the differentiated relationship but this transition itself, from crucifixion to resurrection, as an essential aspect of the self-revelation of the very being of God.
77   Ibid.

the same structural type though essentially unrelated. The basis of the relatedness and similarity of these two problems lies not in something exterior to them, but in the inner essence and secret of the problem. Their similarity lies in the fact that the Holy Spirit is the power and bond which brings the impossible relationship (transition) into being and sustains it. Thus, the problem cannot be reduced to an inner-worldly solution. The transition of which we speak can in no way come about through created powers and processes. It can come about only as a decisive act of God.

It is crucial to understand that Barth sees in this problem a fundamental and irreducible problem. The problem of the transition from Jesus Christ to others in the resurrection is not a meaningless and unrelated problem, making the resurrection a capricious and disconnected act of God in response to an unanticipated result of his primary saving act on the cross. Rather Barth is concerned here to delineate the depth and breadth, the integrity and comprehensive simplicity of God's saving act. In bringing about the reconciliation of human persons with God in Christ, God has not only acted in true accordance with his inner being, but he has also revealed that being to us.

Barth sees the self-revelation of the ontological reality of the divine Trinity in its work *ad extra* in Jesus Christ. He insists that we must give up our notion of God as defined by our perception of excellencies ascribed to him. He is not the sum total of unrelated, eternal attributes. Such a litany of supposed divine characteristics obscures the revelation of God in Christ by translating and thereby transforming it into a description of abstract and timeless features. We must understand God, rather, as he really is, that is, in the terms of his own self-revelation, and more specifically, in the terms of the problem and solution of this transition:

> God in the Holy Spirit, as He acts and reveals Himself between the man Jesus and other men, is the living God, and as such our God, who really turns to us as the One He is and not under a mask behind which He is really another, because in the first instance distance and confrontation, encounter and partnership, are to be found in Himself.[78]

Barth not only counts on the fact that God has his true being in his act, he also shows how this is the case. The truth of the gospel is that God was in Christ reconciling the world to himself. He did this by bringing sinful human being to death in Jesus Christ, thereby rendering fellowship between Christ and sinners utterly impossible. The transition from Christ to others therefore is wholly impossible. Yet this impossibility is overcome only through the surprising and gracious divine act of the resurrection of Jesus Christ in the power of the Holy Spirit. The Holy Spirit lives and acts and has his being between Christ and us in the same manner as he lives and acts and has his being between the Father and the Son. Thus, in the living and acting and being of the Holy Spirit between Jesus Christ and us we have the truth and revelation of the life, act and being of the divine Trinity. In this way Barth makes the move from the economic reality of God to the ontological reality of God, from the revelation of God in his works *ad extra* to the revelation of God in his life and being *ad intra*.

---

78   Ibid., p. 343.

What is more, Barth asserts that the revelation of the being of God in his act is no general and abstract revelation. It is rather the specific being of God in his act *in partnership*. That is to say: 'What was and is and will be primarily in God Himself ... is history in partnership [*Geschichte in Partnerschaft*].'[79] This is, for Barth, not a peripheral truth of lesser importance, but the fundamental truth of the reality of the triune God:

> What is primarily in God is the transition which takes place in that distance, the mediation in that confrontation, the communication in that encounter, the history in that partnership. God is twice one and the same, in two modes of being, as the Father and the Son, with a distinction which is not just separation but positively a supreme and most inward connexion.[80]

For Barth, abstract notions of being and act have no place in our understanding of God. Only as he reveals his being in his act do we know God as he really is in himself:

> There is no rigid or static being which is not also act. There is only the being of God as the Father and the Son with the Holy Spirit who is the Spirit of both and in whose eternal procession they are both actively united. This history in partnership is the life of God before and above all creaturely life.[81]

Thus, there is movement, relationship and reciprocity within God's eternal being. God has properly within himself an eternal history in which Father and Son partner with each other in the bond of the Spirit. Descriptions of being with static attributes or character are insufficient to this internal original dynamism. The true being of God cannot be known apart from this eternal activity, this dynamic and processive reciprocity of Father and Son.

Furthermore, the being and act which God has revealed is that particular being and act in the transition of reconciled being and action in Christ to us in the resurrection through the power of the Holy Spirit. For Barth says,

> The triune life of God, which is free life in the fact that it is Spirit, is the basis of His whole will and action even *ad extra*, as the living act which He directs to us. It is the basis of His *decretum et opus ad extra*, of the relationship which He has determined and established with a reality which is distinct from Himself and endowed by Him with its own very different and creaturely being.[82]

The being-in-act of the Father and the being-in-act of the Son do not require something greater or higher to hold them together. They are held together unproblematically in

---

79   Ibid., p. 344.
80   Ibid.
81   Ibid., p. 345.
82   *CD* IV/2, p. 345. Here again we have the notion of the transition as part of the perfection of the work of reconciliation, for it brings us into harmony with the same reality in the being of the Trinity.

the bond of the Spirit from all eternity. The Father's begetting of the Son and the Son's being begotten by the Father with the common work of the procession of the Spirit is the one reality of the triune God.

What are we to understand in all of this? Precisely this: that the impossible transition of Jesus Christ *in nobis*, the resurrection of Jesus Christ from the dead, the movement from Jesus Christ Crucified to Jesus Christ Head of the church, has its basis in the perfect eternal ontological relation of the Father and the Son in the Holy Spirit. According to Barth:

> What then, on the one side, is the distance, the confrontation, the encounter and the partnership between Himself and the world, Himself and man, but a representation, reflection and correspondence of the distinction with which He is in Himself the Father and the Son? And what, on the other side, is the transition, the mediation, the communication and the history which He causes to take place ... in the execution of the reconciliation of the world with Himself, but again the representation, reflection and correspondence of the union of the Father and the Son in the Holy Spirit as His own eternal living act?[83]

With this Barth returns, full circle, to the insight with which he opened the discussion, namely that our problem of transition finds its primordial form in the relation of the Father and the Son as bound in the Spirit:

> As the Spirit of Jesus Christ He is no other Spirit in this totality of His presence and action than the Spirit of God or the Father or the Lord – the power of the transition, mediation, communication and history which take place first in the life of God Himself and then consequently in our life, in the relationship of the man Jesus to us.[84]

Thus Barth identifies the problem of the infinite distance between Jesus Christ and us, the problem of the transition, of the turn from Jesus Christ *pro nobis* to us, as grounded and anticipated, encountered and already overcome in the inner life of the divine Trinity.

The Riddle of the Double Passage of the Humiliation and Exaltation of Jesus Christ

Startlingly at this stage, Barth makes the claim that 'in all that we have so far said concerning Jesus Christ, and the reconciliation of the world as it took place in Him, ... we have been speaking in riddles.'[85] This riddle is not a result of the inventive genius of the theologian but rather is the antithesis at the heart of the New Testament witness to Christ: 'All Christian errors may finally be traced back to the fact that they try to efface the antithesis either on the one side or the other.'[86] In the antithesis of Christ and others, in the antithesis of the humiliation and the exaltation in the being

---

83   Ibid., p. 346.
84   Ibid., p. 347.
85   Ibid., p. 348.
86   Ibid.

of Christ, in the antithesis of the command of the Father and the obedience of the Son – in each the riddle is the same. To understand this antithesis in its origin and implications is for Barth to guard against all manner of reductionist revisions of this central problem.

Barth asks concerning the glory of God in this antithesis, for in the end God does not deal with his people in riddles. Rather he openly reveals himself to them. The *Deus absconditus* has become in Jesus Christ *Deus revelatus*. He avers that we must not stop at this antithesis as though it were in itself an 'ultimate paradox.' Barth asserts, 'although we have not to seek its removal, we have certainly to seek its basis in the *doxa* of God, which means again in the trinitarian life of God.'[87] We must move on to consider to what extent in this antithesis we have to do with the being of God himself. Barth narrows his focus to 'the riddle of His [Jesus Christ's] existence,' of 'the necessity of the antithesis which is to be found in it,' and also 'its overcoming.' His question concerning the Holy Spirit, and 'concretely of the Spirit of Jesus Christ' seeks the 'basis' of this riddle.[88] And it is a question which must be asked from two distinct perspectives, from the viewpoint of the humiliation of the Son of God and from the viewpoint of the exaltation of the Son of Man.[89]

We begin with the first part, namely, the *humiliation* of God in Jesus Christ. According to Barth:

> He, the divine and human Light, was wrapped in the deepest concealment. He, the divine and human Judge, was judged. He, the living God and the only truly living man, was executed and destroyed, disappearing into the night of death. This is the one antithesis in the existence of Jesus Christ.[90]

The antithesis concerns the radical difference between the supreme height of the eternal Son of God and the unimaginable depths to which he went in his humiliation. The question concerns how this height and this depth are held together. Does not the one nullify the other? Particularly in this case, does not the humiliation of the Son of God negate his original exaltation?[91] Does he not cease to be the one he was? Barth argues that the work of the Holy Spirit as the Spirit of Jesus Christ is to bring men and women to belief and confession that he is at one and the time exalted in his humiliation, in spite of the immense difficulty presented by the antithesis. The Spirit of Christ as the self-presentation of the living Christ brings about this work between him and others.[92]

---

87   Ibid.
88   Ibid.
89   Ibid., p. 346.
90   Ibid., p. 349.
91   Note that this is an antithesis of movement, a dynamic antithesis, in which the passage from height to depth is made. That is, it is to be distinguished from a static antithesis of attributes or states. The riddle concerns the inexplicable reality that the exalted eternal Son of God can become unfathomably lowly, without negating either of these radical extremes.
92   Ibid., p. 350.

A danger lurks at this point, however, to conceive of this 'conversion, faith and confession' as a marvel, a miraculous act of God in which the impossible is rendered possible and actual. Barth warns against a notion of the Holy Spirit as a 'great magician who makes this possible.'[93] We cannot understand this move as a special, unusual and unnatural act of the Spirit of God in which he performs a function required by circumstances external to the reality of God, that is, the circumstance of the distance between Jesus Christ and us others. Rejecting this course of reasoning Barth inquires concerning the underlying foundation of this puzzle, that is, 'the necessity of this antithesis of the existence of Christ, the necessity of keeping to it and not trying to evade it, the necessity with which all Christian faith and confession must relate themselves to it.'[94]

The logic of Barth's argument runs as follows. It is none other than the Spirit of Christ who 'instructs us concerning the necessity of that antithesis in the existence of Jesus Christ.'[95] That is, the Spirit of Christ reveals to us that it is indeed the case that this same Jesus who was crucified is now risen and declared to be the Son of God, and hence it was none other than the exalted eternal Son of God himself who humbled himself completely, taking the path of obedience even to his ignominious death on the cross. The Spirit of Christ leads us to understand and testify that this antithesis, this great height and depth, is in God's action in Christ, and therefore in God himself. Not only so, but the Holy Spirit also instructs us concerning 'all that this means for our existence.'[96] He reveals that all that we are has been gathered up in Jesus Christ and brought with him to its final irrevocable end on the cross. And what can this mean but that what we are in our alien being-in-sin-and-death is under the severest mortal threat? For who we are in Christ is utterly antithetical with who we are in our isolated anthropological sphere.

But the instruction of the Spirit of Christ does not end there for he also leads us to an understanding of 'the overcoming of this antithesis, which means that He leads us to the basis of this matter and sets us on it.'[97] By disclosing the basis of this antithesis in Christ (and therefore in God himself), and establishing men and women upon this firm foundation, he leads us beyond the scandal of the antithesis, so that we no longer recognize it as an untenable impossibility, but see it for what it truly is, namely, the glorious reality of the divine being. The Holy Spirit reveals to us that this humiliation is not a baseless and alien introduction of contradiction into the being of God, but is rather the true, just and gracious way of the Father and the Son in the work of reconciliation. As Barth says, 'He discloses and entrusts to us the will of the Father and the Son, in which the humiliation and death and concealment of the Son of God are resolved.'[98] It is in this way and work that the Spirit of Christ is 'the Spirit

---

93   Ibid.
94   Ibid.
95   Ibid.
96   Ibid.
97   Ibid.
98   Ibid.

of truth' for in him we have the presence, revelation and action of 'none other than the living God, i.e., the trinitarian God.' But this means that:

> the divine freedom of the Father who orders and the Son who obeys is the freedom of the love in which God willed to take to Himself the world and man, and has in fact taken them to Himself in this total way, by His own interposition. This is the twofold but single will of God as it has taken place in the existence of Jesus Christ in that antithesis of exaltation and abasement. For all that it is so puzzling, it is a representation, reflexion and correspondence of the life of God Himself.[99]

In and with this is disclosed the surprising truth that both these realities belong unproblematically to the essential being of God. Both 'the height from which the Father sends the Son, and which cannot be concealed in the human life of the Son as His act of obedience, but necessarily shines out in His existence as the royal man' and 'the depth to which the Father sends the Son, and in which the latter treads the way of His humiliation to the very end as the lowliest of all men'[100] are true and essential and non-contradictory aspects of the being of God. In other words, in the power of the Spirit of Christ, God reveals himself to comprehend within his own essential trinitarian being the freedom for the height of the exaltation and the depth of the humiliation enacted in Jesus Christ in the work of reconciliation. The true God is neither imprisoned in his inexhaustible height of exaltation nor in his unfathomable depth of humiliation.

In Barth's view the Holy Spirit as the Spirit of the Lord is to be understood as 'the power of this witness of the Son of God in His human life as it is declared and received in His resurrection from the dead.'[101] That is to say: 'He is the Holy Spirit ... because He discloses the antithesis which dominates this life in its necessity as the antithesis which is first in God because it is first opened up, but also overcome and closed again, in the will of God.'[102] As the true Spirit, he not only reveals the truth of the reality of the triune God in the work of reconciliation but also brings men and women into a true grasp of and response to this revelation of the being and act of God in Jesus Christ.[103]

Barth moves on to consider the second part of the answer to this riddle, namely, that which concerns the *exaltation* of the royal man Jesus.

> The riddle of the existence of Jesus Christ is not only that of His humiliation but also of His exaltation. ... It is not only that of His death, but also of His resurrection and life. The second aspect of His existence is that the eternal Son of God is self-demonstrated in the

---

99   Ibid., p. 351.
100   Ibid., pp. 351f.
101   Ibid., p. 352.
102   Ibid.
103   Ibid.

exaltation of the man Jesus of Nazareth; that He has revealed the secret of His identity with Him.[104]

Again Barth begins with the understanding that by the work of the Spirit of Christ in revealing the transition from Jesus Christ to us others we know and confess that we are indeed Christians. Easter is our origin and light. There the Spirit of Christ reveals the identity of the Son of God with the Son of Man exalted on the cross, and hence in him the antithesis of the lowliness of the Son of Man and the height of the Royal Man. Again, Easter is not an 'alien marvel' at which we 'gape and stare,'[105] but rather it is the sure place of revelation in which is disclosed the genuine coexistence and dynamic teleology of height and depth and depth and height in the true being of the triune God. By the illumination of the Spirit of Christ men and women have been awakened to a knowledge of the covenant 'fulfilled even on man's side.'[106] Barth explains:

> We not only have a *theologia crucis*, but a *theologia resurrectionis* and therefore a *theologia gloriae*, i.e., a theology of the glory of the new man actualised and introduced in the crucified Jesus Christ who triumphs as the Crucified; a theology of the promise of our eternal life which has its basis and origin in the death of this man.[107]

Here again we are to understand that the antithesis inherent in the existence of Jesus Christ is not an alien matter in need of being overcome, but is rather the necessary 'point of reference,' the inalienable substance and foundation of Christian faith and confession.[108] In this antithesis is revealed *the* inescapable matter which undoes and establishes us anew, the fact that 'in the humiliation of the Son of God there is actualised and revealed the exaltation of the Son of Man, and our own exaltation in Him as our Brother and Head.'[109] But again, what can this mean but the utter dissolution of our human being in our isolated anthropological sphere, for this Son of Man has taken our human being and has exalted it, bringing about 'a new beginning of our human being, which is quite beyond us'?[110] How can the antithesis of our exalted human being in him and our human being apart from him mean anything but the destruction of us in our alien and opposed anthropological sphere?

Barth asserts that Jesus 'is the new and true and royal man, who is triumphantly alive even, and especially, in His death.'[111] But how can what ends in death be triumphantly alive? How can we be assured that he did not exalt human being

---

104   Ibid., p. 353. Barth's equation here of exaltation with resurrection, which he explicitly denied in *CD* IV/1, leads us to believe he continues to adhere to some notion of ontological transformation of human being which occurs in the resurrection.

105   Ibid., p. 354.

106   Ibid.

107   Ibid., p. 355.

108   Ibid.

109   Ibid.

110   Ibid., p. 354.

111   Ibid., p. 358.

in vain? Barth's answer at this point is somewhat indirect and unsatisfying. He reminds us that it is none other than the eternal Son of God, who can do nothing in vain, who has done this. Therefore, even in the death of the Royal Man, he is triumphant. Barth concludes: '"Jesus is Victor" is simply a confession of the majesty of the incarnate Son of God.'[112] While we do not dispute this answer, we note it merely asserts, but does not explain how it is, that the conversion of human being is not nullified in its death. We suggest we must look to the resurrection for the guarantee of the effectiveness of this conversion. We will return to this theme in our final chapter.

Barth carries on with the insistence that individual Christian believers and the community of faith alike do not arrive at this 'second, decisive step of faith and confession' by virtue of the exercise of their own theological imagination or will. It is in no sense an accomplishment of the willing and running of human persons in their own strength. Rather: 'They do so as they are stimulated and empowered by the Spirit, in His freedom.'[113] By referring human persons to, and establishing them upon, the foundation of this riddle in the being and history of God himself, the Holy Spirit demonstrates that he is the Spirit of truth:

> [The Spirit of Christ] is the Spirit of truth because He lights up the life of the man Jesus as the life of the Son with the Father and the Father with the Son; and He lights up the antithesis which controls this life in its necessity but also in its unity, in the dynamic and teleology which are first in the living act of God Himself. He awakens true knowledge and faith and confession because, proceeding from the man Jesus exalted at the right hand of God, poured out and given, He is not merely the gift of the Father and the Son and therefore of God, but is Himself God with the Father and the Son, and therefore the Giver and source of truth, *Creator Spiritus*.[114]

That is, the selfsame Spirit of God who is the basis and power of the antithesis and its overcoming in the life of the God-man, and who is therefore revealed to be the basis and power of the antithesis and its overcoming in the life of the Father and the Son, is also the basis and power of the antithesis and its overcoming of reconciled human being as it is in Christ and unreconciled human being as it is in our alien and opposed anthropological sphere. The Holy Spirit is the promise and reality that we are what we are not and what we are not we are; he is and guarantees the movement from our self-alienation to wholeness, from the radical disintegration of two diametrically opposed and discontinuous selves to the healing and integration of that antithesis. The Spirit of Christ is therefore none other than God himself, properly and inalienably, as the basis and power of the transition between Jesus Christ and others. It is for this reason, Barth claims, that the community of believers can be assured of its ground when it 'hears and obeys' the witness of the Spirit of Christ. It cannot 'give itself too

---

112   Ibid.
113   Ibid., p. 355.
114   Ibid., p. 359.

willingly or wholeheartedly to His illumination and direction'[115] for his witness is the truth and actuality of the essential being of God.

The Manner of The Operation of The Holy Spirit

A further question to be addressed is just how the Spirit of Jesus Christ acts effectively. This again is an explication of the reality of the transition of reconciled being and action in Christ *pro nobis* to us which has indeed occurred in the power and operation of the Holy Spirit. The specific nature of the Spirit's operation between Christ and us Barth describes first as the *indication* of the Holy Spirit which points us to a very definite place of departure, that is, the power and lordship of the man Jesus. Second, the Holy Spirit gives warning or *correction* which is a rebuke of our choice of bondage over freedom. The Spirit works effectively through positive *instruction* and exhortation – a definitive, particular command, not something that can be generalized or abstracted, but specific, positive direction. The question about how the Holy Spirit goes about his work, and, therefore, the question of the power and lordship of Jesus, is our concern.

In this discussion we will return to an investigation of the second major criticism advanced against Barth's doctrine of the Holy Spirit mentioned earlier, namely, that the role of the Holy Spirit so dominates the subjective appropriation of reconciliation as to effectively eliminate all genuine human response. Again, Philip Rosato serves as a prime exponent of such a view.[116] We shall see, however, that Barth has a substantial view of human response as evoked by the Holy Spirit.

Rosato sees the need to restore an interaction between the Spirit of the Creator and the nature of man.[117] Recognizing that Barth sees the Holy Spirit as the transition between the history of God and the history of human beings, Rosato inquires: 'does [Barth] overemphasize the Spirit's role and thus neglect man's part in this process of mediation?'[118] The Spirit's intra-trinitarian function so dominates its economic role that the interaction of human beings and God's Spirit remains underdeveloped. Rosato cannot find a 'new, as yet unrealized future of human nature which man can develop with the aid of God's Spirit'.[119] Says Rosato:

> Barth allows the Spirit Himself, God's eternal mediating principle, to become the sole point of contact between God and man in time as well, so that autonomous human actions lose their right to play even a subordinate part in the divine–human interaction.[120]

---

115 Ibid.
116 Cf. Rosato, chapter 7.
117 Rosato, p. 132.
118 Ibid., p. 135.
119 Ibid., p. 139.
120 Ibid.

The effect of this is 'The Spirit looms so large that man subsequently loses his historical significance in Barth's backward-pointing trinitarian theology.'[121] But our exposition will demonstrate that the large looming of the Spirit in Barth's understanding does not undermine, but rather under girds, the historical significance of the human being.

Barth delineates the specific features of the operation of the Holy Spirit, which possesses the particularity of precisely that transition from Jesus Christ to us. Just as Jesus Christ in his reconciling being and act is a specific and determinate reality, so the transition from Jesus Christ to human persons is a specific and determinate reality drawing its definiteness from the being and act of Jesus Christ himself. Furthermore, the operation of the Holy Spirit in this transition is also distinct and definite as it corresponds to the finished, determinate and differentiated work of Jesus Christ:

> The man Jesus as the exalted and true and new man has definite features, and so too have His power and lordship, so too has the transition from Him to us, so too the power of our participation in His exaltation, and therefore so too the operation of the Holy Spirit.[122]

Barth stresses that this operation of the Holy Spirit is one which has the character of an event that takes place in the relational field of human persons. That is, this operation, because it has to do with the real transition from Jesus Christ to others, has the character of that which occurs between one person and another. It is from this theme – the Holy Spirit as the direction of Jesus Christ to us – that the entire fourth point of paragraph 64 gains its title: 'The Direction of the Son.' It is from the Son of God that direction [*Weisung*] is given to us others.[123]

Indication

Barth defines this direction of the Son through the Holy Spirit in three distinct yet complementary ways. First, 'a direction is an indication, pointing us to a very definite place of departure.'[124] That is to say, the Holy Spirit 'makes the power and lordship of the man Jesus, the fact that He lives, and lives for us, so that we also live in Him, the presupposition which obtains here and now for us.'[125] Barth explicitly denies that persons are placed at the crossroads of decision, for this would be the creation of a 'ghost' and not a true person. The real new human person created by the Holy Spirit corresponds to the definite existence of the true man Jesus. Because 'decision has already been made in the existence of the man Jesus'[126] concerning all other persons, there is no longer a standing in the throes of decision but only the definite direction of the decision of Jesus Christ (for himself and for us in him). It

---

121 Ibid.
122 *CD* IV/2, p. 361.
123 Ibid., p. 362.
124 Ibid.
125 Ibid., p. 363.
126 Ibid.

is the decision of Jesus Christ taken for all others, according to Barth, which grants the fundamental reference of human identity. It is a pointing to the reality of the true human person in Jesus Christ with the announcement: that is what you are! 'This is the basic indicative of the divine direction to the extent that it is an indication; to the extent that its imperative amounts to a simple: "Be what thou art."'[127]

But if this is indeed the case, how is it that men and women fail to understand themselves as such? Barth's answer to this problem refers to the fact that persons continue to question and doubt the truth and reality which the Holy Spirit established with unshakeable certainty. Persons repeatedly fall away from this understanding, seeking to ground their identity upon a false and therefore ruinous foundation. In Barth's view, the human creature:

> thinks and speaks and behaves and acts in a way which ignores that which he already was and is in virtue of the indicative of the Holy Spirit, which ignores his only possibility, his peace with God, his divine sonship, his obedience and usefulness as a good servant of God, in short his true and actual and exalted humanity.[128]

The Holy Spirit works, asserts Barth, to bring the person back to his or her place of origin 'from which he [or she] lives and alone can live.'[129] The Holy Spirit does not place the human person under the heavy obligation of another 'ought' but rather places that person in the field of a liberating 'may.'[130]

Barth accordingly understands the work of the Holy Spirit to be a 'realistic work' in two respects.[131] With respect to the identity of the Holy Spirit, Barth asserts Holy Spirit is really the Spirit of Christ and hence refers men and women to the real being and action of God in Christ. With respect to the work of the Holy Spirit, Barth declares that the effect of the Holy Spirit's operation in the lives of men and women is both a real (effective and definite) and a realizing (a making real) work, for men and women are made real as they embrace their true selves as they are in Christ. Barth then turns to an account of the biblical texts and calls us to the recollection that in the New Testament there is a 'wealth of aorists and perfects and presents used in the description of their [the elect] being and nature as the presupposition of all the later appeals and prohibitions and promises –the characteristic height which gives to this exhortation its momentum.'[132]

Thus, in the work of the Holy Spirit both the instruction that we are truly Christians, that is, that our true human being is in and after Jesus Christ, and the announcement of our freedom so to live is effectively communicated:

---

127   Ibid.
128   Ibid., p. 364.
129   Ibid., p. 365.
130   Ibid.
131   Ibid.
132   Ibid.

'Be strong in the Lord, and in the power of his might' (Eph. 6;10), is a saying which perhaps expresses the heart and totality of what has to be said from this first standpoint of the direction of the Son of God and therefore of the operation of the Holy Spirit – the ontology and also the dynamic of what we have here called His indication.[133]

Correction

The second distinctive feature of the direction of the Son of God given in the Holy Spirit has to do with the negation of false possibilities. That is, the Holy Spirit operates by granting direction in terms of warning or *correction*. This is the critical aspect of the concept which 'has to do with the possibilities selected and grasped by man, and therefore with the use or non-use of the freedom which he is granted at that point of departure.'[134] According to Barth, on the one hand 'the possibility which is selected and grasped in that freedom and from that point of departure is always only the one possibility – a very definite thinking and speaking and willing and acting and behaviour.'[135] However, on the other hand, 'the possibilities selected and grasped in a lack of freedom are always characterised by the fact that they are many, the one being preferred to the other by accident or caprice, rationally or irrationally.'[136]

In Barth's view 'We are already free in Jesus' although we conduct ourselves 'as if we were not free, ... as if we ourselves were not already exalted and renewed and sanctified in the man Jesus.'[137] The tendency is to revert to our place and condition apart from Christ. 'We place ourselves under the judgment and rejection which Jesus has borne for us too, and from which we too are liberated in Him.'[138] It is in the operation of the Holy Spirit, says Barth, that both the possibility of false humanity rejected in Jesus Christ and the possibility of true humanity created and accepted in Jesus Christ are distinguished and made manifest:

> The Holy Spirit knows and distinguishes and separates in the man to and in whom He works the new man ... from the old man who is already superseded in the existence of the man Jesus, who continually stirs and moves in us as if he still had a right and place there, with all the reason and unreason, the cleverness and folly, of his enterprises and adventures, with the whole range of his activity and indolence.[139]

At issue here, claims Barth, is the matter of the transition from Jesus Christ to us, the matter of the recognition and embrace of this transition and of the new human reality as its definite consequence.[140] Says Barth:

---

133   Ibid., pp. 366f.
134   Ibid., p. 367.
135   Ibid.
136   Ibid.
137   Ibid.
138   Ibid.
139   Ibid., p. 368.
140   Ibid., p. 369.

In Him we have both our justification and sanctification, both our regeneration and conversion. All this has been done and is in force. ... What is at issue in the fellowship and operation and direction of the Holy Spirit is that we should accept this, so that it is just as true and actual in our lives as it is in itself.[141]

The operation of the Holy Spirit has to do with both the rejection of the old and false human being in the existence of men and women and the actualization and acceptance of the new and true human being in the existence of men and women. In this way the Holy Spirit's operation is one both of negation and affirmation, of correction and, as Barth brings out more clearly in the third part of his answer, instruction.

Instruction

The third distinguishing feature of the direction of the Son of God given in the operation of the Holy Spirit has the character of *instruction*. It is the positive aspect of this indication, which the New Testament calls exhortation (παράκλησις). Barth is quick to make clear that this instruction is not limited merely to the information or considerations the Holy Spirit advances. The Holy Spirit in his operation of giving instruction 'actually reveals and makes known and imparts and writes on our heart and conscience the will of God as it applies to us concretely here and now, the command of God in the individual and specific form in which we have to respect it in our own situation.'[142] In carrying out his work of instruction the Holy Spirit embarks upon and accomplishes what we, even in our best theological ethics, can only manage to request. What is more, the instruction given by the Holy Spirit is, in Barth's understanding, a highly fixed and determinate one:

> What we are given in it is not merely general principles and lines of action which leave plenty of room for selection in detailed interpretation – as if it were not the details that really matter! On the contrary, He shows us the only good possibility which there is for us here and now in the freedom of our point of departure and which we not only may but must select and grasp in all circumstances.[143]

But the Holy Spirit's critical work of correction is not to be dissociated from or held in tension with his positive work of instruction. The two are differentiated aspects of one and the same operation of the Holy Spirit as the direction of the Son of God: 'As instruction the direction of the Holy Spirit says Yes and Forward at the very point where in its capacity as correction it says No and commands us to halt and retreat.'[144]

In speaking of the life which corresponds to this threefold operation of the Holy Spirit Barth refers to the biblical injunction of walking worthy of Jesus as the Lord:

---

141 Ibid.
142 Ibid., p. 372
143 Ibid.
144 Ibid., p. 374.

> The life demanded and created by the Holy Spirit is one which is 'worthy' of Jesus as the κύριος (Col. I:10), of the Gospel concerning Him (Phil. I:27), of our calling by Him and to Him (I Thess. 2:12). That is to say, it is one which stands in an appropriate and responsible relation to the archetypal and exemplary life of this man. ... Corresponding to the definition of baptism (I Pet. 3:21), it is one long request to God for a good conscience [through] the resurrection of Jesus Christ.[145]

Thus, the power and operation of the Holy Spirit, in Barth's view, is the utterly particular power and operation of the transition of Jesus Christ *in nobis*. In the form of indication, correction and instruction the Holy Spirit lives between Jesus Christ and us causing us to be seized by that which is ours in Jesus Christ, and causing us to seize the same. It is the Holy Spirit who sets us free in the specific freedom of reconciled being and action.

Conclusion

The question with which we began this chapter was 'If the event of the crucifixion of Jesus Christ precludes penetration to its inner truth, as the reality of the utter concealment of death entails, how are we to know and take ourselves as included in it?' Barth's answer, as we have said, is the resurrection of Jesus Christ (and us in him). The resurrection of Jesus Christ then constitutes the transition from the narrower christological sphere to the anthropological sphere in the life and power of the Holy Spirit. Barth has made it clear that the resurrection of Jesus Christ is not to be seen as the sign of his exaltation. It is rather to be understood as the effective revelation of reconciled being and action in Jesus Christ, the transition of this from him to us. What is concealed in Christ in his crucifixion is reconciled human being and action. This concealment is not partial and therefore able to be 'seen through' from our side. It is rather concealed utterly and completely by divine act. However, this concealed reality is not content in its concealment, not content to remain distant and unknown. It is rather truth pressing for subjectivization. It is an active power, seeking expression in the anthropological sphere opposed to and contradicting it. But this is no impersonal and indefinite power. It is rather miraculous, resurrection power, and therefore none other than the power of God. Thus it is the power of the Holy Spirit, the same Spirit of Jesus Christ. The Holy Spirit of Jesus Christ empowers the transition from Jesus Christ to us, just as he does the transition between God the Father and God the Son. Thus this transition is not merely a problem brought about by the atoning work of Jesus Christ and solved in his self-revelation in the power of his Spirit. It is the very transition in which God lives as God. The resurrection transition is of the same order and profound nature as the otherness and reciprocity between Father and Son in the Holy Trinity, for the same Holy Spirit has his life, being and action in and as these transitions. Thus the problem of the transition from Christ to us is not original, but is grounded in the transition of the Father and the

---

145   Ibid., p. 375.

Son in the Holy Spirit. The Holy Spirit effects the transition from Christ to us in the concrete particularity of the revelation of reconciled being and action in Christ to us. In all of this Barth has asserted that the resurrection of Jesus Christ is his effective turning to us, embracing us and being embraced by us in the encounter grounded, established and sustained by his Spirit.

Chapter Seven

The Resurrection as the Presence and Promise of the Future

In Barth's discussion of 'The Promise of the Spirit'[1] he comes once again to the question of the transition from the christological sphere in the narrower sense to the anthropological sphere. Beyond doubt is the conviction of the New Testament that this transition of Jesus Christ *in nobis* is real and effective. What has yet to be expounded is the crucial truth that the Reconciler is not only the Justifier and the Sanctifier, but he is also the Mediator of this reality. That is, Jesus Christ, in his own being and action, glorifies himself in and among and through human beings, such that the human being is ordered and set free for a receptive and active participation in his glory. As Barth summarily pronounces:

> He discloses and manifests and announces and imparts Himself, moving out from Himself to where He and His being and work are not yet known and perceived, to where there is not yet any awareness of the alteration in Him of the situation between God and man.[2]

Leaving no uncertainty as to the significance of the resurrection in this turn, Barth affirms, 'it is the reference to the living Jesus Christ risen from the dead which makes it possible and necessary for us to give this particular answer to our question.'[3] Once again, the focus of our attention shall be Barth's understanding of the resurrection as the transition from Jesus Christ to us, and specifically in this chapter, in the light of his mediatorial activity.

As is the case with the first two christological aspects of the doctrine of reconciliation, so with the third (from the standpoint of the Glory of the Mediator), Barth takes the resurrection of Jesus Christ as the point of departure for his subsequent development of the doctrine of pneumatology, soteriology, sin, vocation, the church and the Christian life. At almost every point in the development of this theme, asserts Barth, there is 'urgent cause to return to this starting-point and to realize how far we do actually begin here and how far everything that is to be noted in detail is to be understood in the light of it.'[4] But, we may ask, what is the content and meaning of this turning of the Crucified to us? How does it come about? What peculiar shape does it take? These are the questions Barth addresses in this section.

---

1   *CD* IV/3, §69.4.
2   *CD* IV/3.1, p. 280.
3   Ibid., p. 281.
4   Ibid., pp. 275f.

The primary theme which Barth develops in this regard is the revelation of the primal glory of Jesus Christ in his resurrection. Jesus Christ in his completed being and action is not content to remain enclosed within himself, concealed in the darkness of his crucifixion. The nature of his being is such that it reaches out beyond itself, illuminating and embracing the sphere of other men and women, revealing to them his own identity, and hence the true identity of other men and women in him, with the result that these others respond in a corresponding embrace of him and themselves as they are in him, and in so doing participate in his newness of life. The event of the resurrection is the specific act of this revelation in which Jesus Christ is at once the sovereign subject of this revelation and its peculiar content.

The implications of this comprehensive statement are varied and profound. The first that we shall consider here is the manifestation of the teleological determination of the being of Jesus Christ. That is, in the revelation of his own reconciled being and action he has historical density. His is not a static, timeless reality, but one with and in time. We shall then consider the specific content of this teleological determination of reconciled human being and action, a theme which Barth explicates under the banner of the *parousia* of Jesus Christ. That is to say, the mediation of reconciled being and action in Jesus Christ is a protracted event, an historically extended act with its own distinct beginning, middle and end. Barth takes the resurrection to be the first and basic form of the *parousia* of Jesus Christ, claiming that the resurrection of Jesus Christ is in a manner of speaking a self-transcending event, a reality which opens up a new history, a history which moves towards its new and definite end. The third and final implication which occupies us in this chapter, concerns the nature of the freedom of human persons as they respond to their encounter with the living Word of God. In this section we turn our attention to Barth's handling of the question of the meaningfulness of the delay of the final *parousia* of the Lord. We see how Barth views this delay as the creation of the conditions necessary for free human subjective response to the objective accomplishment of reconciliation in Jesus Christ. Jesus' resurrection is that event which opens and conditions the new history of the transition of reconciled human being and action from Jesus Christ to others, such that others as independent subjects, genuinely and freely correspond to their objective reality in Christ. Let us now turn to a fuller description of these notions.

The Resurrection as the Revelation of the Primal Glory of Jesus Christ

According to Barth, Jesus' resurrection is the revelation of the glory of Jesus Christ in its rudimentary and essential form. The resurrection is not properly understood merely as one salvific event among others; it is rather the defining revelatory event. In it the eternal glory of Jesus Christ is manifested without limitation or defect, the man Jesus of Nazareth is declared and recognized to be the Son of God.

The significance of the resurrection of Jesus Christ can be duly appreciated only when understood as that revelation which moves out from this perfect centre, comprehending and embracing on its way all created reality. From this centre and by the power of its own illumination this glory lights up the whole of history, constituting and revealing all things to be what they are:

> It is to this event that the New Testament witness refers, and on this that it builds, when it speaks of the universality of the particular existence of Jesus Christ, of the inclusiveness of His specific being and action, of the continuity in which He has His own special place but reaches out from it to embrace ours too, to comprehend us men, to address and claim and treat and illumine us as His own people which we are in virtue of His being and action, and thus to find a form among us and in us.[5]

The particular existence of Jesus Christ has universal significance not because it plays into some supposed general quality or characteristic or process of our human being and condition, as though the resurrection of Jesus Christ had captured our reality in some mythical manner. Nor can it be accounted for as the triggering of some powerful law or mechanism hidden deep within the ontological structure of our reality, thereby inciting the transformation of our reality from forces latent within our reality. Rather its universal significance is grounded in the fact that this resurrection revelation moves out from its own perfect centre in Jesus Christ to embrace the reality of other men and women of other times and places. It is only in this particular, purposive, personal movement from Jesus Christ to us that we apprehend and embrace our reconciled being and action in him.

Consistent with his earlier emphasis, Barth's innovative treatment of the resurrection as the way of the Crucified to others underscores the completeness of the work of Christ on the cross. His resurrection does not augment or fulfil his life and death, his completed being and action.[6] The situation between God and the human person was altered and settled once for all in his death. Nothing need be nor can be added. Yet, according to Barth, the culmination of his humiliation in his death, being the full expression of death, involved even the extinguishing of its own light. Hence the great accomplishment made actual in his death would have remained concealed within impenetrable darkness. His completed being and action 'would have remained shut up in Him.' The disciples, the world and we ourselves would have remained irretrievably sealed off from this accomplishment, unaware of it and unaided by it. Without the resurrection event the alteration of the situation between God and human beings accomplished in him 'would have lacked the glory and revelation and therefore the prophetic character of His being and action.' Barth continues by saying that though the life of Jesus would still unquestionably have been the life of the world 'it would not have been light shining in this world and illuminating it.'[7] Barth asserts then that if Jesus Christ had not risen from the dead we are left with the paralysing conclusion:

---

5   *CD* IV/3.1, p. 281.
6   Ibid., p. 282.
7   Ibid.

The world reconciled to God in Him would then be practically and factually unreconciled as though nothing had happened, for it would be in no position to know Him as its Reconciler and therefore itself as the reconciled world, and thus to wrestle positively or negatively with what had taken place for it in Him, and to reconstitute itself as such.[8]

Barth remains indefatigable in his assertion that the alteration of the situation between human beings and God was brought to its completion in Jesus' death, yet he asserts equally strenuously that this alteration is neither declared nor known, and has none of its universal effect, apart from the resurrection event.

Congruent with Barth's depiction of the resurrection event as the revelation of the primal glory of Jesus Christ is his development of the doctrine of revelation in resurrection terms. That is to say that just as was his practice in his development of the objective accomplishment of reconciliation in Jesus Christ, so in his depiction of its outward movement to and embrace of the anthropological sphere, Barth disenfranchises all theological ideas which are not concretely grounded in the reality of Jesus Christ. Such abstract concepts can have no primacy of place in the explication of a theological vision which attempts to hold at its centre the constitutive and representative being and act of Jesus Christ on behalf of all men and women. Contrariwise, Barth sees all theological language as informed and relativized by the reality of Jesus Christ himself. Thus it is that Barth redefines even the notion of revelation by subordinating it to the specific reality of Jesus Christ. Revelation, then, for Barth, is not a loose term derived from a general notion of the noetic traversing of the infinite divide between divine and human spheres. Rather revelation has the specific nature and character of resurrection:

The particular event of His resurrection is thus the primal and basic form of His glory, of the outgoing and shining of His light, of His expression, of His Word as His self-expression, and therefore of His outgoing and penetration and entry into the world and ourselves, of His prophetic work.[9]

That is, the revelation of Jesus Christ has its primordial origin, determination and power in his resurrection from the dead. The substance and meaning of revelation is wholly derived from and relative to the turn of Jesus Christ to us others. Revelation is then, not a superior or more comprehensive reality which in this instance happens to take the concrete form of resurrection. Rather, the revelation of Jesus Christ, in Barth's view, arises from, is wholly commensurate with and exhaustively determined by, indeed, is identical with, the resurrection of Jesus Christ.

The kind of revelation spoken of here then is not that merely of facts demanding acknowledgement or assent, but a revelation demanding fullest appropriation ontologically as well as epistemologically. Revelation, because it has this particular character, cannot be conceived as the simple communication of ideas or experiences. It is rather the communication of Jesus Christ himself, the personal encounter of the

---

8   Ibid.
9   Ibid, p. 281.

crucified and risen Jesus Christ with other human beings. It is, in Barth's terms, a 'noetic with all the force of an ontic.'[10]

At this point the philosophical terms which Barth had employed to explicate the movement of Christ from his crucifixion to his resurrection break apart under the strain. While the ontic-noetic rubric served well to safeguard the notion of the completion of the reconciling work of Christ in his crucifixion and death, preventing us from viewing the resurrection as an addition to that work, Barth's depiction implies that a development of the resurrection of Jesus Christ as merely the noetic counterpart of the ontic reality of reconciliation culminating at the cross is insufficient. But it would be unwise of us at this point to move too swiftly to charge Barth with inconsistency, for this is an instance in which the theological reality breaks free of the constraints of philosophical thought. Barth claims that while the resurrection is the noetic truth corresponding perfectly to the ontic reality of the crucifixion and death of Jesus Christ, the resurrection also has a distinct ontic character and force. This noetic cannot be properly understood apart from its own ontic weight.

In this Barth is in no way admitting a limit to the power of the life and death of Jesus Christ *pro nobis* to effect the fullest ontological transformation of human being such that it stands utterly reconciled to God. Quite to the contrary, Barth is acknowledging that the power of the transition from the Crucified to us is so great that, while it remains inextricably grounded in the ontic reality of reconciled human being and action in Jesus Christ, it confers not only the knowledge of that reality but also the new being corresponding to that reality.

As a result Barth makes the astonishing claim that the resurrection is the movement of the ontological reality of reconciliation in Jesus Christ to others such that it encounters others and in that encounter empowers others to receive and embrace at the same time both its being and the truth of its being. Again, the revelation of this being, because this being – Jesus Christ – is not simply its own being but is as such the origin of all being, also involves the conferring of new being upon those who encounter and receive it. The revelation of reconciled being and action in Jesus Christ not only brings men and women into a knowledge of this reality, but also brings them into a new mode of being which is commensurate with this knowledge.

Again this is not an instance of some greater reality, such as a supposed greater and more general notion of revelation. Barth here reasons from the supreme height and determinateness of the revelation act of Jesus Christ in his resurrection. It does not require to be classified with other similar revelations as instances of an abstract law of revelation. It is rather this resurrection revelation in its utter concretion which is as such the zenith, the quintessential revelation.

The matter may be further clarified by stating once again that, in Barth's view, the doctrine of reconciliation has to do with not only the objective work of Jesus Christ on behalf of men and women, but also with the subjective appropriation of

---

10   Ibid, p. 297.

the same in the world of other men and women. And according to Barth this has a clear and distinct meaning:

> He not only was what He was for the world, *pro nobis* and *pro me* ... but also that, according to the distinctive Easter term, He appeared in this being and action of His, coming forth and showing Himself as ... reconciliation revealed and not hidden ... as not merely the reality of the alteration accomplished in Him but also its eloquent truth. In the event of His resurrection from the dead, His being and action as very God and very man emerged from the concealment of His particular existence as an inclusive being and action enfolding the world, the humanity distinct from Himself and us all.[11]

While Barth does speak of the resurrection as the triumph of life over death, he does not look for the meaning of the resurrection by attempting to understand the difference between death and life as mutually delimiting ideas. Rather he views the resurrection as the revelation of that ontological reality, already established and actual, achieved in the death of Jesus Christ, and as something more. While he is reticent to speak of a further ontological transformation, that from death to life, beyond the death of Jesus, for fear of inadvertent introduction of limitations to the scope and power of the atoning action of Jesus Christ for us, Barth's development does involve a new ontic aspect of the noetic revelation of reconciliation. The cosmos is, for Barth, fundamentally and finally altered in the death of Jesus Christ quite apart from his resurrection. It is without defect reconciled to God. But, at the same time Barth also insists that in the resurrection we have the new creation, the new theatre of time and space, which is a necessary result of the noetic revelation of reconciled human *being*. The resurrection, in Barth's view, does have to do with the power of being, and not only the power of knowing: 'To know Him as ours, as our Lord ... is thus to know the power of His resurrection.'[12]

The risen Jesus Christ is understood to be the power of transition. It is he himself, in person as it were, who comes and reveals himself and in himself us others.[13] This transition then is not simply an epistemological or subjective one, but also an ontological or objective one. The resurrection as such cannot be reduced to a fact or an idea or an historical event or any other humanly reproducible reality. According to Barth if we clearly understand the resurrection we will know that it is never under our control, and therefore we can never cease to be astonished by it. The resurrection will always be the primordial reality, the point from which all our being and thinking and willing and acting begins:

> If it is clear that a positive answer to our question can be based only upon the reality of the living Jesus Christ manifested and known in this way, but that it really is based upon this as God's own act, then this positive answer ... necessarily acquires and has the stamp of the axiomatic, the first and the last, and therefore the self-evident.[14]

---

11   *CD* IV/3.1, p. 283.
12   Ibid.
13   Cf. ibid., p. 286.
14   Ibid., p. 288.

The resurrection is not simply an event which reveals, even as an act of God in vindication of his Son. It surely is this, but it is more. It is the unique, all-determining and unsurpassable event of the turning and revealing of the crucified Jesus Christ *in nobis*.

Resurrection and Hope: The Future Orientation of Reconciled Being

In further exposition of Barth's understanding of the way of the Crucified to us, we must add that the radiance of the glory of the mediator in the resurrection of Jesus Christ also reveals its *teleological* aspect. Here we note that for Barth the revelation of reconciled human being and action in Jesus Christ is not that of a static and timeless reality. It is rather a reality in and with time. More than that, it is an historicizing reality, that is, a reality which creates a new historical reality in which it has its own past, present and future. Consequently it is a reality which orients the human person in hope, laying hold of reconciled human being and action here and now but also eagerly awaiting its certain and final manifestation in the return of Christ. Our understanding of this teleological dimension of Barth's doctrine of the resurrection will be enhanced first by a review of Barth's essential claims with respect to the third christological aspect of the doctrine of reconciliation, to be followed up by an exposition of it as it pertains to the question of the turn from Jesus Christ to others.

Barth's development of the third christological aspect of the doctrine of reconciliation undertakes to explicate 'the teleological determination of the being of man ... in Jesus Christ.'[15] That is, going beyond Luther's contrast of Law and the Gospel and Calvin's 'dialectic of justification and sanctification' and Schleiermacher's sequential treatment of 'regeneration ... and then of sanctification,'[16] Barth develops a third sphere which he describes as 'the moment of the promise given to man in Jesus Christ.'[17] Barth departs from Protestant Orthodoxy's typical description of the calling of God as 'the basis of the entry into the specific state of grace,'[18] taking what he believes to be a view more in keeping with the New Testament, that human being in Jesus Christ is rather 'a being under and with the promise', that is to say 'a being which in its totality is teleologically directed, an eschatological being.'[19] On this view 'calling is man's forward direction to God as his future.'[20] According to Barth we must not fail to give due attention to this 'prophetic element of the being of man reconciled with God in Jesus Christ.'[21]

---

15   *CD* IV/1, p. 108.
16   Ibid.
17   Ibid.
18   Ibid., p. 109.
19   Ibid.
20   Ibid.
21   Ibid.

In Barth's view the restoration of the covenant between God and human beings in the atonement is complete in terms of the justification and the sanctification of the human being as a faithful covenant partner. But though complete in itself, it is not to be understood as an end, but as a beginning. For 'just as God's creation was perfect as the beginning of all His ways with the created order,'[22] so also 'reconciliation, the being of man converted to God in Jesus Christ, is as such a beginning.'[23] Far from merely a *restitutio ad integrum*, the reconciled being of human persons in Jesus Christ is 'a being which is still open for God, open for that which has not yet happened in the restoration of the covenant as such, for that which has yet to happen on the basis of that restoration.'[24] What Barth has in view here is the fact that 'the perfection of the being in Jesus Christ ... has a further extension.'[25] For Barth, justification and sanctification cannot be understood apart from their purpose and goal. Thus Barth understands the 'calling' of the human being as 'a thing apart and additional to his justification and sanctification.'[26] That is, in this calling we are confronted with the grace of God in a still 'new and particular form,' that in addition to making the human being his faithful covenant partner, 'He wills to make something of him, He has for him a purpose, an end.'[27] This dimension of reconciled human being Barth calls 'eternal life.'[28]

Such an understanding of the historical density of the revelation of God in Jesus Christ has specific ramifications for no less a theme than the being of God himself. The implications of this revelation of the historical being of God prevents trading thoughtlessly upon a non-Christian notion of divinity. Barth appropriately warns:

> we must be careful not to form pagan conceptions of God ... as though at bottom God was a supreme being with neither life, nor activity, nor history, in a neutrality which can never be moved or affected by anything, a being with which man can ultimately be united only in rest or in some kind of passive enjoyment or adoring contemplation.[29]

Such a notion of a supposedly supreme being is quite contrary to the New Testament depiction of God. Thus, Barth explains, 'God is historical even in Himself, and much more so in His relationship to the reality which is distinct from Himself. He is the lord of His kingdom, deciding, acting, ruling, doing good, creating peace, judging, giving joy, living in His will and acts.'[30] And thus Barth claims that the human person is given a promised future in this 'as yet unrevealed depth of fellowship with

---

22   Ibid.
23   Ibid., p. 110.
24   Ibid.
25   Ibid.
26   Ibid.
27   Ibid., p. 111.
28   Ibid.
29   Ibid., p. 112.
30   Ibid.

God.'[31] Referring to Luke 20:36, Barth summarizes his description of this complete fellowship, this eternal life, as a being 'like that of the angels in that it is a being in the service of God.'[32]

In addition to this Barth explains that this hope is not an indeterminate one, but rather is the particular hope granted in Jesus Christ:

> Jesus Christ is the divine pledge as such. ... He is the man who lives not only under the verdict and direction of God but also in the truth of His promise. He is not merely righteous and well-pleasing to God and the object of His love, but beyond that He is taken and used by Him, standing in His service and at His side, working with Him, living eternal life, clothed with His honour and dignity and glory.[33]

Jesus Christ is not only the promise and proclamation of our hope, he is also its content.[34] To view Jesus Christ as 'only a means or instrument or channel' for the quite other hope we have, would reduce our idea to nothing more than 'an anthropological concept.'[35] Rather, according to Barth, 'the divine promise of the future of the being of man is ... in every way ... enclosed in Him and indeed identical with Him.'[36] Thus it is that while our reconciled being and action is firmly rooted in the objective accomplishment of Jesus Christ *pro nobis*, it is in his resurrection, in that action in which he turns and moves to the as yet unaffected anthropological world, that the teleological dimension of our reconciled being is revealed, and hence, that time and space is created for the free and independent response of others.

At this point an important clarification is required. We must inquire of Barth wherein lies the basis of this 'new and particular form' of the grace of God. We must determine whether Barth understands this teleological aspect of reconciled human being as secured in the crucifixion and death of Jesus Christ, or as a new aspect of reconciled being conferred in the resurrection of Jesus Christ as an act of the Father upon the Son (and us in him). While Barth's language is somewhat unclear here, it would appear that he is referring to this teleological dimension as a grace conferred in the resurrection. It is difficult to see how it could be otherwise if death was the real goal of the life of Jesus. How could this death be real, if there remained some eschatological aspect of his being? While we must acknowledge that on the one hand Barth claims in the resurrection (and in the prophetic office of Christ) nothing is added to the reconciliation accomplished fully in the crucifixion and death of Jesus Christ *pro nobis*, we must also take into account that on the other hand Barth understands the outward reaching of the reconciliation event, inclusive of its teleological dimension and determination, as a reality grounded in the resurrection of Jesus Christ from the dead.

---

31   Ibid.
32   Ibid.
33   Ibid., p. 115.
34   Ibid., p. 116.
35   Ibid.
36   Ibid., p. 117.

Barth has repeatedly claimed that in the death of Jesus Christ the work of reconciliation has been fully accomplished. But how are we to make sense of this in light of Barth's description above of the resurrection of Jesus Christ as a 'divine noetic with all the force of a divine ontic'? Surely this is an acknowledgement that the Father's act upon the Son is a divine act accomplishing something above and beyond the death of Jesus Christ, and hence that the work of reconciliation also involves the unique work of the Father, the declarative act in which Jesus Christ is raised and vindicated and revealed. Is the resurrection not an ontological transformation effected upon Jesus Christ at the hand of the Father? Does the raising from death to life not qualify as an act in addition to that which was accomplished in the vicarious death of Jesus Christ? Is it not this act alone, quite apart from the crucifixion and death of Jesus Christ, which creates and guarantees genuine human subjectivity other than that of Jesus Christ? Does not Barth's use of the term 'ontic' to describe the force of this divine act suggest that in his understanding we have in the resurrection an event of transforming power of equal ontological weight and significance with the crucifixion? Is it not necessary to view the resurrection as the conferring of this new teleological determination first upon the Son and then upon others in him?

It is perhaps for this reason that Barth's development of the resurrection of Jesus Christ and of his prophetic office have such great similarity, for both have to do with that further ontological transformation – which appears to follow sequentially the justification and sanctification of human being in Jesus Christ – established and revealed in the resurrection, in which human beings are granted new life, that is, new space and time, in which to offer genuinely free and independent, and therefore appropriate, subjective response to the objective accomplishment of reconciliation in Jesus Christ, and at the same time to serve as true partners with God in the fulfilling of this reconciliation. The teleological determination of reconciled being and action must be taken then as a new aspect of the being of Christ conferred by the Father in the resurrection.

What, one may ask, does this have to do with the turn of the Crucified to others? How does this teleological dimension of our reconciled being and action revealed in the resurrection answer the question of the genuineness of the subjective human response *extra Christum* to the objective achievement of reconciliation *intra Christum*? Our answer must be that it is precisely in address of this question that Barth develops the material as he does. Barth underscores the fact that the Father acts upon the Son in the resurrection and in this makes his declaration to the world. Hence, only in the Son is there the reality and the promise of the resurrection of the dead for all other men and women. Therefore, the transition from the objective accomplishment of reconciliation to its subjective appropriation is focused christologically in the particular act of the Father upon the Son. In addition the specific shape of this transition takes the form of declaration, and as declaration, takes also the form of promise, for the declaration itself is a declaration of what is real and true in Jesus Christ but which has still to be experienced as real and true in the as yet 'unevangelized' anthropological world. According to Barth, this inalienable aspect of our reconciled being, this teleological determination, this 'being in a co-operation of service with God' is an aspect of our reconciled being which we lay hold of *in hope*. That is to say, our new being is a coming being. It will be 'a being by the side of God, the participation of man in the being and life of God, a willing of what He wills and a doing of what He does. It will be a being not only as object, but as an active subject in the fellowship of God with the created world and man.'[37] Thus, it is in the teleological dimension of our reconciled being, conferred and revealed in the resurrection, that time and space is created for free and independent human response[38] to the objective accomplishment of reconciliation in Christ.

Resurrection and Ascension

The teleological determination of reconciled human being and action in Jesus Christ requires further explication in terms of the *parousia* of Jesus Christ. We shall turn to this in our next section. But it will prove valuable first to examine Barth's understanding of the relationship of the exaltation of Jesus Christ to his ascension, since Barth shifts significantly from the position of the Reformers in this regard.

Barth takes great care to distinguish between the exaltation of Jesus Christ and his ascension to the right hand of the Father. This he does in contrast to the earlier view of the two as a single occurrence, the ascension having been understood as the visible sign of the exaltation. Barth's correction of the received view rests upon his conviction that the states of Jesus Christ – His exinanition and exaltation – are in no way incidental to his being, but are rather secured in the ontological integrity of his being. That is, human beings do not just happen to occupy an exalted position in Christ, but rather they are reconstituted in Christ in their essential being as those who are exalted. They cannot therefore be removed from this exalted state without ceasing to be the human beings they are. The transformation of human being from humiliation to exaltation, from the condition of sinner to the condition of faithful covenant keeper, according to Barth, is brought about in the reconciling work of Jesus Christ from Bethlehem to Golgotha. In the cross of Jesus Christ this transformation arrives at its culmination and completion. It is thus that human being is reconciled to God. But human being is not only restored to its original covenant keeping condition. It is also set free and empowered to live in free partnership with God. The ascension of Jesus Christ as Lord to the right hand of the Father, from which he reigns over heaven and earth, marks for Barth the calling of human beings into this free partnership with God. Thus, as we shall see in greater detail later, the ascension has, for Barth, real and specific historical significance in the Easter history of Jesus as the transition from the initial to the middle form of the *parousia*.

Not all agree with Barth in this understanding, of course. Among the most cogent objections to Barth's view of the resurrection is that of Douglas Farrow.[39]

---

37   Ibid., p. 113.

38   *CD* IV/3.1, p. 332.

39   Douglas B. Farrow, *Ascension And Ecclesia: On the Significance of the Doctrine of Ascension for Ecclesiology and Christian Cosmology* (Grand Rapids: William B. Eerdmans

In distinction to Barth's notion of the resurrection as the revelation of the history (past, present, and future) and power of reconciliation, Farrow sees the resurrection as a synecdoche, standing for the sum and substance of Judeo-Christian hope. Farrow criticizes Barth for conflating the ascension and the resurrection, and for undervaluing the importance of the absence of Jesus Christ for the church.

In sum, Farrow's critique of Barth stands upon three legs: i) that Barth's largely Chalcedonian christology identifies soteriological verticality with ontological verticality, and thus affirms the chiastic scheme of the descent of God and the ascent of human being; ii) that Barth conflates the resurrection and ascension, and hence does not permit the ascension to speak as a distinct and meaningful historical event; and iii) that Barth has no Jesus-history beyond the resurrection, leaving us with an ambiguous Christ on account of the fact that he is too definitely circumscribed in his history from Bethlehem to Golgotha. The third point follows logically from the second, and both stem from a serious misreading of Barth. The first point is the more substantive one in as much as it accurately represents Barth's position as far as it goes, but it stops short of accounting for this teleological aspect of the being and action Jesus Christ.

It would be wholly inaccurate to suggest, as it would appear Farrow does, that Barth has little or no conception of a meaningful Jesus-history following upon the crucifixion other than the resurrection as simply the revelation of Jesus-history, for Barth's understanding of post-Easter Jesus-history is indeed both substantial and extensive. We must reject Farrow's accusation that Barth conflates the resurrection, the ascension, and the heavenly session of Jesus Christ, insisting that just the opposite is the case. What Farrow himself conflates, Barth's understanding maintains as clear and distinct.

Of concern here is the challenge Farrow's argument presents to Barth's understanding of the simultaneous double movement of the God-man from Bethlehem to Golgotha. What is in danger in Farrow's development of the U-shaped movement of Jesus-history is the affirmation of the sanctification of human being and action in Jesus Christ completed upon the cross. Farrow seeks to emphasize the exaltation of human being into the fellowship of the Godhead, thus averting a docetic view of the resurrection and ascension. Hence, Farrow sees a sequential movement from humiliation to exaltation in Jesus-history, that is, in the movement of humiliation from presence with the Father to the cross and in the subsequent movement of exaltation through the resurrection and ascension to presence with the Father once again. Farrow's challenge to Barth consists in an uneasiness with the notion of the resurrection and post-Easter history of Jesus Christ as simply the revelation of that which was accomplished in fullness in the death of Jesus Christ on the cross. Farrow believes this leads to an understanding of the ascension as little more than the ascension of the Mind, that is, a view of the return of Jesus Christ to the Father without sufficient accounting for his full humanness. Of importance here is the question as to whether the work of Jesus Christ done on the cross was

Publishing Company, 1999).

sufficient to reconcile human beings with God. If this is so – and we must assert it is – Barth insists we must then see this work as inclusive of our sanctification and not only of our justification. If Jesus Christ is our sanctification, and if this work is completed upon the cross of Calvary, then we must acknowledge the work of Jesus Christ in elevating human being and action from the condition of covenant breaker to the condition of covenant keeper in the course of his obedient life from Bethlehem to Calvary. Does such a view of the exaltation of human being in Jesus Christ necessarily lead to the conflation of resurrection with post-Easter Jesus-history, thus undervaluing the ascension and the resultant tension between *Christus praesens* and *Christus absens* as Farrow suggests? In Barth's view it surely does not. Farrow does not seem to have grasped Barth's understanding of the resurrected Jesus as not signalling something beyond himself, but himself in his own beyond.

Of greatest concern for us is Farrow's insistence upon the necessity of 'disentangling ontological verticality from soteriological verticality.'[40] Here, once again, the sufficiency of the work of Christ on the cross is endangered. And this is what Barth works so fastidiously to avoid. Farrow appears to desire the full-scale rejection of the Chalcedonian schema of the two natures of Jesus Christ as in any way equated with his humiliation and exaltation. That is to say, Farrow rejects the strict coordination of any aspect of Jesus' being with his history: 'The only way to break out of this circle and get back on track with the biblical story is to repudiate altogether the identification of states with natures, returning to the more primitive notion of the decent and ascent of the God-man.'[41] We must rather view Jesus-history at every stage as the history of the God-man (God as man) passing through humiliation to exaltation. And thus, Barth's notion of the humiliation of God coincident with the exaltation of human being, culminating on the cross in the death of Jesus Christ is to be rejected. But again, with Barth, we must ask, in what way is the already exalted God further exalted? And in what way is fallen humanity further humiliated? Or are we to think of the God-man as neither exalted (like God) nor humiliated (like human beings), and therefore as some sort of *tertium quid*? Also, Barth's notion of Jesus Christ perfecting human being by offering full obedience from Bethlehem to Golgotha makes sense of the conversion (and hence exaltation) of human being, but in what sense is human being transformed in Farrow's notion of the exaltation of the God-man as the ascension of Jesus to the right hand of the Father? Isn't Farrow attending more to the God-man's presence with the Father? And does this not precisely presuppose the ontological conversion of humanity at the cross? Still further, can we be satisfied with a notion of the resurrection as a synecdoche of Judeo-Christian hope? Is this the resurrection without which Paul says Christian faith is futile, humanity is still in its sins, and Christian believers are of all peoples most miserable? Is this the resurrection by which we have the powerful revelation of Jesus Christ as the Son of God? Thus, while he may have a point that Barth gives relatively brief attention to the ascension, it is doubtful whether Farrow

---

40   Ibid., p. 247.
41   Ibid., pp. 249f.

duly appreciates the profundity of Barth's insight that the humiliation and exaltation of Jesus Christ is not incidental to his being.[42]

Let us now return to our exposition by recalling that Barth's reason for developing the doctrine of the resurrection in the manner he does is that he might explicate the real transition from Jesus Christ to us. If we do not see the exaltation of the Son of Man as coincident with the humiliation on the Son of God, culminating in his crucifixion and death, we shall surely miss the significance of the transition from the crucifixion to the resurrection of Jesus Christ. To conceive of the exaltation of Jesus Christ as a state of being subsequent to and following upon his humiliation is to misconstrue the character and force of the underlying antithesis. And this in turn is to lose the force and power of the real transition brought about in the resurrection of Jesus Christ. In the other words this would not be a genuine transition based upon the free and gracious will of God to act yet again on our behalf; it would not be congruent with the notion of the being and work of Jesus Christ as completed in his death; it would not reflect the gulf between Christ and us but that between the unfinished work of Christ and its completion apart from and external to him.

In Barth's understanding, this transition from Jesus Christ to us, from his crucifixion to his resurrection, necessitates that his reconciling work be complete upon the cross. That is to say, the transition has not to do with the exaltation of Jesus Christ but rather the powerful revelation of Jesus Christ. The revelation of Jesus Christ, and us in him, is a different kind of transition, which has to be seen in distinction from his humiliation and exaltation. This transition has to be seen as that which makes manifest that the humiliation of the Son of God and the exaltation of the Son of Man has indeed occurred in Jesus Christ, and is available and pressing to be apprehended as such in our remaining anthropological sphere.

Resurrection and *Parousia*: The New Coming of the One Who Came Before

We now return to our analysis of Barth's development of the teleological determination of Jesus Christ. And we begin with Barth's lament that in Christian

---

42   For a fuller assessment of Farrow's proposal see Andrew Burgess, *The Ascension in Karl Barth*, pp. 135–61, and Paul D. Molnar, *Divine Freedom and the Doctrine of the Immanent Trinity*, pp. 64–8, 304–6. Oliver O'Donovan offers a much more balanced and accurate interpretation of Barth, claiming that he 'distinguished the resurrection and ascension as "two distinct but inseparable moments in one and the same event": the resurrection is Jesus' "coming from" perdition and death, the ascension is his "going to" heaven and the Father (IV/2, pp. 150ff.).' O'Donovan shows he shares our understanding of Barth in the following comment: 'It is also correct…to focus our attention *primarily* on the resurrection in attempting to comprehend the twofold event as one, for the ascension is an unfolding of the significance of the resurrection, and is included, as it were, in its scope.' Oliver O'Donovan, *Resurrection and Moral Order: An Outline for Evangelical Ethics*, (Grand Rapids: William B. Eerdmans Publishing Company, 1986, 1994), p. 57. Cf. also Paul Molnar, *Scottish Journal of Theology*, Fall 2000, pp. 396–9.

worship and theology, the resurrection of Jesus Christ, despite the great attention paid to it, is not seen in light of its preeminent importance. It is, he claims, rather 'constantly regarded as merely one particular saving event among the many others which constitute the so-called history of salvation.'[43] However, in Barth's view, neither as the demonstration of Christ's deity, nor as the crowning of his life in the conquering of his death, nor as the prototypical model 'of all incomprehensible renewals in the sphere of the creaturely life of nature and spirit, and particularly in that of individual human existence,'[44] nor even in light of the benefits received from it, is the resurrection seriously understood in its particular scope and greatness. The resurrection must be taken, rather, as 'the immediate and perfect prophecy, by a new and specific divine act.'[45] That is to say: 'the Easter event, as the revelation of the being and action of Jesus Christ in His preceding life and death, is His new coming as the One who had come before.'[46] The One who has lived the course of his life from Bethlehem to Golgotha, now, in full possession of that life, has been made the contemporary of all.[47] Jesus Christ, in the fullness of his being and action, has come to us once again. In the power of his resurrection he has not remained aloof and unknown, but he has turned toward us, crossing the great divide between himself and us, presenting himself among us effectively and without reserve. It is in this new coming of the same Jesus Christ, that he encounters us and we others are drawn into free correspondence to him. But his new and effective presence is not undifferentiated. The teleological determination of his new being and ours in him comes to expression. His *parousia*, his 'effective presence,' has a threefold form, in each of which the Easter reality comes to a new and glorious manifestation.

Three Forms of the Parousia

The Easter event, in Barth's development, is the first form of the *parousia* of Jesus Christ, which, though a single reality, takes three forms. The first form is the resurrection, the primal revelation of the glory of the Risen Lord. The form which the *parousia* takes in the time of the community is the revelation of the glory of the Lord through the impartation of the Holy Spirit. This is the form of the *parousia* after the Easter revelation and before the final *parousia* of Jesus Christ. The final *parousia* is the full visible return of Jesus Christ in yet a third form of the unveiling of his eternal glory. According to Barth in each of the three forms of the *parousia* of Jesus Christ we are confronted with the same reality. It is not the case that in one form more or less is revealed than in another. Rather Jesus Christ reveals his eternal glory in various modes or forms: 'Always and in all three forms it is a matter of the fresh

---

43 *CD* IV/3.1, p. 290.
44 Ibid.
45 Ibid.
46 Ibid., p. 291.
47 Ibid.

coming of the One who came before. Always and in different ways it is a matter of the coming again of Jesus Christ.'[48]

Thus for Barth the Easter event, as the first form of this threefold event of the *parousia* is not less significant than the other forms. Rather, 'the one and total coming in its other forms has its primal and basic pattern in the Easter event, so that we might well be tempted to describe the whole event simply as one long fulfilment of the resurrection of Jesus Christ.'[49] Barth refrains from yielding to this temptation, but nevertheless maintains his insistence that, 'there can be no question that in all its forms the one totality of coming again does really have the character, colours and accents of the Easter event. There can also be no question that this is only the first if also the original form of this one totality.'[50] Barth understands the period of the forty days as the first form of the *parousia*, which arrives at its culmination and conclusion in the ascension of Jesus Christ. During this time the revelation of what had taken place in Jesus Christ from Bethlehem to Golgotha was being put into effect and the church in this new life was being established.

With the end of this form of the *parousia* of Jesus Christ comes its second form – His living present and presence in the form and power of his Holy Spirit. This is the time from the ascension and Pentecost to the time of his final apocalypse. Barth maintains the emphasis upon the active presence of Jesus Christ, yet this presence is quite clearly marked by its invisible, inaudible and imperceptible character. Says Barth:

> There began a time in which He was and continues to be and ever again will be directly present and revealed and active in the community by His Spirit, the power of His accomplished resurrection. ... There began a time in which ... Christians ... can recognize in themselves as in others an altered world only in relation to Jesus Christ, only according to the verdict of the Holy Spirit, only by faith and not by sight.[51]

In this second form of the *parousia*, Jesus is present, revealed and active in his community through his Spirit. This, for Barth, is not a detriment or deficiency. It is still the active presence of the risen Christ, though now distinctly in the form of his own Spirit. This form too is the glorious presence of the Mediator. His bodily absence in no way infers that he is not with his own. Rather he is this in the glorious mode which is apprehended only in faith and hope. Hence the light which shines is the light of promise, the sufficient indication of what has already taken place but is

---

48   *CD* IV/3.1, p. 293.

49   Ibid.

50   Ibid., p. 294. Barth discusses the New Testament texts which speak of the *parousia* in the excursuses of pp. 292, and 294f., and from this he develops the *parousia* as the 'effective presence' of Jesus Christ. Cf. also p. 296, where Barth speaks of the three forms of the *parousia* of Jesus Christ in analogy to the doctrine of the Trinity along the lines of a kind of *perichoresis*.

51   *CD* IV/1, pp. 318f.

yet to be made manifest. According to Barth, it is in this time of the Spirit that the promise is universally given, though it is not yet universally manifest:

> The light is shed abroad, of course, over the events of all times, and to that extent it is the indication of the comprehensive alteration of the human situation which has already taken place. It is not yet, however, the ... time of the resurrection of all the dead. Obviously, therefore, it is not yet the time of the fulfilment of the resurrection which has come to them in Jesus Christ.[52]

In the second form of the *parousia*, then, we have not the full light of the altered cosmos but we do have its certain and clear promise. The second form of the *parousia* of Jesus Christ anticipates the third and final form of this *parousia* when he comes in fully disclosed glory and majesty.

According to Barth the time of the community in the world and the development of the New Testament belongs to this time, the second form of the *parousia*, and recognizes itself as such. It remembers both the life and death of Jesus as seen in the light of the first form of the *parousia*:

> It understands and attests the Crucified, therefore, as the Resurrected, the One who for us took His place for ever at the right hand of the Father, ... who from there speaks and acts and works on earth, in human history, by His Spirit, in the power of His resurrection.[53]

And, in Barth's view, the New Testament 'understands and reveals Him ... on the clear presupposition that He is no longer present and revealed to his own time as He once was in the forty days.'[54] For the Early Church, then, there was 'no question of appealing to His remembered form' abstracted from the verdict of the Father declared in the resurrection. Barth is quite opposed to any understanding of the faith of the early community of believers which does not have as its basis the time of the first form of the *parousia*, the forty days in which the Resurrected One was revealed and present. It was in the light of this time that the disciples came to understand the meaning and significance of the life and death of Jesus. This is the explanation, says Barth, why it is that 'the interest and art and rules of the historian do not matter' to the composers and editors of the Evangelical narratives. 'What matters is His living existence in the community and therefore in the world. What matters is His history as it has indeed happened but as it is present and not past.'[55] While the ascension marks the beginning of the time in which the manner of the presence of the Crucified is differentiated, it in no way affects 'the action and revelation of the Crucified as He was made eternal and therefore always present in His resurrection and for every age from the days of His resurrection.'[56] Rather according to Barth it indicates that the authors of the New Testament distinguished between the time of Jesus Christ

---

52   Ibid. p. 319.
53   Ibid.
54   Ibid., p. 319f.
55   Ibid., p. 322.
56   Ibid.

and their own, between the eschatological aspect of the presence of Jesus Christ and his presence in our present time in the power of his Spirit: 'The time of Jesus Christ is marked off from their own as not merely present but future, the time which has still to come but is expected and hoped for. And their own time ... becomes to them a time between the times.'[57] It is the time in which the church, understandingly and openly, and the world, unknowingly and secretly, exist in hope of the third and final form of the *parousia*.

But, we may ask, what is the significance of this characterization of our time as a time between the times? How is it that there is a distinction in the forms of his *parousia*? Barth reminds us that the resurrection already makes clear that Jesus Christ is the Lord of time. He understands the threefold form of the text in Revelation not as an analysis of the concept of time but as a witness to Jesus Christ as the Lord of time: 'The verdict of God pronounced in His resurrection tells us that He not only was and is but also will be, not only at the end of time, but as Himself the end of time.'[58] And hence, he is not just one future after which there might be another and then another. Rather, 'He is the absolute and final future.'[59] That is to say:

> The verdict of God forbids the men of the New Testament ... to hope only for continuations of His present in the mode in which He now is the One He was. ... The verdict of God ... commands that they should look afresh to Himself as the final future of the world and man, their own ultimate and definitive future.[60]

From this it is clear that any understanding of Barth's eschatology as merely the history of the revelation of the history of Jesus Christ from Bethlehem to Golgotha, is quite mistaken.

In Barth's view, in the second form of the *parousia* of Jesus Christ, in which we are, there is 'a limitation of His being with us and ours with Him' which cannot be denied.[61] In this time we have 'an indirect and historical connection with Him' and 'there is the isolation of the community which confesses Him in faith and serves Him in love in a world in which He appears to be and remain a stranger.'[62] And so Barth asks: 'Where is the alteration of the human situation, the peace and joy of man converted to God? ... Where is the kingdom of Jesus Christ as it has come on earth in virtue of His resurrection?'[63] Answering, he claims, 'The New Testament was well enough aware of the limitation of its own time and all that is in it.'[64] But this limitation was not the basis of the eschatological expectation of the New Testament writers. Rather the firm promise of a third and final form of the self-revelation of Jesus Christ

---

57   Ibid., p. 323.
58   Ibid., p. 324.
59   Ibid.
60   Ibid.
61   Ibid., p. 325.
62   Ibid.
63   Ibid.
64   Ibid., p. 326.

is inherent to the resurrection itself. It was not the limitation, but the surpassing promise of the resurrection which gave rise to this eschatological expectation.

Dissatisfied with an account of this time between the times which rests contentedly on the absence of Jesus Christ as its basis, Barth looks once again to the resurrection of Jesus Christ, to the revelation of his primal glory, and sees there already an abundant hope in the prior light of which the absence of Jesus Christ is to be understood and embraced. According to Barth, the verdict of God commands that the people of the New Testament look forward to Jesus Christ 'beyond the whole future of their present being in and with Him,' to him as their 'absolute and final future.'[65] Thus, not only is the resurrection the beyond of the crucifixion of Jesus, but within the resurrection order itself there is a beyond, the promise and fullness of the second and third forms of the *parousia*.

The New Testament community lived with a longing for the, as yet, future liberation and redemption, not as a form of escape from a hostile present, but in genuine hope of immediate, unhindered and unbroken fellowship with the Lord, and with him of the fullness of Gentiles and Jews, of the manifestation of their own adoption as sons, and of the general resurrection of the dead:

> The eschatological perspective in which Christians see the Crucified and Resurrected and the alteration of their own situation in Him is not the minus-sign of an anxious 'Not yet,' which has to be removed, but the plus-sign of an 'Already,' in virtue of which the living Christ becomes greater to them and altogether great, ... so that believing in Him and loving Him they can also hope in Him.[66]

Thus, this time between the times, for all its joy, advance and expectation, is a provisional time. But though provisional, it is not contradictory. There can be posited no fundamental antithesis between this time between the times and the future final time. The altered human situation is not further altered: 'There can, therefore, be no question of understanding the alteration as more real and complete in its final form and less real and complete in its provisional.'[67] It merely has a different manifestation in this time from its manifestation in that final time, yet with a forward orientation to and hope for the final time.[68]

The transition of reconciled human being and action from Jesus Christ to us has then this particular character. Jesus Christ has elected to be with us in this threefold manner and form, in which he is fully present and effective, and yet still on his way to us. Thus this movement occurs in the nexus of space and time. It has the properties of historical extension, with its distinct beginning, middle and end. And it is apprehended as such in this in between time only by faith and in hope.

It is important to observe here that Barth's fundamental rejection of what is commonly called historicism – despite its near all-pervasive presence – comes

---

65   Ibid. p. 324.
66   Ibid., p. 327.
67   Ibid., p. 328.
68   Ibid.

clearly into view. He casts off the notion that the world is infinitely extended in time, and its sweeping inference that all possibilities of history are contained immanently within history. Denying that all teleology may be reduced to historical teleology, Barth insists upon a Christic teleology. The end or goal toward which all things move is neither a purely historical reality nor is it generated by purely historical forces. Not all process is purely historical process. For Barth it is crucial that history be taken seriously as history, but when history is called to carry more weight than it can bear, being transformed into the comprehensive interpretive framework for all meaning and value, it loses its status as history.

The Significance of the Resurrection as the First Form of the Parousia

Understanding that the resurrection of Jesus Christ is the commencement of his new coming, we may ask the question of the specific contribution made by this first form of the *parousia*. The answer can be explicated in four parts, in Barth's view, the first having to do with the specific meaning of the resurrection revelation, the second with its historical character, the third with its unlimited scope, and the fourth with its 'absolute newness.'

Barth begins with the assertion that in the resurrection we have the irreversible self-revelation of God in Jesus Christ. Again we note that, though Barth's language here does not emphasize the distinction as sharply as it does in 'The Verdict of the Father' (*CD* IV/1), he sees a dual aspect in this self-revelation. There is surely that side of this singular revelation event which concerns the active self-manifestation of Jesus Christ. This is clearly expressed in the following statement: 'His self-declaration, and in it His coming into the world, to us and all men, has taken place once for all and irrevocably in His resurrection.'[69] But there is also another side of this event, the side which emphasizes the pure act of God the Father upon Jesus Christ, as the presupposition of his resurrection appearances. That is to say, the very fact that Jesus Christ now has power to reveal himself as alive from the dead also reveals that God has acted irrevocably in raising him from the dead. The act of the Father's raising of the Son becomes visible in the Son's manifestation of himself in the newness of his eternal life. This revealing act of the Father has its own specific content, which Barth describes in the following manner:

> In Jesus Christ God has not merely acted as man's Judge and Liberator, restoring and renewing him. In so doing He has acknowledged this action in the resurrection of Jesus Christ. And this means supremely that He has publicly bound and committed Himself to man. ... What we have is a divine noetic which has all the force of a divine ontic. He has spoken in acting. Hence He has spoken unequivocally, once for all and irrevocably.[70]

Thus, God the Father has openly, undeniably and irrevocably announced his divine approval upon Jesus Christ by raising him from the dead. Jesus' resurrection is then

---

69   *CD* IV/3.1, p. 296.
70   Ibid., p. 297.

in this sense the revelation of the irreversible commitment of the Father to Jesus Christ and to all men and women in him.

At this point the question arises as to the sufficiency of the christological concentration of Barth's presentation. Have we, in coming upon Barth's assertion of the act of the Father upon the Son prior to the Son's revelation of the same in his resurrection appearances, identified an extra-christological aspect of the resurrection of Jesus Christ? Does this portion of Barth's theological understanding fall to the charge of christomonism, because he too rigorously defines the resurrection as the turn of Jesus Christ to others when in fact the resurrection clearly involves the action of the Father upon the Son? Our answer to both questions here must be an unequivocal No. The very development of Barth's thought here opposes such an accusation. It is beyond doubt from this passage that Barth's theological understanding involves a subject quite distinct from Jesus Christ himself – namely, God the Father – and hence, rules out any christomonism. However, we must assert that Barth's development of this material accurately reflects the christological concentration of the New Testament, for it is consistent with the New Testament claim that the Father acted exclusively upon the Son. The New Testament knows nothing of an act of the Father which is not first and foremost an act upon the Son. Only in and with his act upon the Son does the Father act upon all human persons. In other words, now that all men and women have been reconciled to God through Jesus Christ the Father does not act upon them independent of their representative, Jesus Christ. He does not raise them all from the dead independently and immediately. Rather he raises Jesus Christ from the dead, and in that act declares the resurrection of all creation in him. That is even in death, in the complete expression of his passion, in his utter powerlessness, Jesus Christ remains the representative of all human persons. Barth's christological concentration in this respect is justified.

The second point which according to Barth must be made regarding the significance of the resurrection of Jesus Christ as the first of three forms of his *parousia* is that as the Easter event took place 'it became a link in the chain of cosmic occurrence.'[71] By this Barth affirms that the resurrection of Jesus Christ is a real and definite event within the nexus of space and time, of immeasurable consequence in human history.

> [T]he divine noetic, God's self-declaration as the One He is in the being and action of Jesus Christ, the prophecy of the divine-human Mediator, has the full force of the divine ontic. ... Now that Jesus Christ is risen from the dead, no man who has lived or will live is the same as he would have been if Jesus Christ had not risen.[72]

---

71   Ibid., p. 298. T.F. Torrance is quite right to note that in sharp contrast to the 'transmutation of revelation into the subjectivities of religious consciousness and Christian experience' of Modern liberal christology, 'Barth's insistence upon the corporeality of the resurrection has the effect of confirming the corporeality, and thus the ontological realism, of the Word made flesh and so of the whole self-revelation of God in Jesus Christ from his birth to his death and resurrection.' (T.F. Torrance, *Biblical*, p. 108.)

72   Ibid.

That is to say, what has taken place in Jesus' resurrection extends beyond the alteration of the relation between God and human persons as already accomplished through the high-priestly and kingly activity of Jesus Christ. The resurrection of Jesus Christ includes also the 'real outworking' and 'manifestation' of this transformation through the exercise of his prophetic office. What has taken place is the fundamental alteration of the cosmos itself:

> [I]n the Easter event it has taken place once for all and irrevocably that God has acknowledged the reconciliation of the world to Himself accomplished in Jesus Christ, and that the world and every man has therefore received a new and positive determination. … Hence we can and should conclude that the new creation has taken place in the resurrection of Jesus Christ.[73]

We may say, then, of the way of the Crucified to us, that it is a creative movement, that is, a transition with all the power of the act of creation, a bringing into being that which was not. That is, in the turn of Jesus Christ to us we have nothing less than the beginning of a processive new creation in which all things are being made new. Again, this is not an instantaneous happening, but an event in and with time recreating all things as it moves outward from its centre, Jesus Christ.

To the question 'what precisely took place in the Easter event between God and the world?' Barth answers that the world has been irrevocably impressed with a total, universal and definitive determination. The significance of the resurrection reaches out to the furthest extremity of the cosmos:

> What the disciples came to see in the appearances of the Resurrected was … the full extent of His work and influence as achieved in His life and death. In its totality, universality and definitiveness it then passed into the reality of world-occurrence, of human existence both in detail and as a whole, of the cosmic being and life which are the presupposition and sphere of human existence.[74]

In Barth's view the specific determination given the world and human persons by the event of the resurrection is a comprehensive one, not merely a possibility but an actual happening in the process of fulfilment. Rejecting the notion that Jesus has come to inaugurate a little 'religious, moral or political agitation or movement,'[75] Barth asserts this determination is 'the work which He has done in place of all men, and God in Him on behalf of all men.'[76] In other words 'the kingdom of God became visible, and came into effective action as this link in the chain of world-occurrence, not under certain restrictions or diminutions, but in total power.'[77]

This determination is furthermore a universal one. Jesus' resurrection was not a private satisfaction given to the disciples alone. Rather the Resurrected appeared to

---

73   Ibid., pp. 299f.

74   Ibid., p. 301.

75   Ibid.

76   Ibid.

77   Ibid., p. 302.

them in order that they may go into the whole world in missionary enterprise. With respect to the universal significance of the resurrection Barth notes that its substance and its manifestation was the risen Lord's 'going out into the world, into all the world.'[78] Barth continues:

> [T]he mission of the community has its ontological ground, its practical basis and its sure point of departure in the universalism of the Easter revelation itself, in which in the impartation of salvation to the whole world has already been effected by the One who alone has authority and power to do it. Heaven and earth, angels and men and all creatures, are already in the resurrection of Jesus Christ set in the penetrating and transforming light of His person and work; ... In the Easter event is grounded the necessity of Christian mission. A Christianity with no mission to all would not be Christianity. For it would not be derived from this event. It would not be gathered and upbuilt by the Jesus Christ risen for all.[79]

Thus the Easter event, the turning of the Crucified to us, has the particular result of establishing and sending the church in its universal mission. That is, as the Crucified himself goes out into all the world, he establishes a people who go with him in this way and mission.[80] This being gathered into his mission is at the same time a free and independent response to his mission.

The determination given to the world in the Easter event of Jesus Christ is moreover a definitive one. By this Barth means that it holds true and good from its beginning through its course to its end. Nothing can interrupt the process of the development of the seed which has been planted. It moves unhindered through its course to its full fruition. Furthermore, 'Neither humanity nor the cosmos as a whole can be given any more excellent determination than that which is given with the planting of the seed of the resurrection of Jesus Christ.'[81] What remains beyond the initial revelation of the glory of the Mediator is simply the timely maturation and fruition of this seed.

We must also note, in Barth's view, that the self-impartation of Jesus Christ in the Easter revelation is absolutely new:

> There did not merely recur a recollected picture of Jesus; He Himself came again. ... The event of Easter Day was that He Himself came again, and that He summoned and awakened men to faith in Him rather than faith in their own faith, and to the proclamation

---

78   Ibid., p. 303.

79   Ibid., p. 304.

80   Of course, as aptly pointed out by David Demson, the gathering, upbuilding and sending of Jesus' disciples – and hence, of the being and mission of the church – has its basis within the identity of Jesus himself. As his identity is revealed in the resurrection, so is that of the church. Cf. David E. Demson, *Hans Frei and Karl Barth: Different Ways of Reading Scripture* (Grand Rapids: William B. Eerdmans Publishing Company, 1997).

81   Ibid., p. 306.

among Jews and Greeks, not of their faith, but of His name and action, of the kingdom drawn near in Him.[82]

It must be asserted that Jesus really did come again from death after death:

> If we are not to be guilty of Docetism in our exposition of the Easter story, to grasp and estimate the new feature in this coming we must see and accept the fact that the glory of God is here present in the personal, real, visible, audible and even tangible coming again of this man. Both as true God and also as true man Jesus Christ was again present in the midst of world-occurrence.[83]

As the Lord risen from the dead Jesus came 'from beyond the frontier of all creaturely life.'[84] To speak of the resurrection, as Christians must, is to speak in the shock of surprise appropriate to the revelation of that which is beyond that which encloses, seals in, and maintains death as the final end of all creaturely possibility. It is imperative that we do not slip into a mode of thinking which would reduce the severity of death as end:

> Death is far too radically serious and sharp a limitation of all human being and action … for us to try to understand the resurrection and return of a man from the dead, and his appearance after death, merely as a human or creaturely possibility integral at some deep physical or metaphysical level to the material or spiritual cosmos.[85]

How then are we to speak of the resurrection? Can we speak of an expanse beyond the boundary of boundaries? In Barth's view the resurrection proclaims something absolutely and continually new, something which appears from beyond the horizon of all human being and existence:

> The radically new thing in the coming again of the man Jesus who obviously died on the cross was not a prolongation of His existence terminated by death like that of every other man, but the appearance of this terminated existence in its participation in the sovereign life of God, in its endowment with eternity, in the transcendence, incorruptibility and immortality given and appropriated to it in virtue of this participation for all its this-worldliness.[86]

The radical newness of the coming again of Jesus into the range of human being and experience cannot but be perceived as absolute anomaly. No scheme of thought and no way of being can comprehend it. It continually breaks apart any and all categories by which one might hope to grasp it. It demands the ongoing surrender to its newness.

---

82   Ibid., pp. 308f. Barth writes here in clear contrast to Bultmann. Cf. p. 308, bottom paragraph.

83   Ibid., p. 312.

84   Ibid., p. 309.

85   Ibid., p. 310.

86   Ibid., pp. 311f.

The work of Jesus Christ – His obedient life and death – has brought about the reconciliation of the world such that it is no longer lost in sin and alienation but has been restored to righteousness and fellowship with the Father. What is made clear in the light of the revelation of the resurrection is that as this world reconciled to God it cannot carry on as it had earlier. The reconciliation of the world to God entails a call to advance. In Barth's words:

> in the appearance of the one man Jesus in the glory of God there was made immediately present as a new but concretely real element in the existence of the world the goal given to the world in and with its reconciliation to God, its future of salvation as redemption from the shadow of death and the antithesis which pursues it.[87]

The radical newness of the resurrection demands the conformity of the world to this newness. The chaos of the cosmos cannot overcome this altogether new ordering reality, but rather must be fundamentally reordered, or better, recreated, in full conformity with this reality which is both new and new-making.

The Possibility of a Post-Easter History

But if all that has been said concerning this determination is true we are faced with the great problem of how we are to do justice to this overwhelming understanding. The problem, according to Barth, is the apparent 'almost complete invisibility'[88] of this determination. How is it that such an extensive determination does not completely and immediately overwhelm us? How is it that this transition does not completely supplant human subjectivity in one sudden overcoming act?

> How was it possible that the world's future already made present there in that event should not at once engulf the whole world like a tidal wave, engulfing with its presence all the men of all times and places whose future had become present there in the appearance of the risen Jesus Christ?[89]

Barth's question is not intended to challenge the reality of post-resurrection history, but to understand it in light of the supreme significance of the resurrection event. He freely acknowledges that in spite of the Easter event there is an opposition, a persistence of the previous form of death resisting the new eternal form of life given to the world in God. But how can this be? What really oppresses the world despite Jesus' resurrection is not 'a lack or failure or absence of its efficacy but simply the fact that this is not evident to us, and therefore its apparent absence.'[90] In Barth's view what God sees is really quite different. The world is already made new and established aright. The apparent non-conformity of the world with its new

---

87   Ibid., p. 315.
88   Ibid., p. 307.
89   Ibid., p. 316.
90   Ibid., p. 317.

reality is simply that – appearance. We do not see it because we do not see reality in the way that God does. That is to say, we do not see the ensuing redemption and consummation which follows upon the accomplished reconciliation of the world through Jesus Christ. God however does see this.

Barth points out that we are confused by the fact that:

> in the Easter event we have to do only with a commencement of the revelation of reconciliation and its fruit in the ensuing redemption and consummation, but not with this revelation in its full development. ... The future of salvation both for ourselves and the world is already present in the resurrection of Jesus Christ. It is present in all its fulness. But this does not mean that it has ceased to be the future in another sphere outside this event, i.e., in the sphere of our own existence and that of the rest of the world.[91]

The possibility of a post-Easter history exists because the introduction of the new into the old is the introduction of a new historifying reality, which does not immediately supplant the old world and history, but recreates it from within. It has been granted a new *fundamentum*, which does not have its full and certain effect instantaneously and without opposition, but which rather unfolds gradually and even contestedly through the course of time, proceeding from its beginning to its inevitable completion.

In coming to answer this question Barth acknowledges that the event of Jesus' resurrection, the presence of the future of salvation, is not entirely invisible and intangible. We must be careful not to 'overlook that which has already visibly and continually followed from the resurrection of Jesus Christ in the form of effects upon world-occurrence and the lives of countless individuals.'[92] In particular Barth points to the *kerygma* and the Christian faith created by the return of Jesus Christ, and the establishment of the Christian community. Barth asserts that the church is itself 'the eschatological fact *par excellence*.'[93] But even this, Barth allows, cannot be 'unequivocally seen and known and experienced in a way which is even approximately similar to that of the resurrection itself.'[94]

The Immeasurable Power of the Light

In a summary paragraph,[95] Barth notes that his development of the doctrine of the resurrection thus far brings us full circle, leading us back to the original question of the power of transition from the crucified Jesus Christ to others. It has become necessary to view the resurrection of Jesus Christ as 'the event in which His glory moved out to grasp the world and us men, in which it became and made history, in which He who came before but was concealed now came again and declared Himself and His work in the world.' In this unique event, argues Barth, we have

---

91   Ibid., p. 318f.
92   Ibid., p. 320.
93   Ibid., p. 321.
94   Ibid., p. 322.
95   Ibid., pp. 323f.

arrived at 'the concrete answer to our question,' specifically, that in his resurrection 'Jesus Christ was declared and became effective as the Word of God in the world reconciled to God with all the power of God and therefore once for all, totally, universally, radically and with definitive newness.' But in and with this answer has come a 'strange and disturbing discovery,' namely, that in this same resurrection:

> the question raises itself again with new vigour in face of this primal and basic form of the self-revelation of Jesus Christ. ... It raises itself as the question of the operation of this power and therefore of the enlightening of our own and all created existence as it does actually take place in virtue of this event.[96]

Furthering his description Barth speaks of the resurrection of Jesus Christ as in some respects a self-transcending reality. The real problem is not that the power of the resurrection revelation is too little, but rather, that it is too great, that is, 'too great to be limited to the one event which took place then and there ... too high, too deep, too comprehensive to be the power of this one event alone.'[97] The power of the resurrection event is so great and so utterly glorious that it immediately throws off the constraints of place and time, determining and filling up every day from this first to the last day:

> As the power of this one event it points beyond it. It bursts through its isolations. It transcends its spatial and temporal limits. It must work itself out in another event filling and controlling all times and places. ... It makes and characterises Easter Day as the day of the proclamation and indeed the commencement of the day of all days, of the last day, of the day of the final return of Jesus Christ.[98]

But how it is that the resurrection can be the revelation of the full accomplishment of Jesus Christ in its complete form and yet not be fully known in our world? Why does the resurrection have this particular form and content? The answer has to do with the nature of the revelation with which the risen Lord has chosen to manifest himself: 'In His revelation as the Resurrected from the dead, Jesus Christ encounters us as the One who ... finds Himself in movement or on His way as the divine-human Mediator, striding from His commencement to the goal already included and indicated in it.'[99] That is, he has chosen to disclose himself not in punctiliar fashion but through the course of an unfolding history, with a beginning, middle and end, all of which is assured from its genesis:

> In His prophetic work He moves from the one Easter Day to the day of all days, to the last day, to the day of His final and conclusive return. In the commencement of His work

---

96   Ibid.
97   Ibid., p. 324.
98   Ibid.
99   Ibid., p. 326.

He already has this goal. ... In this commencement, however, the goal is not yet reached except in Him. It is not yet reached in the situation of the world and man.[100]

In exercise of his lordship, Jesus Christ has elected that the perfection of reconciliation already accomplished in him should find its expression in the anthropological world in the form of an extended historical mediation. The coming of Jesus Christ to his own has a commencement distinct from yet consistent with its goal, as the germ of this goal. The commencement is related to the goal such that the goal is guaranteed in the commencement, nevertheless the commencement is not the goal, but its origin and primal form.

But because the prophetic work of Easter day moves from that commencement to its goal in the day of all days, it must be understood that the anthropological world is not yet at its goal as it is in him. Barth acknowledges ours is a day in which wickedness, evil, suffering and death are still pronounced. In this time between the times, darkness continues to press in against the light:

> It is indeed a fact that the world reconciled to God in Him is far from being a redeemed and perfected world, that wickedness, evil and death are still rampant in it and in each individual. ... But it is only the reflection or epiphenomenon of the fact that our reconciliation and that of the world to God in Jesus Christ is indeed accomplished, and even perfectly revealed in His resurrection, yet that it is not yet at the goal in its character as revelation, but is still on the way, Jesus Christ Himself in His prophetic work as light being still engaged in conflict with the darkness which contests the peace established in Him.[101]

Barth notes that it is Jesus Christ as the resurrected from the dead who primarily and in the first instance endures the persistent rebellion and wickedness of the cosmos. Hence, it is not primarily an earthly or human problem, but a divine problem, a problem of the resurrected one. And in this context Barth alludes to the intercessory role of the Lord Jesus in the present time:

> In short, it is not in the first instance the world, or the Church, or an individual man suffering under and either rebelling against or in some way enduring the conflict, but He Himself, the Resurrected, who is still on the way, still in conflict, still moving towards the goal which He has not yet reached.[102]

It is this priestly activity which T.F. Torrance among others believes to be inadequately developed in Barth. Such a view is difficult to maintain given that Barth assigns such extraordinary significance and detailed development to the post-Easter intercessory ministry of Jesus Christ.

Barth explains the period of the persistence of evil not as something which is forced upon Jesus Christ the Victor by virtue of the force and power of the defeated

---

100   Ibid., p. 327.
101   Ibid., p. 328.
102   Ibid., p. 329.

enemy, but rather as the result of the fact that it is the will of Jesus himself not to be yet at the goal at which he certainly will be at the last day:

> the provisional nature of our situation has its true basis and determination in the fact that it is the good will of Jesus Christ to move from the commencement of His revelation to its completion, not causing the commencement and the completion to coincide, but Himself first to be provisionally who He is and to do provisionally what He does, giving Himself time and place for combat. The world, the community and we ourselves have thus no option but to participate in the fulfilment of this good will of Jesus Christ, to tread with Him the way which He wills to take, to fight with Him the battle which He wills to fight, in short, to follow Him.[103]

In answer to the question as to why Jesus Christ would choose to delay his final *parousia* Barth refers to the gracious opportunity created thereby for the joyful participation of human persons in the administration of the gospel:

> [I]t is His good will because it has as its aim the granting to and procuring for the creation reconciled to God in Him both time and space, not merely to see, but actively to share in the harvest which follows from the sowing of reconciliation.[104]

That is, the risen Lord was not satisfied that his people should be 'merely the objects of His action' but that we should be 'with Him' as 'independently active and free subjects' engaged in the ministry of reconciliation: 'He wills to preserve the world, to cause it to persist, in its present and provisional form, in order that it should be the place where He can be perceived and accepted and known and confessed by the creature as the living Word of God.'[105]

Hence creation is permitted a fullness of reconciliation which includes even its participation in the declaration of its own truth. It is a glorious aspect of the reconciliation achieved in Jesus Christ, that there should be a commencement, duration and goal to the revelation of Easter day, for this commencement, duration and goal established the nexus of time and space necessary to the active participation of human beings in the declaration of the accomplishment of reconciliation. If genuine reconciliation entails the true and free participation of human subjects in the divine service, then reconciliation must essentially provide the form (time-space extension) in which such subjectivity may be exercised. That is to say, it is the will of the risen Lord that we others:

> should be with Him as independently active and free subjects when it is a question of this harvest, of the redeeming and consummating declaration of His life as given for us, of the illumination ... of the world by the reconciliation effected ... by Him.[106]

---

103   Ibid., p. 330.
104   Ibid., p. 331.
105   Ibid., p. 332.
106   Ibid.

It is for this glorious reason that the Lord chooses as he does to move from there to here, to effect the transition from himself to others, in the form of a movement of historical depth and extension from commencement to goal. Barth describes this as the truly kind and good will of Jesus Christ because God did not ignore or overrule the human person, treating the human person merely as an object of his work. Jesus Christ 'did not despise but expected the joy and gratitude and praise of creation.'[107] He chose to provide the opportunity and impetus for human beings to enter into free and active obedience.

The Resurrection as the Ground of Human Freedom

In further address of the question of the meaningfulness of the delay of the final *parousia* Barth considers the external conditions necessary for human freedom in our present place and situation. Among the positive conditions of independently active and free human response is the fact that Christians and non-Christians alike 'are reconciled to God in Jesus Christ.'[108] And in this reconciliation God 'has not reversed nor destroyed nor even in its goodness diminished the first divine work of creation, but rather confirmed and brought it to light.'[109] So then, human beings are free to 'realize their possibilities, use their powers, move within their limits and perform the great or little actions corresponding to their capacities.'[110] 'Time,' Barth notes, 'is allowed and given to them,' and 'our creaturely existence as such has a teleology.'[111] And each creature 'makes use of its freedom in analogy to the teleology of the revelation of accomplished reconciliation.'[112] And among the negative (critical) conditions is the condition of the persistence of evil: 'the declaration [of the reconciliation of the world with God] is still exposed to the power of evil, which is broken in the accomplished reconciliation, but which can still mount its assaults and temptations and acts of violence.'[113] Death, too, says Barth is a sobering condition of our existence: 'However we demonstrate and express our freedom, we can do so only within this limit, on this side of the sharply drawn line of death which is visible from the very first and which will alone be visible at the last.'[114]

Barth inquires furthermore about the specific freedom of those who are yet 'without of the knowledge of Jesus Christ.'[115] It must be affirmed that the being and action of Jesus Christ *pro nobis* is for them too. They too, asserts Barth, 'live under

---

107 Ibid., p. 333.
108 Ibid., p. 336.
109 Ibid.
110 Ibid.
111 Ibid.
112 Ibid. Cf. John Webster's fine work on this theme: *Barth's Moral Theology*, pp. 110ff.
113 Ibid., p. 336.
114 Ibid., p. 337.
115 Ibid.

the condition given to our whole sphere by His return and revelation.'[116] Hence, 'what must be said of the qualified nature of the freedom of all creatures in the midst of His prophetic work applies in all its fulness to them too.'[117] They, too, have time and space; they have meaningful aspirations and futures. They, too, are pressed by the destructive forces of evil. Their existence, likewise, is brief and transitory, ending in death. However:

> Since they do not know the Jesus Christ who in His revelation strides from its commencement to its goal, it is concealed from them that our sphere ... is the time and place in which we may go with and after Him from this commencement to this goal.[118]

Hence Barth says those who are enclosed within these conditions 'are not merely not yet redeemed, but totally unredeemed.'[119] That is, the statement 'There is no peace for the wicked' describes 'their ontic situation as well as their noetic, their external as well as their internal, their objective as well as their subjective.'[120]

We may summarize the implications of these assertions in the following manner. Barth refuses to see our present place and time as an 'interruption' or 'suspension' of the *parousia*.[121] The notion of our sphere as one 'surrounded and effected ... by the presence and action of Jesus Christ' but in some strange manner also 'by-passed' in such a way 'that it constitutes a kind of vacuum in the centre of this event' is, in Barth's view, entirely foreign to the New Testament meaning of *parousia*.[122] Barth objects to the thought that our sphere 'is not touched by His coming again,' that 'He has temporarily relinquished the discharge of His function in favor of the Christian.'[123] Barth claims that 'many conceptions of the situation in the time between the resurrection of Jesus Christ and the conclusion of His new coming' are entangled with a vague notion of a 'pause' or 'vacuum' in the prophetic activity of Jesus Christ,[124] that is, upon 'the substitution of Christianity for His own living presence and action.'[125] Once again it becomes clear that Barth keeps in view the great gulf between Jesus Christ and us and the transition from him to us in the resurrection. Jesus Christ not only has effected the transition, but he is also on the way in this transition from its commencement to its goal, each aspect of which has its own peculiar glory (having family resemblance with the other expressions of this glory) of the living presence and action of Jesus Christ. Roman Catholicism's substitution of Christianity for Christ in this regard must be rejected. Rather Barth

---

116 Ibid.
117 Ibid.
118 Ibid., p. 338.
119 Ibid.
120 Ibid.
121 Ibid., p. 346
122 Ibid.
123 Ibid., p. 347.
124 Ibid.
125 Ibid., p. 348.

emphasizes that Jesus Christ, who '*is* [presently] the hope of all,'[126] is at work among us: 'Jesus Christ Himself is … the hope of all not merely from a far horizon or as an object of recollection and expectation to be contemplated and respected from a distance, but as One who is in the place where we are on the date which is our day.'[127] Barth insists that the *parousia* of Jesus Christ moves forward 'without interruption' directly affecting our sphere, calling and freeing us to follow 'Jesus Christ Himself from His beginning to His end.'[128] It is from this theme that the title of this subsection is drawn: 'The return of Jesus Christ in this middle form … is His coming in the promise of the Spirit.'

By 'the promise of the Spirit', Barth means two things, namely, that 'Jesus Christ as the hope of all is present to us' as both the one 'who promises' and also the one who 'is promised.'[129] In the first instance this means: 'Jesus Christ in the power of His life as the Resurrected from the dead … gives to men the sure promise of His final appearing … and therefore of the redemption and perfecting of the world reconciled in Him.'[130] And in and with this is the 'sure promise of His presence and assistance in its temporal being directed to this goal.'[131] That is to say, 'the Holy Spirit, i.e., Jesus Christ acting and speaking in the power of His resurrection, [a phrase Barth repeats twice in this context] is present and active and among and with and in certain men.'[132] Furthermore, Jesus Christ is not present for these human persons merely 'in fact and objectively,' but rather they 'know Him as the One He is,' and thus, they 'know His presence and work in subjective correspondence with His objective reality.'[133] And as a result these certain men 'who are not yet themselves redeemed and perfected' nevertheless 'awaken from their sleep and dreams to the knowledge, confession and freedom in which they may be Christians and exist as such.'[134] And again, 'the Holy Spirit, i.e. Jesus Christ Himself in the power of His resurrection, sets them on their way in this world which is not yet redeemed and perfected, and accompanies them on this way with His promise of the eternal kingdom and their eternal life.'[135] 'Jesus Christ is' in this sense 'here and now the hope … of Christians.'[136]

The second meaning of 'the promise of the Spirit' is that 'He is promised.' Barth here speaks of non-Christians 'for whom Jesus is who He is' but 'who do not know Him as such.'[137] Regarding these, Barth says:

---

126   Ibid.
127   Ibid., p. 349.
128   Ibid.
129   Ibid., p. 351.
130   Ibid.
131   Ibid.
132   Ibid.
133   Ibid., p. 352.
134   Ibid.
135   Ibid., p. 353.
136   Ibid.
137   Ibid., p. 354.

It is not as though Jesus Christ did not die and rise again for them. ... It is simply that they have turned away from this benefit so fully and unreservedly proffered to them, so that it is of no avail, but hovers as an unknown quantity in the clouds, remaining non-actual among and with and in them, being in a sense wasted on them.[138]

What is not to be forgotten however is: 'Since Jesus Christ has risen for him, His power and that of the Holy Spirit are already on the way to him and on the point of reaching him, ... of giving him the promise, ... of radically refashioning and continually refashioning his existence.'[139] It is as such that we have the new coming of Jesus Christ into our anthropological sphere.

Barth's underscores the fact that Jesus Christ is present in his prophetic function, which takes place here and now, by way of the promise of the Spirit, and asks yet again:

Why is it ... that a history of the prophecy of Jesus Christ must arise at all in these three forms, and must still be in progress for us in this middle form? Why must there be, between the Easter time and the definitive end time, this intervening time, the time of the promise of the Holy Spirit, the time of Jesus Christ as our hope?[140]

Barth's answers that the return of Jesus Christ in this middle form of the *parousia* has its own distinct and specific glory, and thus God's reason for it is more than merely providing an occasion for human beings to enter into expression of the freedom obtained for them through Christ. So great is the majesty of God that he has no need to demonstrate the full accomplishment of the reconciliation of the world in Jesus Christ only in totalizing or complete and final form, but rather can reveal it in partial fashion through historical dynamic development from its beginning to its certain end in an equally glorious fashion: 'We have only to realise how great God is in the fact that He did not refrain from willing to give, and giving, and continuing to give the history of His dealings and fellowship with the world and us men ... this form as well.'[141] What must be remembered is that this time between the times, this day in the resurrection movement of the crucified Lord to us from Easter day to the day of all days, this day of the promise of the Holy Spirit, is 'also a day of Jesus Christ, a day of His presence, life, activity and speech.' More than this, 'it is concretely a day of His coming again in the full sense of the word, of His new coming in glory.'[142] We must then affirm and lay hold of the 'positive thing' about our lives here and now, namely, 'that we do actually take part in the *parousia*, presence and revelation of Jesus Christ as the hope of us all, in the promise of the Spirit addressed to us all.'[143] And above all we must recall, affirm and embrace the primary purpose of the 'ongoing of the history of the prophecy of Jesus Christ which fills our time' – those who have yet to

---

138 Ibid.
139 Ibid., p. 355.
140 Ibid., p. 360
141 Ibid., p. 361.
142 Ibid., p. 362.
143 Ibid., p. 363.

participate as independent active human subjects, corresponding to their objective reality in Christ:

> It is for their sake that it must go forward, that Jesus Christ as the living Word of God is still on the way to-day. Their conversion from ignorance to knowledge, from unbelief to faith, from bondage to freedom, from night to day, is the goal of His prophetic work so far as it has a temporal goal. He wills to seek and to save those who are lost, who without Him, without the light of life, without the Word of the covenant, will necessarily perish.[144]

Conclusion

Once again we have observed that Barth's chief concern is the immeasurably vast gulf between the crucified Lord and others, a separation brought about in the act of atonement itself. Barth affirms with the New Testament that the gulf has indeed been crossed, the transition effected in his resurrection. There can be no question as to the reality and finality of this crossing. What remains to be explained is the manner in which this does indeed occur. In the light of the third christological aspect of the doctrine of reconciliation Barth discusses this transition, not as a timeless philosophical construct, but as a movement of historical depth and extension, a progression from a particular commencement (the resurrection) through a particular middle form (the age of the Holy Spirit) to a particular goal (the final form of the revelation of Jesus Christ). This christological transition in the being and history of Jesus Christ necessarily establishes and incites the corresponding teleological determination of reconciled human being. That is, other human beings, because their true being is in him, also have this historical depth, this transitional movement from beginning to end.

Furthermore, Jesus Christ himself is the revelation and content of this origin and end, this *archē* and *télos* of human being. This revelation of his primal glory does not merely provide opportunity for other genuine subjective response to his objective reconciling work, but rather grounds, establishes and calls forth this response. The resurrection of Jesus Christ from the dead not only reveals the data of his reconciling being and action *pro nobis* but also constitutes the way in which the crucified Lord comes to the as yet unaffected anthropological world, establishing and guaranteeing our free individual subjective correspondence.

Conceiving of the *parousia* as a reality of threefold form, the relationship of which has characteristics similar to the *perichoretic* relationship of the members of the divine Trinity, Barth develops the doctrine of the resurrection of Jesus Christ as the first, primal and definitive form of the revelation (apocalypse) of Jesus Christ. The resurrection event itself is too magnificent, too glorious to be contained in a single day. It has the quality of an historically self-transcending event. Barth's claim that this transition has historical extension, that is, that it is history, in no way diminishes

---

144   Ibid., p. 364.

the reality of the transition from Jesus Christ to us, even though its visibility and effect from our standpoint is partial and contested. To the contrary it identifies and demonstrates its reality, for it brings to light the specific substance and character of this transition. Thus the transition from Christ to us has and involves this historical extension, in which in each moment the fullness of the revelation of Christ is given, but in peculiar form. This particular form of transition determines the nature and shape of human freedom in this time. This is not an inferior history in which the presence of Christ is actually substituted for in the presence of Christianity or the church. It is a real and worthy aspect of the presence of Christ. Notwithstanding that point, the resurrection is the event in which Jesus Christ is quintessentially present.

Chapter Eight

Criticisms and Proposals

Undoubtedly, in the multiple volumes of his masterful theological contribution throughout the years, Karl Barth has provided us with an insightful, thorough and highly nuanced account of the matter of the resurrection of Jesus Christ from the dead. Yet, despite his rigorous and highly consistent presentation some crucial problems remain. It is to a discussion of the most significant of these that we apply our energies in this chapter.

The Resurrection as an Ontological and Salvific Work of God

One rather unclear yet significant aspect of Barth's exposition which has surfaced frequently – if not directly, in its implications – in the course of this study is that of the place and importance of the *Auferweckung* (awakening) of Jesus Christ in this transition. We have come to understand Barth's usage of *Auferweckung* to refer in most instances to the purely divine act of the Father upon the wholly passive – indeed crucified and dead – Jesus Christ, while *Auferstehung* (resurrection) appears to have a broader range of meaning sometimes encompassing the whole matter of the awakening of Jesus Christ together with his resurrection appearances, and sometimes with near exclusive stress upon the latter. That Barth believes the distinction between the two is an important one is clear from his earlier noted statements in *CD* IV/1. However, the distinction between the two terms appears to be less sharp in the material of *CD* IV/2 and *CD* IV/3. The primary question is whether or not Barth includes the *Auferweckung* in the representative reconciling being and action of Jesus Christ *pro nobis*. It is clear at this stage in our study that for Barth the self-revelation of Jesus Christ (*Auferstehung*) adds nothing materially new to Christ's reconciling being and action as it culminates in his death.

The question may at first glance appear to be one of little consequence, more a matter of splitting theological hairs than offering a look into the main corpus of the material. However, a closer observation will take note that the distinction is indeed a significant one, offering insights into what some have considered to be problematic elements of Barth's exposition. For instance, the charge that Barth allows epistemological issues to so dominate his discussion of the resurrection that it is robbed of all ontological character, and its consequent relegation of all post-Easter history, soteriology and eschatology to mere reflections of the cross, is addressed in this question. So also is the criticism that Barth's depiction is so christologically focused that it is insufficiently trinitarian, or that it results in a truncated pneumatology. Following a closer look at this question we will trace out the implications for these problematic areas.

On the surface Barth appears to be making contradictory claims. On the one hand he locates the basis and power of the transition from Jesus Christ to others in the utterly gracious raising action of the Father upon the purely passive Jesus Christ. Yet on the other hand he emphasizes the full achievement of reconciled human being and action, inclusive of the power of transition, in the crucifixion and death of Jesus Christ, quite apart from his actually being raised from the dead.

On the one hand, if Barth is asserting the completion of reconciliation in the death of Jesus Christ such that the resurrection amounts to little more than the proclamation of the fact, then we must agree with those who decry his insufficient development of the role of the Father and the Spirit in reconciliation, of the significance of post-Easter history, and of the authenticity of subsequent human action. If, on the other hand, however, Barth is contending for an understanding of the resurrection as a decisive reconciling event in addition to the being and action of Jesus Christ culminating in his death such that the significance of his atoning work is made relevant and therefore real and powerful in the sphere of other men and women only by means of some extra-christological agency, then we must agree with those who find inadequate Barth's depiction of the exclusively christological basis of reconciliation, soteriology and new human being. But does Barth's construal force a decision for one of these options? Our answer is that it does not. Barth's position is more nuanced than these options allow, though Barth himself does not always take sufficient pains to keep the distinction clear.

Two options present themselves as possible explications of Barth's underlying theological construal of the resurrection which gives rise to his apparently contradictory expressions of the relationship of the objective and subjective aspects of reconciliation. In each case it is affirmed unequivocally that Barth sees the being and action of Jesus Christ as the necessary, inalienable, and indispensable basis of both the objective accomplishment of reconciliation and its subjective appropriation. In each case the subjective aspect of reconciliation is grounded and secured already in its objective achievement. Similarly, each case affirms that the insuperable completion of this reconciling being and act of Jesus Christ *pro nobis* occurs in his entry into the fullness of death. In his representative death human beings have been utterly – without deficiency and without additional requirement – reconciled to God. The pressing question at this point in our quest to understand Barth is 'Does Barth conceive of the passive reception of the Father's awakening grace conferred upon Jesus Christ in his death as a constitutive element of the reconciling being and action of Jesus Christ *pro nobis*?' This is where the two aforementioned interpretive options differentiate. And we must acknowledge Barth is by no means fully consistent in his consideration of this question. On the one hand, the answer may be 'No,' in which case we can make sense of Barth's insistence upon the completion of reconciliation, the alteration of how it stands between the human being and God, in the death of Jesus Christ quite apart from his resurrection. In this case the human being would be utterly justified and sanctified in Jesus Christ, though with no knowledge of it, and therefore, practically speaking, unaffected by it. This option is congruent with Barth's depiction of the incarnation culminating in the crucifixion as the ontic and the resurrection as the noetic aspect of reconciliation, though in this case we would be forced to admit the possibility of an ontic with no corresponding noetic, which in effect undermines the usefulness of the terms. What remains unintelligible with this option is Barth's depiction of the resurrection as the Father's 'answer' to the crucifixion of Jesus Christ, and similarly, the description of the crucifixion as a 'negative event with a positive intention' and the resurrection as a 'positive event with a negative presupposition.' Each set of terms implies a 'differentiated relationship' in which neither the crucifixion nor the resurrection is what it is except in its relation to the other.

On the other hand the answer to our question may be 'Yes, the resurrection is constituent in Christ's reconciling being and action *pro nobis*,' in which case Barth's insistence upon the resurrection as the gracious act of the Father upon Jesus Christ is rendered intelligible. With this option we may still make sense of the completion of the justification and sanctification of the human being in the reconciling being and action of Jesus Christ culminating in his death, but we must understand that the fullness of reconciliation also involves the revelation of this in the resurrection. And in this sense we say the reconciliation of the human being with God is brought to its full expression in the subjective appropriation of the objective accomplishment which is made possible only in the new and gracious act of the Father in raising Jesus Christ from the dead. What is of concern here is whether the noetic aspect of reconciliation was already present in the being and action of Jesus Christ culminating in his death quite apart from the Father's grace of resurrection or whether this aspect was an added dimension to reconciled human being, granted only in the awakening of Jesus Christ from the dead. At points, such as in Barth's depiction of the ontic reality of reconciled being in Jesus Christ as the basis and power of its own truth, that is, as truth pressing for subjectivization in *CD* IV/2, or Barth's construal of the teleological aspect of reconciled human being in *CD* IV/3, in which he expounds the historical and eschatological character of reconciled human being, Barth appears to be acknowledging the former. Yet at other points, such as in his depiction of the resurrection as a new and gracious act of the Father upon the Son in *CD* IV/1, Barth appears to affirm the latter.

This ambiguity is best clarified by the claim that the dominant tendency of Barth's thought is to include the awakening of Jesus Christ in the reconciling work which brings about the conversion of human being from sinful to reconciled. That is to say, Barth usually understands the reconciling being and action of Jesus Christ to come to its completion in his crucifixion and death so long as we understand his death to include his wholly passive reception of the Father's gracious awakening of him. The *Auferweckung* belongs to the ontic moment of the conversion of sinful human being to reconciled, for it is an action *upon* Jesus Christ bringing about the ontological transformation required for the movement from Jesus Christ to others. Only in the *Auferweckung* does reconciled human being receive its teleological dimension and determination. How can that which is given over to death and non-being have teleological and eschatological depth? Human being may be justified and sanctified in the representative death of Jesus Christ, but human being cannot be called except in the awakening call of the Father upon Jesus Christ (our representative even in this). Hence while justification and sanctification are achieved in the death of Jesus Christ *pro nobis*, vocation occurs only in his being raised *pro nobis*.

This understanding of *Auferweckung*, while largely upheld in part-volume one of *CD* IV, becomes somewhat obscured by Barth's use of *Auferstehung* in part-volumes two and three.[1] As mentioned, *Auferstehung* has a broader semantic range for Barth. Depending upon the context, it may refer to the awakening of Jesus Christ from the dead, to the resurrection appearances (His self-manifestation as the crucified yet risen one), to the entire *parousia* in primordial form, or to some composite of these nuances. Most commonly, however, Barth appears to use *Auferstehung* in connection with an emphasis upon the noetic aspect of the reality of the reconciliation, that is, the active self-revelation of the crucified Lord. Our conclusion here is that the logic of Barth's depiction of the doctrine of the resurrection as the transition of reconciled human being and action from Jesus Christ to others trades upon a rather strict and sustained distinction between the *Auferweckung* (the awakening) and the *Auferstehung* (the self-manifestation) of the resurrected one, which his presentation does not often enough make explicit. Whereas in the first part-volume, Barth's use of *Auferstehung* tended to be broad enough to include the Father's gracious act of ontological transformation *upon* the purely passive Jesus Christ, his later use of the term narrows the focus to the self-revelation of the awakened one. Consequently in these contexts the ontic force of the *Auferweckung* is underplayed.

Further support for this claim may be adduced from Barth's unusual use of the terms 'ontic' and 'noetic.' Barth's idiosyncratic use of ontic and noetic categories calls into question the adequacy of these terms in their own right and suggests that his understanding is informed not by the precise philosophical meaning of these terms, but by the theological reality of reconciliation, the depiction of which these terms are called upon to serve. We have already underscored the fact that Barth himself appears to have abandoned strict usage of these terms in favor of a more pliable one. Thus, the ontic reality of reconciled human being and action in Jesus Christ culminating, completed and concealed in his crucifixion and death does not exhaustively account for the full reality of the ontological transformation that occurs to human being in the reconciling work of Jesus Christ. As Barth sees it, the raising of Jesus Christ from the dead at the hand of the Father adds a new and distinct teleological dimension to the reality of reconciled human being in Jesus Christ. While Barth's use of the term 'ontic' – describing the reality accomplished in the being and action of Jesus Christ in his death – serves well to guard against the requirement of any *extra-christological human* work in the achievement of reconciliation, it diminishes the significance of the very important ontological transformation which occurs in the further divine act of the Father in awakening Jesus Christ from the dead. But as long as we understand

---

1   Though even in the later part-volumes the distinction remains firm. Cf., for example, *CD* IV/2, p. 152.

the *Auferweckung* as the awakening of Jesus Christ and of others *only in him*, there is no reason to fear, as Barth appears to do, the admittance of some extra-christological human agency in the objective accomplishment of the conversion of human being. The sufficiency of the representative work of Jesus Christ is not threatened by this.

Barth's use of the term 'noetic' also demonstrates a significant reworking of its meaning, in as much as he is constrained to describe the resurrection not merely as the noetic aspect of the ontic reality, that is, the revelation of the truth of the objective accomplishment of reconciled human being and action in Jesus Christ, but as *a noetic with all the force of a divine ontic*. That is, this noetic carries with it the force and power of ontological transformation. Thus, some further ontological transformation is accomplished in the resurrection which is not accomplished in the death of Jesus Christ, and hence, the resurrection cannot be appropriately conceived of as merely the revelation of the reality accomplished at Golgotha. Though Barth's language appears at times to point in this direction, it is simply inadequate to claim that Barth reduces the doctrine of the resurrection to a consideration of the epistemological consequences of his theory of the atonement. A more consistent depiction of the passion (awakening) and action (self-revelation) of Jesus Christ in his resurrection by Barth might not only have prevented a good deal of misunderstanding, but also provided opportunity to develop the transition of reconciled human being from Jesus Christ to others more thoroughly.

The Resurrection as the Revelation of the Trinity

A further instance in which the matter is clarified when we understand the *Auferweckung* of Jesus Christ as belonging to the reconciling being and action (and passion) of Jesus Christ is that of the role of the Trinity in the transition from Jesus Christ to others. Barth has explicated the resurrection as *the* primordial revelation of God, and while he lays the trinitarian foundation for this, he does not expound it fully. We begin with a closer look at the Father's distinct action. According to Barth, the awakening of Jesus Christ is a purely divine act in which the Father alone is active while Jesus Christ is willingly and wholly passive. Despite his emphasis upon the unity of the divine Subject, Barth insists we must not shy away from the fact that in this event the Father acts upon the Son in grace. But in what manner may we speak of the Father's gracious act upon the Son without violating God's unity as Subject? And does this not imply that we are to speak of the being of the Trinity as not only a being in love, but also a being in grace? We will comment on these in turn, but for the moment we insist that apart from this gracious action of the Father the transition from Jesus Christ to others would be impossible. That is to say this transition of reconciled being and action from Jesus Christ to others cannot be understood as an act of Jesus Christ as the exclusive subject, that is, in the revealing of himself and the sending of *his* Spirit. The Father's participation as subject of this transition is also demanded. Thus, on Barth's account this transition can be accounted for only as a matter involving the full trinitarian reality of the Godhead.

It is surprising that Barth did not do more to develop the connection between the doctrine of the Trinity and the doctrine of the resurrection, for there are striking insights and correspondences which seem to be mutually illuminating. His well-known placement of the doctrine of the Trinity, in distinction even to the Reformers, at the head of his dogmatics, reveals his view of the precedence and preeminence of the doctrine, a view remarkably similar to that which he held as regards the doctrine of the resurrection. As such, the resurrection takes the form of the revelatory and scientific point of departure for his theology, while the doctrine of the Trinity governs its form and content. Similarly, both are seen to be at the focal center of the identity and being of God, and both are at the heart of Barth's understanding of divine revelation. We have already thoroughly discussed Barth's notion of the resurrection as the supreme revelation of God. With this is to be coordinated Barth's resolute conviction that the doctrine of the Trinity is thoroughly bound up with the doctrine of revelation. So convinced is Barth of this that he identifies a trinitarian structure in revelation, as expressed in the famous threefold statement: '*God* reveals Himself. He reveals Himself *through Himself.* He reveals *Himself.*'[2] For Barth, the problem of revelation stands or falls with the problem of the doctrine of the Trinity.[3] Thus in Barth's account of the resurrection we are led to expect the revelation of the depths of God's trinitarian life.

But perhaps because he allows the epistemological rubric of the movement from Jesus Christ to others to so dominate the subject matter of the resurrection, Barth does not take up and develop in full measure his insights regarding the reality of the divine being in the resurrection. As already noted Barth saw the problem of the transition between Christ and others as rooted in the altogether prior problem of the transition between Father and Son in the life of the Holy Trinity, but he develops this in terms of a unity-in-difference in the Godhead without augmenting the description to include the divine being in its own eternal becoming. That is, Barth does not take the next step to extend the parallel of the Father's work in the resurrection into the intratrinitarian dynamic of the Father's eternal begetting of the Son. While Barth sees the resurrection as a matter of the unity-in-difference of Christ and his church, he sees it as grounded in but not tantamount to the problem of the eternal generation of the unity-in-difference of the Trinity. Our contention here is that if we take Barth seriously as regards his understanding of the rooting of the problem of the resurrection within the reality of the immanent Trinity itself, and as regards his unswerving assertion that God in his work is not to be distinguished from God in his being, then we must conclude that the resurrection is an act of God of the same character and effect as that of the eternal trinitarian self-differentiation of his own being. That is, the matter of the resurrection of Jesus Christ corresponds to the matter of the will and way of the eternal God to be God as Trinity. To further clarify our meaning it will be necessary to be reminded briefly, and by no means exhaustively, of the general contours of Barth's understanding of the Trinity.

---

2   *CD* I/1, p. 296.
3   Ibid., p. 303.

For Barth, God's life has a particular and irreducible form, which is characterized by the 'process of generation' in which God is God as Trinity.[4] This is not only one possible, but the only, manner in which God is eternally God:

> As God is in Himself Father from all eternity, He begets Himself as the Son from all eternity. As He is the Son from all eternity, He is begotten of Himself as the Father from all eternity. In this eternal begetting of Himself and being begotten of Himself, He posits Himself a third time as the Holy Spirit, i.e., as the love which unites Him in Himself. As He is the Father who begets the Son He brings forth the Spirit of love, for as He begets the Son, God already negates in Himself, from eternity, in his absolute simplicity, all loneliness, self-containment, or self-isolation. Also and precisely in Himself, from eternity, in His absolute simplicity, God is orientated to the Other, does not will to be without the Other, will have Himself only as He has Himself with the Other and indeed in the Other. He is the Father of the Son in such a way that with the Son He brings forth the Spirit, love, and is in Himself the Spirit, love.[5]

George Hunsinger provides an excellent overview in his 1999 essay, '*Mysterium Trinitatis*: Karl Barth's Conception of Eternity': 'God's life is the process by which he posits himself as the Holy Trinity. His life is a life of free distinction and communion in the *perichoresis* of the Father, the Son, and the Holy Spirit.'[6] According to Hunsinger, Barth understood the Trinity to mean that 'God is self-identical, self-differentiated, and self-unified. God is self-identical in being (*ousia*), self-differentiated in modes of being (*hypostases*), and self-united in eternal life (*perichoresis*).' Or, to put it another way: 'the Trinity is the *perichoresis* of the three *hypostases* in the one *ousia*.'[7] For Barth, it is as this particular trinitarian being that God inalienably *is*:

> The name of Father, Son and Spirit means that God is the one God in threefold repetition, and this in such a way that the repetition itself is grounded in His Godhead, so that it implies no alteration in His Godhead, and yet in such a way also that He is the one God only in this repetition, so that His one Godhead stands or falls with the fact that He is God in this repetition, but for that very reason He is the one God in each repetition.[8]

Hunsinger explains further that God's relatedness to the other is not only a matter of God's eternal will, but also and absolutely, a matter of his eternal being: 'In the trinitarian communion of God's love, the otherness of the other is not lost but enhanced.'[9] In other words, in determining to be God as Trinity, God has so constituted his own eternal being such that his own Godhead involves the positing of

---

4   *CD* II/1, p. 305.

5   *CD* I/1, p. 483.

6   George Hunsinger, *Mysterium Trinitatis*: Karl Barth's Conception of Eternity' in *Disruptive Grace: Studies in the Theology of Karl Barth* (Grand Rapids: William B. Eerdmans Publishing Company, 2000), p. 192.

7   Ibid., p. 190.

8   *CD* I/1, p. 350.

9   Hunsinger, *Mysterium Trinitatis*, p. 190.

the other, who is also completely and without remainder himself. God's own being is ineluctably one of oneness and threeness:

> The threeness in God's oneness is grounded in these relations. This threeness consists in the fact that in the essence or act in which God is God there is first a pure origin and then two different issues, the first of which is to be attributed solely to the origin and the second and different one to both the origin and also the first issue. According to Scripture God is manifest and is God in the very mode or way that He is in those relations to Himself. He brings forth Himself and in two distinctive ways He is brought forth by Himself.[10]

If it is the case that the eternal life of the one God is indistinguishable from his eternal self-differentiation as Father, Son and Holy Spirit, what does this mean for our understanding of the resurrection? With Barth, we must not shy away from the firm reality that the crucifixion of Jesus Christ means his dereliction, that is, his abandonment by the Father and his entry into the full reality of death. And we cannot at this point retract our commitment to the hypostatic union, side with the Docetists, and declare that he entered into the fullness of death in his humanity only, but not in his essential deity. Barth himself speaks explicitly about 'the death of the Son of God on the cross.'[11] It must be asserted that Jesus Christ is as much *vere Deus vere homo* in his death as in his life. But what can his death mean except the utter dissolution of the God-man – not the disintegration of the hypostatic union, but the giving up of the life of this One who is both God and man in indissoluble unity? It is only in this manner that sinful humanity is borne to death in him. God himself has chosen to deal with the plight of humanity in such a manner that he has bound humanity to himself, inextricably linking humanity's destiny to that of the Son of God. As it is for the God-man so it is for the rest of humankind. The death of the Son of God means the death of the humanity he has taken into himself. But this is not the full extent of the threat of the death of the Son of God. It has not only its human-ward implications, but also its God-ward consequence.

The dying of the Son of God must also mean that the perfect unity of the Godhead is threatened. What can we conclude except that the trinitarian being itself is in jeopardy, not apparently but really, not by external constraint but by the free will of God? Barth's understanding of the Trinity involves the notion that God eternally differentiates himself as Father, Son and Holy Spirit. Yet it is precisely God's determination to be God as Trinity that is threatened in the crucifixion of the God-man, for the God-man drinks the full cup of death and in so doing is separated from his Father. The entrance of the God-man into death involves the rejection and removal of this divine other, the turning of the Father away from the Son. It constitutes as such the supreme challenge to God's eternal life, pressing for the reversal of the self-differentiation of God as Father, Son and Holy Spirit. The dying

---

10   *CD* I/1, p. 364.

11   *CD* II/1, p. 663. Cf. also *CD* IV/1, pp. 130, 215, 224, 246f., 253f.; *CD* IV/2, pp. 141, 152, 292f., 399ff.

of the Son of God constitutes a full out assault upon the trinitarian being and life of God.

But still we must ask, if the crucifixion and death of the God-man brings the threat of dissolution to the Trinity, what then do we have in the resurrection? We venture to suggest that the resurrection is the supreme reassertion of God's self-differentiating will and being. That is, the resurrection of Jesus Christ from the dead is to be understood as the reaffirmation, in the face of utter nothingness and dissolution, of God's self-determination to be God as Father, Son and Holy Spirit. This accords remarkably well with Barth's understanding of the Trinity:

> What is real in God must constantly become real precisely because it is real in God (not after the manner of created being). But this becoming (because it is this becoming) rules out every need of this being for completion. Indeed, this becoming simply confirms the perfection of this being.[12]

The resurrection of the Son of God is nothing other than God's reassertion of his own eternal trinitarian being. In the face of death God predicates himself anew as Father, Son and Holy Spirit. The Father, ever and always eternal origin, issues forth his Son in the power of the Holy Spirit. The *Auferweckung* of Jesus Christ stems from this primordial act in the trinitarian life of God. Fully congruent and continuous with the same eternal divine self-differentiation, God reaffirms his trinitarian being in the face of death, whose challenge he has taken because he has bound himself to humanity in its existence under the rule of death. But death cannot extinguish the light of the life of God, for God is God in just the act of freely positing himself and freely positing himself as Trinity. God in his incomparable freedom as God simply re-asserts himself as God, simply wills to be and is the God he is eternally, simply lives in the unitary and self-differentiating existence of the one true God as Father, Son and Holy Spirit. The resurrection of Jesus Christ then is nothing other than the eternal divine life of self-differentiation as Father, Son and Holy Spirit, only now in the face of humanity's great enemy, death. The resurrection of Jesus Christ then is at its root nothing other than the 'intradivine relation or movement' of the Trinity, the '*repetitio aeternitatis in aeternitate*'.[13]

And the fact that the destiny of humanity is bound up with that of the Son of God can mean nothing other than that humanity's destiny is thereby inextricably linked to the eternal life of the Trinity. God thus rescues humanity by taking humanity's death into his own divine life. In his life death's hold upon humanity is broken, for God has so taken humanity to himself in Christ, that humanity through him shares in the eternal life of God, which has as an inalienable aspect of its being the positing of the life of God in self-differentiated and self-differentiating unity. Hence humanity has it as part of its reconciled being the fact that it is unalterably caught up in the eternal life and life-giving reality of God, such that death no longer poses a threat.

---

12   *CD* I/1, p. 427.
13   Ibid., p. 394.

The resurrection is then not only the conquering of the death of Jesus Christ, but the destruction of death, and not for himself alone but for all those gathered in him.

The Resurrection as the Revelation of the Father

Of great significance is Barth's description of the gracious act of the Father as his 'answer' to the crucifixion and death of Jesus Christ. Again the agency of the Father in distinction to that of Jesus Christ is clear, and hence we have the revelation of this transition as a trinitarian act. We differ with Barth, however, in the manner in which he works out the implications of this understanding. Because the resurrection is the Father's answer to the work of Jesus Christ, we are compelled to understand Jesus' crucifixion not only as effecting the condemnation and bearing to death of sinful human being and the perfecting of human being in the obedience of the Royal Man (which too culminates in death), but also as an appeal to the Father's justification of his own eternal trinitarian being, which entails the defeat of death for humankind in Christ. We disagree with Barth then that the Father would have been in the (concealed) right to permit human being, and by implication the Son of God who has bound himself to human being, to remain in the grip of chaos and non-being.[14] To do so would be not only to deny the sanctifying work of Jesus Christ, that is, the conversion of human being in breach of the covenant to human being in faithful fulfillment of the covenant, but also to deny God's own eternal self-differentiation as Trinity. Having rightly earned his reputation as a theologian of the freedom of God, it is not surprising that Barth should make this emphasis. But while it is true that Barth states that 'Godhead in the Bible means freedom, ontic and noetic autonomy'[15], Barth also claims that:

> God's freedom is not an abstract freedom or sovereignty. ... What makes it divine and real being is the fact that it is the being of the Father, the Son and the Holy Spirit, and it is in the fact that they exist in this triune God in His one but differentiated being that God's freedom and love and all His perfections are divine in this concretion.[16]

Certainly at this point Barth is right to stress the freedom of God, effectively refuting every intrusion of the idea of a necessary process of becoming in God, and underscoring the graciousness of this act. But we must ask about the character of the particular freedom of God. Whatever else must be said, the freedom of the Father is surely not a freedom to deny himself. His freedom must be that particular freedom which is true to himself. Barth seems to suggest that the Father would have been perfectly true to himself in this instance, even had he not raised his Son from the dead. It is here that we believe Barth has entertained a notion of the freedom of the Father too far removed from God's original and basic exercise of freedom in his self-disposition to be God in the distinct trinitarian mode of Father, Son and

---

14   *CD* IV/1, p. 306.
15   *CD* I/1, p. 307.
16   *CD* II/1, p. 659.

Holy Spirit. In his early work on the doctrine of God Barth claimed: 'God's eternal fatherhood ... denotes the mode of being of God in which He is the Author of His other modes of being.'[17] How then can Barth also hold that the Father would have been perfectly in the right not to raise his Son from the dead? Is this not tantamount to God's denial of his being as Trinity, for the Father would have been forevermore without his eternal other, his Son? It is in this sense most profoundly that Barth does not sufficiently work out the implications of the resurrection from a trinitarian perspective. Rather at this point Barth should have drawn the implications of his understanding of the eternal life of God as one who differentiates himself in triune existence for his understanding of the resurrection. What we have in the resurrection is God's reassertion of himself in his trinitarian being, but now with the second 'mode of being' of the Godhead inextricably bound up with human being, a union which entails the resurrection of humanity in him.

As a consequence we are furthermore compelled to understand the crucifixion and death of Jesus Christ as in some way a prayerful appeal to the eternal grace of the Father, as a work performed in trust and anticipation of the Father's subsequent act of resurrection. Barth largely overlooks the matter of Jesus entrusting himself to the Father in the face of death. He rather says that Jesus bows his head to death, explicitly passing over the notion that Jesus commits his Spirit to the Father. Barth makes little if not nothing of the faith of Jesus in the Father as he faces the ultimate dissolution of death:

> Anything pointing in this direction [anything suggesting that not everything for the reconciliation of the world with God had taken place at Golgotha], any limitations of the τετέλεσται are quite alien to the New Testament. But the direct continuation of the τετέλεσται in John 19:30 is: και κλίνας τὴν κεφαλὴν παρέδωκεν τὸ πνεῦμα. And the occurrence of Golgotha which is complete in itself consists ultimately in the fact that Jesus 'bowed his head.' What does this mean? In obedience to the will of God? Before God as Father? His obedience consists in the fact that He commends or offers up His spirit, that is, Himself – He delivers up Himself. To whom? To God His Father, to His decree and disposing? Naturally, and this is emphasized in the saying handed down in Luke 23:46: 'Father, into thy hands I commend my spirit,' myself. But there, too, there is the continuation: τοῦτο δὲ εἰπὼν ἐξέπνευσεν. It is therefore to death that He bows His head and commits Himself. In and with the fulfillment there of the will of God it is nothingness which can triumph over Him. ... The reconciliation of the world with God which took place in Jesus Christ had therefore the meaning that a radical end was made of Him and therefore of the world.[18]

Barth argues that while at his death Jesus did bow his head to his Father, it took the particular expression of the bowing of his head to death and non-being, submitting himself without reserve into its grip. Barth chooses this emphasis seeing in it a punctuation of the death of Jesus as the great and final act of his representative reconciling work. The covenant was complete in him in this final act. Nothing further

---

17   *CD* I/1, p. 393.
18   *CD* IV/1, p. 306

was required and hence there could be no need of any further arrangement with or appeal to the Father.

But what does Barth make of the fact that Jesus also committed his Spirit into the hands of the Father? Surely it cannot be that Jesus did not fulfill completely every aspect of God's reconciling purposes committed to him to do. In this regard his action and passion in this life is complete – 'It is finished!' What then is the significance of the commending of his Spirit into the hands of the Father? Can this be understood in any sense other than the committing of his eternal life and being (the Spirit of and in him) to the Father, his expectation in faith that the Father would raise him up from the dead (that is, re-issue the Spirit to him)? It is the handing over of himself without reserve to the grace of the Father in the face of death. And we take note again that this is not grace in any general sense. It is rather the particular grace of resurrection. The Father's raising of the Son is the specific grace of the Father upon the Son. Barth has acknowledged as much. Thus, the Son entrusts himself to the same being, the same life, power, and love of the Father which issues eternally in the trinitarian being of God, with the entailment that he would not abandon him to the grave, but that he would raise him up to newness of life.

For what then is the Son appealing to the Father, except that the Father should restore him (and all who are gathered in him) to eternal life and fellowship with the Father? That is, he commends his Spirit into the hands of the Father in order that he may, by the Father in the power of the Holy Spirit, be raised (that is, begotten as ever and always) into the being and perichoretic fellowship of the Trinity; that he may yet again and despite all assume his place as the Son of God bound eternally both to the Father and to humankind, the God-man who is alive anew and forevermore. This is not to say the Trinity has been dissolved in the death of the Son of God and remade in his resurrection, but that the Son of God has so bound himself to humankind that death's threat against humanity must now also become a threat directly against the trinitarian being of God, a threat which can never be victorious for God simply lives in his freedom to exist as Trinity. The God-man has so bound himself to sinful men that he takes their plight, even their death and destruction, upon himself, such that their end is inextricably bound up with his. Yet it is the very nature of the being of God to will to be God not in isolation, not imprisoned in monadic aloneness, but in fellowship with himself as Father, Son and Holy Spirit. Because it is the will and essence of God to be God in this manner, death has no victory, for God precisely in this moment reaffirms his eternal trinitarian being, this time with human being bound to himself in the being of the second Person. The resurrection is the outward form of God's reaffirmation of himself as trinitarian being. That is God so binds himself to humankind in Jesus Christ that the very trinitarian being of God is threatened, by virtue of the fact that the God–man, the Son of God and the Son of Man, goes into death. The Son of God surely dies, and humankind with him, but not without hope. Because it is the very nature of God to elect himself as Father, Son and Holy Spirit; that is, because God continues to elect himself as the Father who is the fount of the eternal begetting of the Son and the eternal procession of the Spirit, the threat of the dissolution of God as Trinity is utterly – in the grace and freedom of the Father

– nullified. What is more, the threat of the dissolution of creation and humankind is also removed forevermore. In other words, God removes the threat of death against humanity by securing human being in his own trinitarian life, against which death has no avail.

In another sense the resurrection reveals the constancy of the Father's eternal will. It has been the Father's will from all eternity to be in fellowship with human beings. That is, God desires to have his people. Apart from the resurrection of Jesus Christ God would not have his people, who are raised to newness of life only in him. Once again, it appears as a strange thought on Barth's part to suggest that God might have equally been in the right not to move out and gather in his people. God does rather what he had always intended to do, that is, to gather a people to himself. While Barth characteristically asserts that the presupposition of the incarnation is the crucifixion of Christ, he appears reluctant to claim that the resurrection too is the presupposition of the incarnation. Perhaps the reason for this is that Barth sees the New Testament witness focusing on the passion and crucifixion of Jesus. Yet he admits that the incarnation stories are narratives of faith, predicated on the basis and in the conviction of the resurrection of the Crucified. The *télos* of the exinanition of the Son of God is the cross; he took on flesh in order that he might be obedient even to death. However, it is also true that Barth insists upon the *bodily* resurrection of the same Jesus, as the event and sign that God reaffirms his commitment to fellowship with humankind in him. In this sense then the presupposition of the incarnation, the *télos* of the exaltation of the Son of Man, is not only the crucifixion and death of Jesus, but also his resurrection (and ours in him). The resurrection is as such the will of the Father from the beginning.

The Resurrection as the Revelation of the Holy Spirit

Furthermore, an understanding of the *Auferweckung* as belonging to reconciled being in Jesus Christ sheds light upon the charge that Barth's pneumatology is insufficiently developed. A threefold response is required. First, and quite simply, we note that it is not Barth's intention to provide a fully worked doctrine of the Holy Spirit or of the Trinity in his development of the transition of reconciled being and action from Jesus Christ to others, and he does not. Certainly Barth is concerned to develop the manner in which this transition comes to its fullness vis-à-vis the Holy Spirit and the *parousia*, and how it has its ground and basis in the Trinity. But he does not attempt here to develop these points in detail, though the material has many important insights and quite suggestive lines of thought. George Hunsinger judiciously reminds us of Barth's intention to develop his pneumatology most extensively in the projected fifth volume of the *Church Dogmatics*.[19] Thus the accusation that Barth's account of the Holy Spirit in his doctrine of reconciliation is inadequate because incomplete is

---

19   George Hunsinger, 'The Mediator of Communion: Karl Barth's Doctrine of the Holy Spirit' in *Disruptive Grace: Studies in the Theology of Karl Barth* (Grand Rapids: William B. Eerdmans Publishing Company, 2000), pp. 149f.

misguided for it seeks comprehensiveness in the wrong place. The charge may be made responsibly only in view of the entire project of the *Church Dogmatics*.

Second, it must be affirmed that Barth does indeed develop the doctrine of the Holy Spirit in terms appropriate to the discussion at hand. We recall that Barth's primary concern is the transition of reconciled human being and action from Jesus Christ to others. A genuine transition he asserts can be none other than that of the self-mediation of Jesus Christ to others. If it is a matter of the transition of the reconciled *being* of Jesus Christ to others, how can it be achieved by any means other than in the immediate confrontation of *his* being with that of others? But how is this possible? Only as his very own Spirit moves out and encounters these others. Hence the question of the transition of reconciled being and action from Jesus Christ to others demands the explication of the Holy Spirit not in his own right (that is, abstracted from this transition) nor even as the Spirit of the Father – though Barth acknowledges the Scriptures do also speak of the Holy Spirit in this way – but as the Spirit of the Lord. In the explication of the Spirit of the Lord as the Spirit of this transition, the trinitarian life of God is revealed. Barth's development of the Holy Spirit in this way has very important trinitarian content, for he shows how the inner life of the Trinity is reflected in this transition. The antithesis and its overcoming is an essential element in the very being of God. The Holy Spirit is the power of this transition within the ontological Trinity, just as the Spirit of the Lord is the power of this transition from Jesus Christ to others. Barth's development of the doctrine of the Holy Spirit in this context is thus quite appropriate and illuminating.

There is, however, a third matter of consideration in response to this question. The question may be put in this way: 'Is there some aspect of this transition from Jesus Christ to others which requires explication in terms of the *Creator Spiritus* rather than the Spirit of the Lord?' Put in other words, the question is: 'Does Barth's depiction of this transition in near exclusive christological terms sufficiently account for the doctrine of the Holy Spirit in this regard?' Here again we return to Barth's distinction between the *Auferweckung* (awakening) and the *Auferstehung* (self-revelation) of the risen one, in an effort to work out consistently its implications. As Barth makes clear in his treatment of the biblical texts, not only the Father but also the Holy Spirit is understood to be an active agent in the *Auferweckung* of Jesus Christ. That is, the Holy Spirit is not only the active subject in the self-revelation of Jesus Christ, an undeniably important aspect in the transition of reconciled being and action from Jesus Christ to others, but also an agent acting upon the wholly passive Jesus Christ in his awakening from the dead. By this we are prompted to consider the possibility that there is more to be said regarding that aspect of the transition from Jesus Christ to others which concerns the direct agency of the Spirit apart from the self-revelation of the Spirit of the Lord. While Barth's depiction of the resurrection as the Father's pure act upon Jesus Christ lays a fine foundation for this, Barth chooses not to develop the implications in detail. Barth lays a sufficient foundation for a more complete pneumatology when he affirms the Spirit's distinct role in the raising of Jesus Christ. If, in the event of the *Auferweckung* the Spirit is active while Jesus is willingly and wholly passive, we have the basis for a supplementary development of the doctrine of the Holy Spirit as agent of the transition from Jesus Christ to others, not only as the Spirit of the Lord but also as life-giving Spirit. This is not to deny Barth's claim that in the transition from Jesus Christ to others the Holy Spirit is God in his most proper being – that the unity and otherness of Jesus Christ and his own in the self-giving of the Spirit of the Lord reflects the unity and otherness of the Father and Son in the power of the Holy Spirit, the antithesis and communication in which God has his being – but to add that the Holy Spirit also effects the once for all transition from death to life. It is this additional aspect of the Holy Spirit's being and action, which Barth does not develop in detail. Hence, we conclude his doctrine of the Holy Spirit remains incomplete.

What is left undeveloped in Barth's account is an adequate depiction of the Holy Spirit as *Creator Spiritus*, as life-giving Spirit, as the one in whose power and action death is not only defeated but destroyed. His illumination of the antithesis and transition from Jesus Christ to others in the light of the eternal antithesis and communication of the Father and the Son does little to account for the eradication of the antithesis between Jesus Christ and others in his awakening. Once again, if the death of Jesus Christ means the death of the God-man, then the transition required here is somewhat different than the unity-in-distinction Barth has described. In the death of the God-man there is so to speak no longer an other for the Father. Only if the God-man is raised out of death to newness of life can there be a restored antithesis and transition in the Trinity, but now with the Son of God as the God-man in fellowship with the Father. In other words something quite new has taken place in the resurrection of Jesus Christ from the dead. Whereas logically and temporally prior to the crucifixion of the God-man death had no part in the inner fellowship of Father, Son and Holy Spirit, now, because the Son has taken to himself sinful human being, and has borne it to death, the transition which must be overcome in the power of the Spirit includes the overcoming of the death of the God-man in the resurrection. Thus the Holy Spirit acts upon the God-man raising and exalting him to divine life and fellowship with the Father once again, and along with him, distinctly in this event, reconciled human being.

But Jesus Christ died once, and lives again to die no more. Death itself has been defeated, and as death is the concealment and separation of Jesus Christ from others, this too has been destroyed. This requires exposition in terms of the life-giving Spirit to whom it is attributed that he acts in his own right, yet according to the single will of God, upon the wholly passive Jesus Christ, awakening him from the dead so that he lives forevermore. If we are correct in claiming that Barth understands the resurrection as the reality and power of the transition from Jesus Christ to others, then we must conclude his presentation of the antithesis and communication of the Father and the Son as the same sort of transition as that between Jesus Christ and others tends to obscure the New Testament's emphasis upon the once and for all nature of the resurrection of Jesus Christ (His defeat of death). In this he appears to cast Jesus' death and resurrection dangerously in the mold of an eternally recurring death and resurrection (antithesis and transition) in the life of the Trinity. This is not Barth's meaning, but the depiction leaves itself vulnerable in this way, especially if the distinction between *Auferweckung* and *Auferstehung* is not strictly maintained. While we agree with Barth that the being and action of the Holy Spirit mediates the otherness and unity of the Father and the Son in the Godhead, and that this is reflected in the mediation of the relationship between Jesus Christ and others, we must disagree that this adequately accounts for the entirety of the transition from death to resurrection, which as we have argued is an essential aspect of the transition of reconciled being and action from Jesus to others. Death and resurrection have no reciprocity and no mediation. Resurrection means the uni-directional movement from death to life and the consequent final defeat of death. In this manner the resurrection-event guards against any and all abstraction from the specific divine-historical content of this event. The resurrection as an historical event cannot be replaced by a necessary metaphysical scheme or even an independent notion of the Holy Spirit as the power of the transition from Jesus Christ to others. Further development of the *Auferweckung* as the singular event in which this transition occurs as the once and for all transition from Jesus Christ to others in the power of the life-giving Spirit would help to clarify the distinction between the once and for all transition from death to life and the eternal antithesis and transition (otherness and unity) between the Father and the Son. This does not undermine Barth's depiction of the Holy Spirit as the Spirit of the Lord, but merely calls for a supplementary account of the Holy Spirit as life-giving Spirit. Such an account does not jeopardize in any way the primacy of christology in revelation and in reconciliation – the ontic and noetic union between God and the human race is always and only mediated through the God-man Jesus Christ, and hence through the Spirit of the Lord. The being and operation of the *Creator Spiritus* is known only (but truly known, in his being!) by means of the resurrection revelation of Jesus Christ as Lord, and in the power of the transition from him to others.

Still further light is shone upon Barth's understanding of the doctrine of the Holy Spirit when we understand the *Auferweckung* as an essential aspect of the reconciling representative work of Jesus Christ, especially as concerns the question: 'Does Barth distinguish effectively between the resurrection of Jesus Christ and the Holy Spirit?' The poignancy of the question is reinforced by the fact that Barth develops the doctrine of the resurrection, the Holy Spirit and the mediatorial office of Jesus Christ in particular in relation to the question of the transition of reconciled being and action from Jesus Christ to others. Does Barth's development of the doctrine of the Holy Spirit and the mediatorial office of Jesus Christ fulfill the same function as the resurrection, thereby inadvertently rendering the resurrection redundant and unnecessary? Apart from a clear grasp of the importance and meaning of the *Auferweckung* we may be tempted to answer 'Yes' in response to this question. However, it is Barth's certain, though not sufficiently ramified and emphasized, apprehension of the significance of the *Auferweckung* in distinction to the *Auferstehung* which offers some control over the way in which he develops the doctrine of the Holy Spirit. That is, had Barth developed the doctrine of the Holy Spirit primarily from the perspective of a preconceived ontological Trinity – a notion of the Trinity abstracted from that depicted in the history of God in the crucifixion and resurrection of Jesus Christ – he might have undermined the significance of the resurrection altogether. What significance would the resurrection have if the transition of reconciled being and action was characterized as carried out by the Holy Spirit quite apart from his distinction as the Spirit of the Lord? If the Holy Spirit quite apart from this distinction were the subject of this transition, the resurrection would be reduced again to the mere *datum* of the righteousness of Jesus Christ. In no way could the resurrection be understood as the encounter of the risen Christ with his own. In no way could the resurrection be seen as the transition of the reconciled human being and action of Jesus Christ to others. The subjectivity of Jesus Christ in this transition is secured only in the *Auferweckung*. Only as he is raised from the dead is he enabled to act as subject of his own self-revelation. If, as Barth tirelessly insists, the crucifixion and death of Jesus Christ involved his own self-concealment, that is, the closing of the door between himself and others, only on the basis of his awakening is Jesus Christ himself able to open that door once again from the inside. For Barth, it is the *Auferweckung* which demands that this transition be carried out under the auspices of the Spirit of the Lord, for the *Auferweckung* ensures that this transition is an action of the crucified *yet risen* Lord. Hence, for Barth, the awakening of Jesus Christ must be distinguished from the self-revealing action of the Spirit of the Lord and the mediatorial activity of the risen Christ, for it is the basis which makes possible the carrying out of this transition as the action of the crucified yet risen One as living subject. Barth then, though he finds it necessary to expound them in relation to each other, does not conflate the resurrection with the Spirit of the Lord or the mediatorial activity of Jesus Christ. The resurrection remains a distinct and basic aspect of the transition of reconciled being and action from Jesus Christ to others.

The Resurrection as the Victory over Death

A strict distinction between *Auferweckung* and *Auferstehung* also brings further definition to the meaning of Jesus' resurrection as the victory over death. Barth in a certain manner depicts Jesus' death as in itself victory, asserting that in it God and man are reconciled and hence the final battle is won. But does this satisfy as an explanation for the victory of Jesus over death?

The preaching of Peter asserts that 'But God raised him up, having loosed the pangs of death, because it was not possible for him to be held by it.'[20] This text suggests an imprisoning of Jesus in death, from which he is freed only in the act of God raising him up. And this in turn implies that the victory over death comes as a result of the new act of God in raising Jesus from the dead, which follows the preceding act of God in condemning his Son to death. What meaning could this have if in the moment of death death itself is defeated? What threat at all could there be of death 'holding Him' if in the very act of his dying death is defeated and victory

---

20   Acts 2:24, RSV.

is complete? And what are we to make of the New Testament's emphasis upon his having been buried, if not as a sign of his imprisonment in death? Is it not more likely that the New Testament's recognition that his body was not subjected to decay in fulfillment of prophetic expectation, suggests that there was some hold that death had on him such that the threat of bodily decay was real? Paul describes the risen Christ as 'the beginning,' 'the firstborn from the dead'.[21] These terms denote a state of being from which Jesus was raised, that is, that Jesus had not only died, but he was in fact dead, and not only so but was also 'among the dead', prior to the act of his resurrection. It is crucial to see Jesus' death as a submission of himself (and others in him) to the captivity of death for the express purpose of destroying death. In the light of Christ, to die is not necessarily the sting of death; to remain captive to it constitutes its tragedy.

Furthermore, it is to be asserted that it is the action of the Father in the power of the Holy Spirit upon Jesus Christ, and therefore upon the hypostatic union of God the Son and the man Jesus, which really defeats death. The fact that the Son of God entrusted his Spirit to the Father who was able to raise him from the dead, and that the Father did indeed raise him from the dead, marks the defeat of death once and for all. It is the fact that the embrace of the love and grace of the Father is greater than the strangle-hold of death that, death doing its worst, the love and grace of the Father establishes the Son ever anew. Death has no power over God by virtue of the fact that God is his own eternal source and origin. In the trinitarian life of God, the Father is the source of the eternal generation of the Son. For the Son to pass through the real pain of death can only mean the defeat of death, because the life and being of the Son is not his possession alone. It is his truly, but as it has its source in the Father, issues from him eternally. This is what Jesus meant when he said: 'For as the Father has life in himself, so he has granted the Son also to have life in himself'.[22] If, as Barth claims, we cannot ignore the grace of the Father extended to the Son in the raising of Jesus from the dead, can we see this act of grace as in some way non-essential to the being of God? The very fact that the life and being of the Son rests in the hands of the Father means that it is secured even in his passion and death. The power of the life and being of the Son does not rest solely in its own strength. Rather the power of the life and being of the Son rests also in the loving grace of the Father who does not die. Hence he 'did not count equality with God a thing to be grasped'.[23] In the reality of the Trinity, the Son does not have his eternal being in and of himself in isolation from his Father, but rather his is a trinitarianly assured being; that is, the secret of the being and existence of the Son is that it is held purely as a gift of the loving Father in the power of the Holy Spirit. Thus, the Son is able to surrender himself to death entirely and without reserve, because his being does not have its basis in himself alone, but in his relations with the Father and the Holy Spirit, and as such in the life of the Trinity. Thus, against Barth, we must assert that it is not Jesus'

---

21   Colossians 1:8, RSV.
22   John 5:26, RSV.
23   Philippians 2:6, RSV.

death alone, but his death together with his resurrection which constitutes the victory of God over sin and death.

To sum up then, Barth's distinction between the *Auferweckung* (awakening) and the *Auferstehung* (self-revelation) of Jesus Christ, though not consistently maintained, is indeed a trenchant one. In it are signaled some problematic areas of Barth's resurrection thought, which require either further clarification or supplementary development. The *Auferweckung* must be clearly affirmed as an ontological and salvific work of God – in addition to the crucifixion and death of Jesus Christ – in which reconciled human being and action in Christ is granted its teleological determination (clearly an aspect of reconciliation in Barth's depiction). Apart from this act, the work of reconciliation remains incomplete. Furthermore, Barth's development of the resurrection as the primordial revelation-event in which the inner life of the Trinity is fully disclosed, requires further exposition in terms of the resurrection as the reaffirmation of God's eternal self-determination to be God as Father, Son and Holy Spirit. Though Barth's trinitarian theology lays a sufficient basis for this, he himself does not make the connection. So too, Barth's pneumatology requires distinct explication in terms of the life-giving Spirit. Moreover, the work of reconciliation must be developed not only as the victory of God over sin in the crucifixion and death of Jesus Christ but also as the victory of God over death in his *Auferweckung*. And while this is surely an aspect of resurrection theology Barth would have developed under the theme of Redemption, it nevertheless requires expansion in his discussion of Reconciliation, for it is integral to the transition from Jesus Christ to others, as well as to the justification of God with respect to the trinitarian relations of God and the eternal decision of God not to be God without his people.

Conclusion

We affirm that the reconciling being and action of Jesus Christ *extra nos* and *pro nobis* was crucial to Karl Barth's theological understanding throughout his career. What has remained debatable for some, however, is whether the supreme ontic and noetic weight placed upon the divine-human action of Jesus Christ can be upheld without entirely supplanting all genuine human existence outside of him. Does the comprehensive being and action of Jesus Christ take on such universal proportions that it effectively annihilates the very humanity it is purported to save? Is Barth's christology so exclusive that it, at best, relegates anthropology to an indistinguishable aspect of christology, or, at worst, obliterates it altogether? Crucial to the success of his theological enterprise is a satisfying account of the movement from the existence of true human being in Jesus Christ himself to that in others. Failure in this endeavour would mean that Barth's ontic and noetic christocentrism collapses under its own weight for it is unable to provide sufficient basis for the genuine existence of other human beings.

Barth's answer to this charge is that this is precisely the case, if in fact the reality of the reconciling being and action of God in Jesus Christ ends in the crucifixion and death of Jesus Christ, for his death means the death of our human being, and thus, the radical end of every human being. But, Barth insists, his reconciling being and action does not come to its end in his death. There is an astonishing and ultimately inexplicable 'beyond' to his death. That beyond is the glorious resurrection – at once historical and history-making – of Jesus Christ from the dead. The resurrection is for Barth the turn, the way and the power of the crucified Lord to us. Jesus' resurrection is the effective transition of reconciled human being and action from himself (christology proper) to others (anthropology). Barth's doctrine of the resurrection then is his answer to the dogmatic problem of the all-determining reality of Jesus Christ in his incarnation, crucifixion and death. Only in the resurrection is the reality of reconciled human being revealed such that others are empowered to receive and apprehend and embrace it as their own. And only as such do they respond in genuinely free and independent human decision and action. Barth's doctrine of the resurrection is then in large measure an exposition of the fact of this transition and how it is made.

As a result of our study we are compelled to stop and appreciate the simultaneous simplicity and grandeur of Barth's construal of the context and terms for this discussion. For Barth, while the arrangement of the material of the doctrine of reconciliation affords many options, this particular matter – the matter of the transition of reconciled human being and action from Jesus Christ to other human beings – remains the inescapable underlying problem if we take seriously the representative work of Jesus Christ *pro nobis*. Thus he is able to describe this problem as 'the scandal of the gospel.' What many critics take to be a fatal flaw in his theological programme, Barth takes to be the fundamental matter of the gospel of Jesus Christ, that is, Jesus Christ *pro nobis in nobis*, and holds to it as the Archimedean point of his exposition. Thus the doctrine of the resurrection emerges with fundamental implications for every other theological locus – pneumatology, Trinity, Scripture, soteriology, ecclesiology and eschatology, to name a few.

We have demonstrated that Barth develops the doctrine of the resurrection of Jesus Christ from the dead as the way of the crucified Lord to us, the transition of the reality, revelation and power of reconciled human being and action as it is in Jesus Christ *pro nobis* to others who are as yet untouched by it, but who in this encounter are awakened by it and freed to receive and embrace it and to live in genuine independent subjective correspondence to it. Jesus' resurrection accomplishes this for it is the only genuine beyond to the representative crucifixion and death of Jesus Christ. The resurrection is the new, free and gracious act of God upon Jesus Christ following his crucifixion in human history. In this the Father not only demonstrates the righteousness of his judgment upon sinful human being on the cross, but also affirms his election of creation and order to the exclusion of non-being and chaos. The resurrection is furthermore primordial revelation for it is the self-revelation of the God-man Jesus Christ, that the man Jesus is indeed the Son of God. In it Jesus Christ, the Trinity and other human beings are revealed in being and in truth. This resurrection revelation occurs as the miraculous transition of reconciled human being and action from Jesus Christ *pro nobis* in his outward movement to encounter other human beings in the power of his Holy Spirit. Because it is accomplished in the powerful encounter of *his* and no other Spirit, it is a genuine communication and transition of reconciled human being. And in addition, the resurrection of Jesus Christ is the ground, impetus, measure and goal of the eschatological existence of human beings. As the first and primordial form of the threefold *parousia*, the resurrection marks the new beginning in which human persons are granted the necessary conditions in which to embrace their new being in Christ and to enter into free subjective partnership with God.

Karl Barth's doctrine of the resurrection of Jesus Christ is as complex as it is important in the overall scheme of his theological understanding. His early reverent astonishment at the resurrection of Jesus Christ grew with him throughout his career, all the while maintaining a privileged position at the heart of his theological understanding. His development of the doctrine of the resurrection in the context of the transition of reconciled human being and action from Jesus Christ to others tenders an ingenious way of taking the representative atoning work of Jesus Christ seriously and, equally seriously, the transition of reconciled being and action from Jesus Christ to others. Each aspect is a necessary one, apart from which the gospel loses its cohesiveness. Barth's courage and tireless effort reminds us that the way forward in our theological understanding lay not in a reduction or repudiation of the resurrection of Jesus Christ as attested in the New Testament, but in an ever-deepening and faithful exploration of this foundational element of Christian faith.

Bibliography

Bibliographies

Kwiran, Manfred, *Index to Literature on Barth, Bonhoeffer and Bultmann*, Basel: Friedrich Reinhardt Verlag, 1977 (*Theologische Zeitschrift*, Sonderband VII), and index by author and subject to 2823 items of secondary literature on Barth including books, articles, dissertations and book reviews.

Wildi, Hans Markus. *Bibliographie Karl Barth*. Zürich: Theologischer Verlag, 1984.

Wildi, Hans Markus. Bibliographie Karl Barth. Band 2:Veröffentlichungen über Karl Barth. Zurich: Theologischer Verlag, 1992.

Primary Sources

Barth, Karl, *Anselm: Fides Quaerens Intellectum*. London: SCM, Richmond, Virginia: John Knox, 1960 (reprinted by Pickwick Press, Pittsburgh, 1975); Cleveland: World, 1962.

————, *Church Dogmatics,* Edinburgh: T. & T. Clark, Vols. I/1 (1936) –IV/4 (1975), trans. G.W. Bromiley et al. See also *The Christian Life*. Edinburgh: T. & T. Clark, 1981. See also *Church Dogmatics. Index Volume*. Edinburgh: T. & T. Clark, 1977.

————, *Credo,* New York: Charles Scribner's Sons, 1962.

————, *Die Auferstehung der Toten: eine akademische Vorlesung uber I, Kor. 15*, Zollikon-Zuruich: Evangelischer Verlag, 1953, *The Resurrection of the Dead*, trans. H.J. Stenning, London: Hodder & Stoughton, 1933 (1924).

————,*The Epistle to the Romans*, trans. from the Sixth Edition by Edwyn C. Hoskyns, Oxford: Oxford University Press, 1933.

————, *Ethics*, New York: Seabury, 1981.

————, *Evangelical Theology: An Introduction*, trans. by Grover Foley. Grand Rapids: Eerdmans Publishing Co., 1963.

————, 'The Humanity of God,' (1956), trans. by John Newton Thomas, in: *The Humanity of God*, Richmond: John Knox Press, 1972, pp. 35–65.

————, 'Rudolf-Bultmann – An Attempt to Understand Him' in *Kerygma and Myth: A Theological Debate*, 2:83–132, edited by Hans-Werner Bartsch, trans. by Reginald H. Fuller, London: SPCK, 1962.

————, *The Word of God and the Word of Man*, Douglas Horton trans. USA: The Pilgrim Press, 1928.

Barth, Karl and Bultmann, Rudolf, *Letters 1922–1966,* ed. Bernd Jaspert, trans. and ed. Geoffrey W. Bromiley, Grand Rapids, Mich: Eerdmans, 1981 (1971).

Secondary Sources

Badcock, Gary D., *Light of Truth & Fire of Love: A Theology of the Holy Spirit,* Grand Rapids: William B. Eerdmans, 1997.

Balthasar, H.U. von *The Theology of Karl Barth,* trans. John Drury, New York: Holt, Rinehart and Winston, 1971; Garden City, New York: Doubleday, 1972.

Barth Centennial Issue of *Theology Today,* Vol. 43, No. 3, 309–418, October 1986.

Berkhof, Hendrikus, *Two Hundred Years of Theology: Report of a Personal Journey,* Grand Rapids: Wm. B. Eerdmans, 1989.

Berkouwer, G.C., *The Triumph of Grace in the Theology of Karl Barth,* London: The Pasternoster Press, 1956.

Bockmuehl, Klaus, *The Unreal God of Modern Theology: Bultmann, Barth, and the Theology of Atheism: A Call to Recovering the Truth of God's Reality,* Colorado Springs: Helmers & Howard, Publishers, Inc., 1988.

Boersma, Hans, 'Alexandrian or Antiochian? A Dilemma in Barth's Christology', in *Westminster Theological Journal,* Vol. 52, 263–80, Fall, 1990.

Bolich, Gergory C., *Karl Barth and Evangelism,* Downers Grove: Inter-Varsity Press, 1980.

Bouillard, Henri, *Karl Barth: Parole de Dieu et existence humaine,* Première Partie and Deuxième Partie, Aubier: Éditions Montaigne, 1957.

———, *The Knowledge of God,* trans. by Samuel D. Femiano, New York: Herder and Herder, 1968.

Bromiley, Geoffrey W., 'Doctrine of Reconciliation: A Survey of Barth's Kirchliche Dogmatik', in *Scottish Journal of Theology,* Vol. 10, 76–85, March 1957.

———, 'Doctrine of the Atonement: A Survey of Barth's Kirchliche Dogmatik', in *Scottish Journal of Theology,* Vol. 8, 175–87, June 1955.

Brown, Robert F., 'On God's Ontic and Noetic Absoluteness: A Critique of Barth', in the *Scottish Journal of Theology,* Vol. 33, No. 6 (1980), 533–49.

Brown, Colin, 'A Cheer and a Half for Barth', in *The Reformed Journal,* No. 37 (March, 1987), 18–20.

Brown, Raymond E., *The Virginal Conception and Bodily Resurrection of Jesus,* New York: Paulist, 1973 (London: Geoffrey Chapman, 1974).

Brunner, Emil and Barth, Karl, *Natural Theology: Comprising 'Nature and Grace' by Emil Brunner and 'No!' by Karl Barth,* trans. Peter Fraenkel, Introduction by John Baillie, London: The Centenary Press, 1946.

Brunner, Emil, 'The New Barth: Observations on Karl Barth's *Doctrine of Man*', *Scottish Journal of Theology,* Vol. 4, No. 2 (1951), pp. 123–35.

Buckley, James J., 'A Field of Living Fire: Karl Barth on the Spirit and the Church', in *Modern Theology,* Vol. 10, 81–102, Jan. 1994.

————, 'Adjudicating Conflicting Christologies [*Christology in Conflict*, by B. Marshall; bibliog..; replies, pp. 137–58]' in *Philosophy and Theology*, Vol. 6, 117–35, Winter 1991.

————, Christological Inquiry; Barth; Rahner and the Identity of Jesus Christ', *Thomist*, Vol. 50 (1986), 568–98.

Bultmann, Rudolf, *Faith and Understanding*, trans. by Louise Pettibone Smith, Introduction by Robert W. Funk, New York: Harper & Row, Sixth edition, 1966.

————, 'Karl Barth, *The Resurrection of the Dead*,' (1926), in *Faith and Understanding*, Vol. 1, ed. Robert W. Funk, trans. L. P. Smith. London: SCM, 1969, pp. 66–94.

————, *Theology of the New Testament*, English trans. K. Brobel, London: SCM Press, Vol. I, 1952; Vol. II, 1955.

Busch, Eberhard, *Karl Barth: His Life from Letters and Autobiographical Texts*, trans. by John Bowden, London: SCM, 1976.

————, 'God is God: The Meaning of a Controversial Formula and the Fundamental Problem of Speaking about God', in *The Princeton Seminary Bulletin*, New Series, Vol. 7, No. 2, (July 1986), 101–13.

————, *The Great Passion: An Introduction to Karl Barth's Theology*, trans. by Geoffrey W. Bromiley, Grand Rapids: William B. Eerdmans Publishing Company, 2004.

Casalis, Georges, *Portrait of Karl Barth*, Garden City, New York: Doubleday, 1963.

Carnley, P.F., *The Structure of Resurrection Belief*, Oxford: Clarendon Press, 1987.

Childs, Brevard S., *Biblical Theology of the Old and New Testaments: Theological Reflection on the Christian Bible*, Minneapolis: Fortress Press, 1993.

Conzelmann, Hans., *1 Corinthians: A Commentary on the First Epistle to the Corinthians*, trans. by James W. Leitch, Philadelphia: Fortress Press, 1975.

Crawford, R., 'Theological Method of Karl Barth', in *Scottish Journal of Theology*, Vol. 25, 320–36, August 1972.

————, 'Resurrection of Christ', in *Theology*, Vol. 75, 170–76, April 1972.

Crossan, John Dominic, *The Historical Jesus: The Life of a Mediterranean Jewish Peasant*, San Francisco: Harper, 1991.

Cullman, Oscar, *Immortality of the Soul or Resurrection of the Dead?*, London: Epworth Press, 1958.

Dalferth, Ingolf U., 'Theologischer Realismus und realistische Theologie bei Karl Barth', *EvTh*, Vol. 46 (1986), pp. 402–22; Translated as 'Karl Barth's Eschatological Realism' in Stephen W. Sykes, ed., *Karl Barth: Centenary Essays*, Cambridge: Cambridge University Press, 1989.

————, *Der auferweckte Gekreuzigte: Zur Grammatik der Christologie*, Tübingen: J.C.B. Mohr (Paul Siebeck), 1994.

————, *Theology and Philosophy*, Oxford: Basil Blackwell Ltd, 1988.

————, 'Karl Barth's Eschatological Realism' in Stephen W. Sykes, ed., *Karl Barth: Centenary Essays*, Cambridge: Cambridge University Press, 1989.

Demson, David E., *Hans Frei and Karl Barth: Different Ways of Reading Scripture*, Grand Rapids: William B. Eerdmans Publishing Company, 1997.

Evans, C.F., *Resurrection and the New Testament*, London: SCM Press, 1970.

Farrow, Douglas B., *Ascension And Ecclesia: On the Significance of the Doctrine of Ascension for Ecclesiology and Christian Cosmology*, Grand Rapids: William B. Eerdmans Publishing Company, 1999.

Ford, David, *Barth and God's Story: Biblical Narrative and the Theological Method of Karl Barth in the 'Church Dogmatics'*, Frankfurt am Main: Lang. 1981.

Frei, Hans W., *The Doctrine of Revelation in the Thought of Karl Barth, 1900 to 1922*, Ph.D. dissertation, Yale University, 1956.

———, *The Identity of Jesus Christ: The Hermeneutical Bases of Dogmatic Theology*, Philadelphia: Fortress Press, 1975.

———, 'Theological Reflections on the Accounts of Jesus' Death and Resurrection' (pp. 45–93) and 'Of the Resurrection of Christ' (pp. 200–206), in *Theology and Narrative: Selected Essays*, eds George Hunsinger and William C. Placher, New York: Oxford University Press, 1993.

Fuller, Daniel P., *Easter Faith and History*, Grand Rapids: William B. Eerdmans Publishing Company, 1965.

Godsey, John D., 'An Introduction to Karl Barth's Church Dogmatics: Part A: The Architecture of Karl Barth's Church Dogmatics', in John D. Godsey recorder and ed., *Karl Barth's Table Talk*, Edinburgh: Oliver and Boyd, 1963.

Gollwitzer, Helmut ed., *Karl Barth: Church Dogmatics: A Selection*, Edinburgh: T. & T. Clark, 1961; New York: Harper & Row, 1962.

Green, Clifford E., *K. Barth, Theologian of Freedom*, London: Collins, 1989.

Gunton, Colin E., *Becoming and Being: The Doctrine of God in Charles Hartshorne and Karl Barth*, Oxford: Oxford University Press, 1978.

———, 'No Other Foundation: One Englishman's Reading of Church Dogmatics, Chapter V', in Nigel Biggar ed., *Reckoning With Barth: Essays in Commemoration of the Centenary of Karl Barth's Birth*. Oxford: Mowbray, 1988.

———, 'Karl Barth and the Development of Christian Doctrine', in the *Scottish Journal of Theology*, Vol. 25, No. 2 (May 1972), 171–80.

Hartwell, Herbert, *The Theology of Karl Barth: An Introduction*, London: Gerald Duckworth & Co., Ltd, 1964.

Harrisville, Roy A., 'Karl Barth and *Romerbrief* [was it Exegesis?]', in *Dialog* (Minnesota), Vol. 28, 276–81, August 1989.

Hart, Trevor, 'Revelation' in *The Cambridge Companion to Karl Barth*, ed. by John Webster, Cambridge: Cambridge University Press, 2000.

Hendry, George S., 'Nothing', in *Theology Today*, Vol. 39, 274–89, October 1982.

———, 'Freedom and God in the Theology of Karl Barth', in *Scottish Journal of Theology*, Vol. 31, No. 3, 229–44, 1978.

———, 'The Dogmatic Form of Barth's Theology', in *Theology Today*, Vol. 13, No. 3 (October 1956), 300–314.

———, 'The Transcendental Method in the Theology of Karl Barth', in the *Scottish Journal of Theology*, Vol. 37, No. 2 (June 1984), 213–27.

Herzog, Frederick, 'Theologian of the Word of God', in *Theology Today*, Vol. 13, No. 3 (October 1956), 315–33.

Hunsinger, George, 'Beyond Literalism and Expressivism: Karl Barth's Hermeneutical Realism', in *Modern Theology*, Vol. 3, No. 3 (April 1987), 209–23.

———, *How to Read Karl Barth: The Shape of His Theology*, New York: Oxford University Press, 1991.

———, *Karl Barth and Radical Politics*, Philadelphia: Westminster Press, 1976.

———, 'The mediator of communion: Karl Barth's doctrine of the holy spirit', in *Cambridge Companion to Karl Barth*, ed. John Webster, Cambridge: Cambridge University Press. 2000.

———, '*Mysterium Trinitatis*: Karl Barth's Conception of Eternity', pp. 186–209, in *Disruptive Grace: Studies in the Theology of Karl Barth,* Grand Rapids: William B. Eerdmans Publishing Company, 2000.

Hunsinger, George, ed., *For the Sake of the World: Karl Barth and the Future of Ecclesial Theology*, Grand Rapids: William B. Eerdmans Publishing Company, 2004.

Janes, Burton K., 'Taking a Step Toward Pentecost: The Holy Spirit in the Thought of Karl Barth', in *Paraclete*, Vol. 25, 24–8, Winter 1991.

Jaspert, Bernd ed., and Geofrey Bromiley trans. and ed., *Karl Barth/Rudolph Bultmann Letters 1922–1966*, Grand Rapids: Wm. B. Eerdmans, 1981.

Jeanrond, Werner G., 'Karl Barth's Hermeneutics', in Nigel Biggar ed., *Reckoning With Barth: Essays in Commemoration of the Centenary of Karl Barth's Birth*, Oxford: Mowbray, 1988.

Jenson, Robert W., *Alpha and Omega: A Study in the Theology of Karl Barth*, New York: Thomas Nelson and Sons, 1963.

———, 'Karl Barth', in David F. Ford ed., *The Modern Theologians*, Vol. 1. Oxford: Basil Blackwell, 1989.

———, 'Re-review: Karl Barth's *The Word of God and Word of Man*, *Modern Christian*, Vol. 25, No. 4, 52–4, 1983.

———, *The Triune Identity: God according to the Gospel*, Philadelphia: Fortress, 1982.

———, 'You Wonder Where the Spirit Went', in *Pro Ecclesia*, Vol. 2, 296–304, Summer 1993.

Johnson, William Stacy Jr, *The Mystery of God: Karl Barth and the Postmodern Foundations of Theology*. Louisville: Westminster John Knox Press. 1997.

Jüngel, Eberhard, *Barth-Studien*, Zurich: Benziger, 1982, trans. as *Karl Barth: A Theological Legacy* by Garrett E. Paul. Philadelphia: The Westminster Press, 1986.

Kahler, Martin, *The So-Called Historical Jesus and the Historic, Biblical Christ*, English trans. and ed. Carl E. Braaten, Philadelphia: Fortress Press, 1964.

Kant, Immanuel, *Critique of Pure Reason*, edited and trans. by Norman Kemp Smith, New York: St Martin's Press, 1965.

———, *Religion Within the Limits of Reason Alone*, trans. by Theodore M. Greene and Hoyt H. Hudson, New York: Harper and Row, 1960.

Kaufman, Gordon, *Systematic Theology, A Historicist's Perception*, New York: Charles Scribner & Sons, 1968.

Klappert, Bertold, *Diskussion um Kreuz und Auferstehung*, Zur gegenwärtigen Auseinandersetzung in Theologie und Gemeinde, Wuppertal: Aussaat, 1967.

———, *Die Auferweckung des Gekreuzigten. Der Ansatz der Christologie Karl Barths im Zusammenhang der Christologie der Gegenwart*, Neukirchen-Vluyn: Neukirchener Verlag, 1971; 1981, x–424, p. DM 19, 80 pg.

———, 'Die Rechts-, Freiheits- und Befreiungsgechichte Gottes mit dem Menschen: Karl Barths Versonungslehre (KD IV/1–3),' in *Evangelische Theologie*, Vol. 49, No. 5, 460–78, 1989.

Klooster, Fred H., 'Karl Barth's Doctrine of Reconciliation [in Church Dogmatics], in *Westminster Theological Journal*, Vol. 20, 170–84, May, 1958; Vol. 24, 137–72 (1962).

———, 'Karl Barth's Doctrine of the Resurrection of Jesus Christ', in *Westminster Theological Journal*, Vol. 24, 137–72, May 1962.

Kung, Hans, *Justification. The Doctrine of Karl Barth and A Catholic Reflection*, (includes response by Karl Barth), Philadelphia: Westminster, 2nd edn, 1981.

———, 'Karl Barth and Postmodern Paradigm', in *Princeton Seminary Bulletin*, New Series, Vol. 9, No. 1, 8–31, 1988.

Künneth, W., *The Theology of the Resurrection*, trans. James W. Leitch, St Louis, Mo.: Concordia, 1965 (1933, new ed. 1951); London: SCM Press, 1965.

Lee, Jung Young, 'Karl Barth's Use of Analogy in His Church Dogmatics', *Scottish Journal of Theology*, Vol. 22, No. 2 (June, 1969), pp. 129–51.

Lehmann, Paul L., 'Barth and Brunner: The Dilemma of the Protestant Mind', *Journal of Religion*, Vol. XX, No. 2 (April 1940), pp. 124–40.

———, 'The Changing Course of a Corrective Theology', in *Theology Today*, Vol. 13, No. 3 (October 1956), 332–57.

Lorenzen, Thorwald, *Resurrection and Discipleship: Interpretive Models, Biblical Reflections, Theological Consequences*, Maryknoll, NY: Orbus Books, 1995.

Lüdemann, Gerd, *The Resurrection of Jesus: History, Experience, Theology*, London: SCM Press Ltd, 1994.

Macquarrie, John, *Jesus Christ In Modern Thought*, Philadelphia: Trinity Press International, 1990.

Maimela, Simon S., 'The Philosophical–Phenomenological Presuppositions of the Theology of Karl Barth [bibliog]', *Th Er*, Vol. 18, No. 2, 66–72, June 1985.

Mangina, Joseph L., *Karl Barth on the Christian Life: The Practical Knowledge of God*, New York: Peter Lang, 2001.

———, *Karl Barth: Theologian of Christian Witness*, Louisville: Westminster John Knox Press, 2004.

Marshall, Bruce Davis, *Rhetoric*, Spring, 1994.

———, '*Particular Identity and Method in Christology*', Yale University, 1986.

Marxsen, Willi, *Jesus and Easter: Did God Raise the Historical Jesus from the Dead?*, trans. by Victor Paul Furrish, Nashville: Abingdon Press, 1990.

McCormack, Bruce L., *Karl Barth's Critically Realistic Dialectical Theology: Its Genesis and Development, 1909–1936*, Oxford: Clarendon Press, 1995.

McCormack, Bruce L., 'Revelation and History in Transfoundationalist Perspective: Karl Barth's Theological Epistemology in Conversation with a Schleiermacherian Tradition' in *Journal of Religion*, Vol. 78 (1998), pp. 18–37.

McGrath, Alister E., *The Making of Modern German Christology: From the Enlightenment to Pannenberg*, Oxford: Basil Blackwell, 1986.

Migliore, Daniel L., 'How Historical is the Resurrection: A Dialogue', in *Theology Today*, Vol. 33 (1976), pp. 5–14.

Molnar, Paul D., 'Some Problems with Pannenberg's Solution to Barth's "Faith Subjectivism"', *Scottish Journal of Theology*, Vol. 48 (1995), pp. 315–39.

————, *Divine Freedom and the Doctrine of the Immanent Trinity: In Dialogue with Karl Barth and Contemporary Theology*, London: T. & T. Clark, 2002.

Moltmann, Jürgen, *The Crucified God. The Cross of Christ as the Foundation and Criticism of Christian Theology*, trans. R.A. Wilson and John Bowden, London: SCM, 1974 (1973).

Mueller, David L., *Foundation of Karl Barth's Doctrine of Reconciliation: Jesus Christ Crucified and Risen*, Toronto Studies in Theology, Vol. 54, New York: The Edwin Mellen Press, 1990.

Nash, Ronald H., *Christian Faith And Historical Understanding*, Grand Rapids: Zondervan, 1984.

Niebuhr, Richard R., *Resurrection and Historical Reason*, New York: Scribner's, 1957.

O'Collins, Gerald, S.J., *Christology: A Biblical, Historical, and Systematic Study of Jesus*, New York: Oxford University Press, 1995.

————, 'Karl Barth on Christ's Resurrection', *Scottish Journal of Theology*, Vol. 26, 1973.

————, *Jesus Risen: An Historical, Fundamental and Systematic Examination of Christ's Resurrection*, New York: Paulist Press, 1987.

O'Donovan, Oliver, *Resurrection and Moral Order: An Outline for Evangelical Ethics*, Grand Rapids: William B. Eerdmans Publishing Company, 1986, 1994.

Pannenberg, Wolfhart, *Jesus – God and Man*, trans. Lewis L. Wilkins and Duane A. Priebe. Philadelphia: Westminster, 1968 (1964).

————. *Systematic Theology*. Grand Rapids: Eerdmans. Trans. Geoffrey W. Bromiley, Vol. 1 (1991 [1988]), Vol. 2 (1994 [1991]).

Placher, William C., ed., 'Barth in the Nineties', *Toronto Journal of Theology*, Vol. 10, 7–52, April 1994.

Richardson, Kurt Anders, *Reading Karl Barth: New Directions for North American Theology*, Grand Rapids: Baker Academic, 2004.

Roberts, Richard H., 'The Ideal and the Real in the Theology of Karl Barth', in S. Sykes and Derek Holmes, eds, *New Studies in Theology I*, London: Duckworth, 1980.

Robinson, James M., ed., *The Beginnings of Dialectical Theology*, trans. Keith R. Krim and Louis De Grazia, Richmond, Virginia: John Knox Press, 1968.

Robinson, N.H.G., 'Barth or Bultmann?', Religious Studies, Vol. 14 (1978), pp. 275–90.

Rosato, Philip J., The Spirit as Lord: The Pneumatology of Karl Barth, Eidnburgh: T. & T. Clark, 1981.

Rumpeltes, Hans, 'Bibliographie (bis 1973 – about the resurrection)', in Hildegard Temporini und Wolfgang Haase, Hg., Augstieg und Niedergang der Römischen Welt. Geschichte und Kultur Roms in Spiegel der Neueren Forschung, II.25.1: Religion (Vorkonstantinisches Christentum: Leben und Umwelt Jesu; Neues Testament [Kanonische Schriften und Apokryphen]). Hg. Wolfgang Haase. Berlin/ New York: Walter de Gruyter, 1982, pp. 844–90.

Schilling, S. Paul, Contemporary Continental Theologians, New York: Abingdon Press, 1966.

Schurr, George M., 'Brunner and Barth on Life after Death', in Journal of Religious Thought, Vol. 24, 2, 95–110, 1967–68.

Shuster, Marguerite, 'The Preaching of the Resurrection of Christ in Augustine, Luther, Barth and Thielicke', in The Resurrection, ed. by S. Davis, 1997.

Schwöbel, Christoph, 'Theology' in The Cambridge Companion to Karl Barth, ed. John Webster, Cambridge: Cambridge University Press, 2000.

Spykman, Gordon, Reformational Theology: A New Paradigm for Doing Dogmatics, Grand Rapids: William B. Eerdmans Publishing Company, 1992.

Sykes, Stephen W., 'Introduction', in H. Martin Rumscheidt ed., The Way of Theology in Karl Barth: Essays and Comments, Pennsylvania: Pickwick Publications, 1986.

———, 'Barth on the Centre of Theology', in S.W. Sykes ed., Karl Barth: Studies of His Theological Method, Oxford: Clarendon Press, 1979; New York: Oxford, 1979.

———, Karl Barth: Centenary Essays, ed. by S.W. Sykes, Cambridge: Cambridge University Press, 1989.

———, Karl Barth: Studies of His Theological Method, ed. by S.W. Sykes, Oxford: Clarendon Press, 1979; New York: Oxford, 1979.

Thiselton, Anthony C., 'Barr on Barth and Natural Theology: A Plea for Hermeneutics in Historical Theology', [Biblical Faith and Natural Theology, by J. Barr, 1993; review article], in Scottish Journal of Theology, Vol. 47, No. 4, 1994.

———, 'Luther and Barth on 1 Corinthians 15: Six Theses for Theology', in The Bible, the Reformation and the Church, ed. by P. Stephens, 1995, Luther and Barth on 1 Corinthians 15: Six Theses for Theology in Relation to Recent Interpretation, ed. by P. Stephens, The Bible, the Reformation and the Church, pp. 258–89, 1996.

Thompson, John ed., Theology Beyond Christendom: Essays on the Centenary of the Birth of Karl Barth, Allison Park, Pennsylvania: Pickwick Publications, 1986.

———, The Holy Spirit in the Theology of Karl Barth.,Oxford: Oxford University Press, 1991.

Torrance, Alan, 'The Trinity' in the Cambridge Companion to Karl Barth, John Webster, ed., Cambridge: Cambridge University Press, 2000.

Torrance, Thomas F., *Karl Barth: An Introduction to His Early Theology 1910–1931*, London: SCM Press Ltd, 1962.

———, *Karl Barth: Biblical and Evangelical Theologian* Edinburgh: T & T Clark, 1990.

———, 'Introduction: The Place of Christology in Biblical and Dogmatic Theology', in T.H.L. Parker ed., *Essays in Christology for Karl Barth*, London: Lutterworth Press, 1956.

———, 'The Legacy of Karl Barth (1886–1986)', in *Scottish Journal of Theology*, Vol. 39, No. 3, 289–308, 1986.

———, 'The Modern Eschatological Debate', in *Evangelical Quarterly*, Vol. 25, 45–54; 94–106; 167–78; 224–32, January–October, 1953.

———, *Space, Time and Resurrection*, Grand Rapids: Eerdmans, 1976.

———, *Reality and Evangelical Theology: The Realism of Christian Revelation*, Downers Grove: Intervarsity Press, 1982; 1999.

Waldrop, Charles T., 'Karl Barth's Concept of the Divinity of Jesus Christ', in *Harvard Theological Review*, Vol. 74, 241–63, July 1981.

———, 'Karl Barth's Christology', 1984.

———, 'Revelation, Redemption, and the Divinity of Jesus Christ', in *Scottish Journal of Theology*, Vol. 31, No. 6, 501–15, 1978.

Wallace, Mark I., 'Karl Barth's Hermeneutic: A Way Beyond the Impasse', in *Journal of Religion*, Vol. 68, No. 3 (July 1988), 396–410.

Watson, Gordon, 'A Study in St Anselm's Soteriology and Karl Barth's Theological Method', in *Scottish Journal of Theology*, Vol. 42, No. 4, 493–512, 1989.

———, 'Karl Barth and St Anselm's Theological Programme', in *Scottish Journal of Theology*, Vol. 30, No. 1, 31–45, 1977.

Weathers, Robert A., 'Barth's Epistemology as a Postmodern Paradigm: A Reconsideration', in *Perspectives in Religious Studies*, Vol. 21, Summer 1994.

Webb, Stephen H., *Re-figuring Theology: The Rhetoric of Karl Barth*, Albany, NY: State University of New York Press, 1991.

Weber, Joseph C., 'Feuerbach, Barth, and Theological Methodology', in *Journal of Religion*, Vol. 46, 24–36, January 1966.

———, 'Karl Barth and the Historical Jesus', in *Journal of Bible and Religion*, Vol. 32, 350–54, October 1964.

Webster, John B., 'The Finest Grasp of the Real: Barth on Original Sin', in *Toronto Journal of Theology*, Vol. 4, 19–29, Spring 1988.

———, '"Assured and Patient and Cheerful Expectation": Barth on Christian Hope as the Church's Task', in *Toronto Journal of Theology*, Vol. 10, 35–52, Spring 1994.

———, 'On the Frontiers of What is Observable: Barth's Romerbrief and Negative Theology', in *The Downside Review*, No. 105 (July 1987), 169–80.

———, 'Recent work on Barth since 1975', Themelios, Vol. 7, No. 3 (1981), 31–5.

———, *Barth's Ethics of Reconciliation*, Cambridge: Cambridge University Press, 1995.

————, *Barth's Moral Theology: Human Action in Barth's Thought*, Grand Rapids: William B. Eerdmans Publishing Company, 1998.

————, *Karl Barth* (Second Edition), New York: Continuum, 2000; 2004.

Wells, Harold G., 'Karl Barth's Doctrine of Analogy', in *Canadian Journal of Theology*, Vol. 15, 203–13, July–October 1969.

Wenham, John, *Easter Enigma: Are the Resurrection Accounts in Conflict?*, Grand Rapids: Academie Books, 1984.

Williams, Rowan, 'Barth on the Triune God', (pp. 147–93) in *Karl Barth – Studies of His Theological Method*, ed. S.W. Sykes, Oxford: Clarendon Press, 1979.

Wingren, Gustaf, *Theology in Conflict: Nygren-Barth-Bultmann*, trans. by Eric. H. Wahlstrom, Philadelphia: Muhlenberg Press, 1958.

Wright, N.T., *The Resurrection of the Son of God*, Minneapolis: Fortress Press, 2003.

Index